Great Women
of Islam

Who were given the good News of Paradise

Table of Contents

Publishers Note

All praises are due to Allâh the Almighty, the Lord of all that exists. May Allâh's peace and blessing be upon His final Prophet and Messenger, Muhammad, his family and his Companions.

Darussalam is pleased to present this valuable book, 'Great Women of Islam, who were given the good News of Paradise'. It was compiled in the Urdu language by a great scholar and a compiler of Islamic books, Mahmood Ahmad Ghadanfar, and translated by our Islamic sister Jamila Muhammad Qawi.

This book is about the life stories of the Mothers of the believers and sixteen Prophet's women Companions. They were those pure and virtuous women of Islam who were honored during the very lifetime of the Prophet ﷺ with the prediction that they would live forever in Paradise in the Hereafter.

All the Mothers of the believers were of very noble character and conduct and pleased Allâh so much that He sent special greeting for Khadijah رضــــي الله عنـها. 'Aishah رضي الله عنها had a brilliant mind and a remarkable memory, and had the distinction of being the source of many Ahâdith because of her long association with the Prophet ﷺ. Her knowledge of the many branches of religion like Tafsir, Hadith, Fiqh and Shari'ah, her wisdom in interpretation, her mastery of the teachings of the Prophet ﷺ – all these qualities made her one of the most remarkable personalities of the time.

Female Companions were very active in religion as well as in politics and business. They were so courageous in the battlefield that their services like giving medical aid to the soldiers, nursing the wounded on the battlefields, and providing food and water to the wounded and thirsty can be found in history. They spread the message of Islam and it is proved by many of the instances that converted many of the disbelievers to Islam.

There are many more stories likes this that will encourage our Islamic sisters to get more knowledge about such great women. I hope that they will study this book thoroughly and try their best to follow these noble women of Islam.

Pray' to Allah the Almighty that He grants them all - the writer, translator and editor and everyone else who participated by any means - the best reward in this world and in the Hereafter, for having supported in the completion of such a valuable book. *Ameen*

Exploits and Achievements
of the *Sahâbiyât*
(Women Companions)

Exploits and Achievements of the *Sahâbiyât* (Women Companions)

The *Sahâbiyât* (Women Companions) were the noble women who were the contemporaries of the Prophet Muhammad ﷺ. They were the pure, virtuous crusaders of Islâm, and were honored during the very lifetime of the Prophet Muhammad ﷺ with the prediction that they would live forever in Paradise in the Hereafter. Their achievements and influence are found in every sphere of that momentous period in the history of the world, when the whole of humanity would be transfigured forever. They were as active in religion as in politics, as courageous in war as in the peaceful and persuasive propagation of the teachings of Islâm. These noble selfless women could be found in the battlefields among the foremost ranks of those taking part in *Jihâd*. They were to be found in the political arena, in the field of education, in the courts of Islâmic jurisprudence, in the interpretation of *Shari'ah*,[1] in trade and commerce, in agriculture, in medicine and in nursing. In short there was no sphere that did not benefit from their intellect, their wisdom and their gentle yet firm strength of character.

Religious Achievements

Among the many services that one can render to Islâm, is to fight in the battlefields. Few, if any, examples of such zeal, determination,

---

[1] The collective body laws as revealed by Allah ﷻ.

perseverance and courage can be found in history. When the disbelievers attacked the Muslims during the Battle of Uhud, only a few devoted followers were left to fight with the Prophet Muhammad ﷺ. At this critical stage the Women Companion Umm 'Ammârah ﵞ shielded him with her body and warded off the enemy with her sword as well as her bow and arrows. When Qaniah got within striking distance of the Prophet Muhammad ﷺ, it was she who bore the brunt of his attack. She had a deep wound on her shoulder, yet she continued to attack him with her sword. But he was well protected and she could not make a dent in his armor. Against Mussailmah Kaththâb she fought so courageously that she suffered a dozen wounds and lost an arm.

In the battle of Ahazab (the battle of Trench), the Companion Safiyyah ﵞ displayed brilliant military strategy in handling the Jewish attack, and slew one of the Jews. In the Battle of Hunain Umm Salim ﵞ set out to attack the enemy with her sword.

In the battle of Yarmook, Asmâ' bint Abu Bakr, Umm Abbân, Umm Hakeem, Khawlah, Hind and the Mother of believers Juwairiah رضي الله عنهم displayed extraordinary valor. Asmâ' bint Yazid ﵞ killed nine enemy soldiers. In the year 28th after Hijrah, Umm Harâm ﵞ took part in the attack on Cyprus.

The Mohter of the believers 'Aishah, Umm Salim and Umm Salit رضي الله عنهـن were among those who were very proficient at nursing the wounded.

The *Sahâbiyât* usually accompanied the Prophet Muhammad ﷺ on his military expeditions and took part in battles both on land and at sea. Besides taking an active part in the war, there were many other services that the *Sahâbiyât* performed, like giving medical aid to the soldiers, nursing the wounded on the battlefields and providing food and water to the wounded and thirsty. Standing side by side with the soldiers they would hand them arrows, nursing the wounded and generally help to keep up the morale of the army. They also helped to carry the martyred and the wounded back to Al-Madinah. Umm 'Atiyah ﵞ took part in seven battles, and fought during the rule of the Caliphs 'Umar Farooq ﵞ, the women and even the children helped to bury the dead.

They spread the message of the new religion and through example converted many of the disbelievers to Islâm. It was Fâtimah bint Khattâb 🌸 who converted her brother 'Umar bin Khattâb ﷺ; he was to become one of the bravest and most faithful of the Companions of the Prophet Muhammad ﷺ. It was Umm Salim 🌸 who influenced Abu Talhah ﷺ, and it was Umm Hakim 🌸 who convinced her husband, Ikrimah to accept Islâm. Umm Shareek Dosiah 🌸 very discreetly worked among the women of the tribe of Quraish to spread Islâm.

Another aspect of missionary work is to preserve the religion in its pristine form, and protect it from any modifications, impurities and innovations that may creep in because of cultural or traditional practices already prevalent in society. This very important work of preserving the purity of Islâm was performed by many of the *Sahâbiyât*; most prominent among whom was 'Aishah 🌸 .

In the year 35th after Hijrah, when Caliph 'Uthmân ﷺ was martyred and there was chaos and confusion over who was next in the line of succession, it was she who brought unity into the ranks by influencing the Muslims of Basrah (Iraq) and Makkah.

Leading the prayers and calling the *Athân,* or the call for prayer, is another important aspect of religious life. Although women cannot lead men in prayers, they can do so with assemblies of women. Many women contemporaries of the Prophet Muhammad ﷺ performed this task as well. 'Aishah, Umm Salim, Umm Waraqah and Sa'dah bint Qamâmah رضي الله عنهن were some of the most prominent among these. In fact, Umm Waraqah 🌸 turned her house into a place of prayer for women; the *Athân*[1] was given there by a lady *Mu'aththin*[2] for the women's congregation, and Umm Waraqah 🌸 performed the duties of the *Imâm* in lea the prayers.

Political Achievements

The *Sahâbiyât* (Women Companions) played a prominent role in politics as well. Caliph 'Umar ﷺ so valued Shifa' bint 'Abdullâh 🌸 for

---

[1] The call to prayer given 5 times during the day.

[2] The *Mu'aththin's* duty is to give the *Athân*.

her political intelligence and insight that he very often consulted with
her. He often gave her the responsibility of running the affairs of state
relating to trade and commerce. Before the Hijrah (migration) of the
Prophet Muhammad ﷺ to Al-Madinah, the disbelievers wanted to lay
siege to his house, it was Ruqayyah bint Saifee ﷺ who warned him.
The Prophet Muhammad ﷺ then secretly left for Al-Madinah, leaving
'Ali ﷺ asleep in his place. Vast political rights are granted to women
in Islâm. A woman even has the right to grant shelter to an enemy, if
she so wishes. A historian, Abu Dawood relates that Umm Hâni ﷺ,
the sister of 'Ali ﷺ, had given refuge to an enemy disbeliever and the
Prophet Muhammad ﷺ said,

> "If you have guaranteed sanctuary and safety to a person, then
> we stand by you."

This is the law of Islâm that the *Imâm*[1] or leader has to stand by the
guarantee offered by the woman.

Education, Knowledge and the Fine Arts

There are various subjects, an understanding of which are essential for
a thorough knowledge of Islâm and its tenets. *Qirâ'at*[2] interpretation
and commentary, *Shari'ah, Fiqh,* study of *Hadith,* all are important
aspects of Islâmic studies. Many of the women Companions were
experts in these fields. 'Aishah memorized the Qur'ân as did Hafsah,
Umm Salmah, Umm Waraqah رضى الله عنهن. Hind bint Aseed, Umm
Hishâm bin Harithah, Zaidah bint Hayyân; Umm Sa'ad bint Sa'ad رضى
الله عنهن all knew portions of the Qur'ân by heart. The latter used to
regularly lecture on the Qur'ân. In the sensitive interpretation of
Hadith, all were expert, but 'Aishah and Umm Salmah رضى الله عنهما were
exceptional masters of interpretation and commentary. With the
former, 2,210 *Ahâdith* are associated and 378 with the latter.

'Aishah ﷺ was an expert on interpretation and commentary due to her
close association with the Prophet Muhammad ﷺ. Much of the Book of
Tafsir in *Sahih Muslim* contains narrations from her.

---

[1] The *Imam* leads the prayer in the congregation.

[2] The correct way of reading the Qur'ân – elocution and enunciation.

Asmâ' bint Abu Bakr (sister of 'Aishah), Umm 'Atiyah, Umm Hâni and Fâtimah bint Qais رضي الله عنهن also had extensive knowledge of *Ahâdith*.

In Islâmic jurisprudence or *Fiqh* 'Aishah's ﷺ verdicts could fill several volumes. The same could be said of Umm Salmah's ﷺ recorded verdicts.

The invaluable verdicts of Safiyyah, Hafsah, Umm Habibah, Juwairiah, Fâtimah (the Prophet's daughter), Umm Shareek, Umm 'Atiyah, Asmâ' bint Abu Bakr, Laila bint Qâi'f , Khawlah bint Tuyait, Umm Dardâ, 'Athikah bint Zaid, Sahlah bint Sohail, Fâtimah bint Qais, Zainab bint Jahash, Umm Salmah, Umm Aiman, Umm Yusuf رضي الله عنهن could fill several volumes.

'Aishah ﷺ was also well versed in the law of inheritance and many renowned and respected Companions consulted her on the finer points of the law.

Besides being masters of Islâmic law and of the finer points of *Fiqh*, the women Companions had skill and ability in other branches of knowledge. Asmâ' bint Yazid bin Sakan ﷺ was an expert in making speech; Asmâ' bint 'Umais ﷺ was famous for her interpretation of dreams. Several Companions were noted for their skill in medicine and surgery. Aslamiah Umm Mattâ'a, Umm Kabshah , Hamnah bint Jahash, Mu'aâthah, Ammaimah, Umm Ziad, Rabi'a bint Mu'awath, Umm 'Atiyah, Umm Salim رضي الله عنهن were some of them, well known for their skills. Rufaida Aslamiah's ﷺ tent, set up as a surgery with all the necessary instruments, was situated close to the Prophet's Mosque at Madinah. The arts were not neglected by any means. Some of the most noted poetesses were, Sa'adi, Safiyah, 'Atikah, Bint Zaid, Hind bint Athâthah, Umm Aiman, Kabashah bint Râfi'a, Ummâmah Maridiah, Hind bint Hârith, Zainab bint 'Awâm Azdi, Maimoonah and Ruqayyah رضي الله عنهن. A book of verses by Khansâ' ﷺ, the best known among them has been published.

Industry, Trade and Commerce

The women Companions also practiced the practical or survival skills as we know them today. Agriculture, business, trade and commerce, writing, editing, cottage industries like weaving, manufacture and designing of clothes - all these are mentioned in the *Musnad* (collection of *Ahâdith*) of Imâm Ahmad. Agriculture was not so common, but was mainly practiced in the rural fertile areas around Al-Madinah, especially by the women of the *Ansâr*. Among the immigrants, or Muhâjir as they were known, Asmâ' also practiced farming. The era before the advent of the Prophet ﷺ was known as the age of illiteracy, but some of these worthy women were highly educated and skilled in the arts of penmanship and calligraphy. Shifâ' bint 'Abdullâh ﷺ learned to read and write even during these dark ages and was celebrated for her skill at this art. Hafsah, Umm Kulthum bint 'Uqbah and Karimah bint Miqdâd رضــي الله عنــهن were all literate. 'Aishah and Umm Salmah رضي الله عنــهما could not write but they could read. Both of them were blessed with remarkable memories and inquiring minds; and because of their close association with the Prophet ﷺ many of the authentic *Ahâdith* originated from them.

Some of the *Sahâbiyât* also ran businesses. Khadijah ﷺ was a very successful businesswoman and used to send trading caravans to different countries. Khawlah, Maleekah, Thaqafiyah, and Bint Fakhariyah رضي الله عنهن used to trade in the oriental oil-based perfumes known as *'Itar*. Saudah ﷺ operated a leather tanning industry. The daughters of the Ansâr would compose verses and poems for festive occasions and sing. According to the *Hadith* narrated by Fri'âh bint Ma'auth ﷺ, they recited their poems in the presence of the Prophet ﷺ, who had appreciated their literary skills.

Umm Salmah ﷺ used to recite the Qur'ân with *Tajweed*, which was a difficult skill and much appreciated.

Thus there was no sphere of activity - social or cultural – that was not influenced and assisted by the presence of these great ladies. May Allâh ﷺ have Mercy on their souls!

Allâh will be pleased with them and they with Him.

امـهـات المؤمـنين

Mother
of the
Believers

Khadijah bint Khawaylid رضي الله عنها

Narrated Abu Hurairah ﷺ: Jibrîl (Gabriel) came to the Prophet ﷺ and said, "O Allâh's Messenger! This is Khadija, coming to you with a dish having meat soup (or some food or drink). When she reaches you, greet her on behalf of her Lord (Allâh) and on my behalf, and give her the glad tidings of having a palace made of *Qasab* in Paradise, wherein there will be neither any noise nor any toil (fatique, trouble, etc.)." (*Al-Bukhâri*)

Khadijah bint Khawaylid رضي الله عنها

The strength of character and noble qualities of Khadijah ﷾ earned her the honor of being greeted by Allâh ﷻ through his Angel Jibril ﷿.

An image of faithfulness, integrity, truth, modest good manners and nobility; generous, wise and understanding, nurtured in an atmosphere of wealth and luxury. She was the first person to have an abiding faith in the utterances of the Prophet ﷺ and to accept Islâm as her religion and her way of life. She was blessed with the distinction of having been greeted with *Salâm* by Allâh ﷻ and the Angel Jibril ﷿. She was the first lady ever to be so honored. She was the first wife of the Prophet ﷺ, and he did not marry again during her lifetime. They lived together in peace and harmony for more than 24 years. It was in her house that the Prophet ﷺ received the revelations of Allâh ﷻ, through the Angel Jibril ﷿. During the siege that Prophet ﷺ underwent in Makkah, in the Shi'ab Abi Tâlib, she was there by his side, constantly supportive and sacrificing all the comforts of life.

When she passed away, the Prophet ﷺ was heartbroken at the loss of a dedicated companion who stood by him during the most difficult period of his life. He personally supervised the preparation of her grave, and climbed down into it to check it out. He then lowered her body into the grave himself. Thus ended the life of the lady who was the greatest supporter of Islâm in its earliest days. She who was the mother of Fâtimah ﷾, the First Lady of Paradise, the grandmother of the beloved grandchildren of the Prophet ﷺ, Hasan and Hussain رضي الله عنهما

who are to be the foremost of the youths in Paradise.

❀❀❀❀❀

'Abdullâh bin 'Abbâs ﷺ narrated that one day the Prophet ﷺ drew four lines on the earth and asked his Companions if they understood what these lines stood for. They respectfully replied that he knews better. He then told them that these lines stood for the four foremost ladies of the universe. They were Khadijah bint Khawaylid, Fâtimah bint Muhammad, Maryam bint Imrân, the mother of the Prophet Isa ﷺ, and 'Âsiah bint Mazâhim رضي الله عنهن (the wife of the Pharaoh).

The first named has the distinction of being the mother of all the believers, or practicing Muslims; the second Fâtimah, the daughter of the Prophet ﷺ was given the glad tidings that she would be the leader among the women of Paradise. Maryam ﷺ, the Pure and Chaste is the only woman to have given birth to 'Isa ﷺ, a Prophet of Allâh without having been touched by any man.

'Âsiah the long suffering and righteous wife of the evil Pharaoh had advised her husband to adopt the infant Moses (ﷺ). This was at a time when infanticide was the law of the land. All the newborn boys of the tribe of Israel were being murdered because of the prediction that one of them would finally overthrow the Pharaoh and destroy him. She not only nurtured him in the very palace of Pharaoh, but also was one of the first to accept Islâm, as preached by Moses (ﷺ).

❀❀❀❀❀

'Aishah ﷺ narrates that whenever the Prophet ﷺ talked about Khadijah ﷺ, it was in terms of the highest praise. One day her innate feminine envy overtook her sense of decorum and she spoke in disparaging terms of her, wondering why the Prophet ﷺ missed her when he was blessed with a better, younger wife by Allâh ﷺ. This displeased him, but forbearing as he was, he just sighed and answered,

> "I have not yet found a better wife than her. She had faith in me when everyone, even members of my own family and tribe did not believe me, and accepted that I was truly a Prophet and a Messenger of Allâh ﷺ. She converted to Islâm, spent all her wealth and worldly goods to help me spread this faith, and this too at a

time when the entire world seemed to have turned against me
and persecuted me. And it is through her that Allâh 🕸 blessed
me with children."

🌼🌼🌼🌼🌼

Khadijah 🕸 was born in Makkah in the year 556 CE. Her mother's
name was Fâtimah bint Zâ'ed, and her father's name was Khawaylid
bin Asad. He was a very popular leader among the tribe of Quraish,
and a very prosperous businessman who died while fighting in the
famous battle of Fujjâr. Khadijah 🕸 thus grew up in the lap of luxury.
She married Abu Hâlah Malak bin Nabash bin Zarrarah bin At-
Tamimi. She bore him two children, Hâlah and Hind. She wanted to
see her husband prosper and financed him in setting up a big
business. But unfortunately he passed away. Some time later the
young widow married 'Atique bin 'Aith bin 'Abdullâh Al-Makhzomi,
and she had a daughter by him as well named Hindah. But the
marriage soon broke up on grounds of incompatibility. After this all
her attention was devoted to the upbringing of her children, and
building up the business she inherited from her father. Her astuteness
and business ability made hers one of the most widespread businesses
among the Quraish. Her policy was to employ hardworking, honest
and discriminating managers to deal on her behalf. There was no
network of travel and communication as there is today and a lot
depended on the integrity of the employees who traveled far and
wide on her behalf. She exported her goods to far away markets like
Syria, and her managers bought goods from those markets to be sold
at home. Makkah being strategically located on the trading caravan
routes and the centre of international trade fairs, was a very profitable
market for the goods brought back. The managers would get fifty
percent of the profit, and this was enough incentive for them.

Khadijah 🕸 had heard of the integrity, honesty and principled
behavior of the Prophet 🕸, and sent a job offer to him to head her
trading caravans. He gladly accepted the offer and started working for
her. Khadijah sent him on a business trip; her old and trusted slave
Maisarah being delegated to accompany and serve him.

This trip proved to be an extremely profitable venture and Maisarah
was astounded by some very remarkable scenes he witnessed on this

trip. He was impressed and completely won over by the Prophet's ﷺ integrity, strength of character, adherence to principles, his amicable dealings and his business abilites. On the way back from Syria, the Prophet ﷺ lay down under a tree to rest for a while. Nestora, a Jewish monk, noted for his knowledge of religion and for his insight saw him and asked Maisarah who he was. Maisarah told him all about the Muhammad ﷺ and his reputation for honesty and intelligence. Nestora then told him that this man would be elevated to Prophethood in the future, as no man had ever rested under that particular tree but Prophets.

Tradition has it that Maisarah saw two angels bearing a cloud over Prophet's head to protect him from the glare and heat of the sun. He was stunned and overcome by a sense of gratitude that he had been given the opportunity of benefiting from the close companionship of this man soon to be chosen by Allâh ﷻ as his Messenger.

When he returned home Maisarah reported to his Khadijah all that had taken place on the trip to Syria. She was deeply moved and impressed, and started thinking of proposing marriage to Muhammad ﷺ. But how could she express her thoughts to him? She already rejected several proposals of marriage from men belonging to some of the noblest families of the Quraish. How would her tribe react? What would her family say? And what was more, would her proposal be acceptable to this young, yet unmarried man of the tribe of Quraish?

As she pondered over these questions and debated within herself, one night she dreamt that the shining sun had descended from the heavens into her courtyard, radiating her home. When she woke up she went for the interpretation of this wonderful dream to her cousin, Waraqah bin Nofal, a blind man noted for his skill in interpreting dreams, and for depth of his knowledge, particularly of the Torah and the Injil. When he heard her dream, he gave a serene smile, and told her not to worry, as this was a very promising dream. The glorious sun she saw descending into her courtyard indicated that the Prophet ﷺ whose advent had been predicted in the Torah and the Injil was to grace her home and she would gain from his presence in her life.

After this meeting with Waraqah she became stronger in her desire to marry Muhammad ﷺ. But she was still not sure how to go about it.

One of her very close friends, Nafeesah bint Manbah knew of her inclination. One day she told Khadijah 🌸 that what was bothering her so much was not a major problem, and she herself would help her to solve it. She went immediately to Muhammad 🌺, and without much ado she requested his permission to ask him a very personal question. When he said he had no objection, she asked why he had not yet got married. He said he did not have the financial resources. Then she asked him if he would be willing to marry a beautiful lady from a noble and wealthy family, who was inclined towards marriage with him. He asked whom she was referring to; when he learnt her identity he said that he was willing, provided she was willing to marry him. Of course Khadijah 🌸 was overjoyed. The Prophet 🌺 was then twenty-five years of age and Khadijah 🌸 was forty years old. (According to one tradition, she was twenty-eight). The two uncles of the Prophet 🌺, Hamzah 🌺 and Abu Tâlib approached her uncle, 'Umar bin Asad, with the formal proposal. It was accepted and the date was fixed. The two families began preparing for the wedding. On the date that had been fixed, the families and friends gathered and the marriage was solemnized. Halimah Sa'adiah who nursed the Prophet 🌺 in his infancy was specially invited for the wedding and traveled to Makkah from her village. When she left after the festivities, Khadijah presented her with household goods, a camel and forty goats as an expression of gratitude to the lady who had taken such good care of Muhammad 🌺 in his infancy.

❀❀❀❀❀

Khadijah was very blessed in the marriage, and had six children. First two sons, Qâsim and 'Abdullâh; then followed the daughters, Zainab, Ruqayyah, Umm Kulthum and Fâtimah رضــي الله عنــهم. They were wonderful, intelligent children and it was a very happy, peaceful and content household. But all this did not seem enough. Muhammad 🌺 felt something was missing, and he was extremely restless. He would retire for a month once a year to the cave of Hira to dedicate himself entirely to prayer and meditation. One day he felt the presence of another being who held him in his arms in a tight embrace. Then he loosened his hold and asked him to read; Muhammad 🌺 answered that he was illiterate. But the person repeated the same act and the phrase again and again. Then finally he read these *Âyât* which are the first revelation of the Qur'ân. They are from *Surah Iqrâ* or *Al-'Alaq* of the Noble Qur'ân.

"Read! In the Name of your Lord Who has created (all that
exists). He has created man from a clot. Read! And your Lord is
the Most Generous. Who has taught (the writing) by the pen.
He has taught man that which he knew not." (96:1-5)

Then the being disappeared. This was such an awesome experience
that the Prophet ﷺ returned home sweating and shaking. He called
out to Khadijah ﷺ asking her to cover him with a sheet or a blanket.
After lying down for some time he became a little more relaxed. When
he had calmed down to some extent, he told his wife that he feared for
his life, and narrated the whole incident to her. Khadijah ﷺ, a picture
of loyalty and serenity consoled him saying that Allâh ﷻ would
surely protect him from any danger, and would never allow anyone to
revile him as he was a of man of peace and reconciliation and always
extended the hand of friendship to all. He never lied, always
hospitable, carried the burdens of others and helped those who were
in trouble. These soothing and encouraging words of sympathy and
understanding from Khadijah ﷺ gave him immeasurable strength and
confidence. She then took him to meet her cousin, Waraqah bin Nofil,
who immediately guessed the identity of the being in the Cave of Hira
as the Angel Jibril ﷺ, the Messenger of Allâh who had visited Moses
(ﷺ) as well. Waraqah ﷺ who was very old wished that he could live
to see the time when the Prophet Muhammad ﷺ would be forced into
exile by his people. The Prophet ﷺ was very surprised and asked if his
people would really do this to him. Waraqah assured him that it was
typical of human beings that they would never appreciate or follow a
Prophet who rose among them. As the proverb has it, "A Prophet is
never honored in his own land." Waraqah added that he wished he
were alive at that time and be able to help him. He added that if what he
had been told were true then surely it meant that her husband was the
Prophet of Allâh whose advent had been mentioned in the scriptures.

The Prophet ﷺ had six children by Khadijah ﷺ - four daughters and two
sons. The four daughters grew up to be faithful and courageous daughters
of Islâm. They were named Zainab, Ruqayyah, Umm Kulthom and
Fâtimah رضي الله عنهن. They all migrated to Al-Madinah, with the Prophet ﷺ.
Zainab ﷺ was married to Abul 'Aas bin Rabee'ah and Ruqayyah ﷺ was
married to 'Uthmân ﷺ. When she passed away he married Umm
Kulthom ﷺ; Fâtimah ﷺ was married to 'Ali bin Abi Tâlib ﷺ. The first

three daughters died during the lifetime of Muhammad 🕮, and his beloved daughter Fâtimah 🕮 lived just six months after he passed away.

The Prophet 🕮 had three sons, two by Khadijah 🕮 and Ibrâhim, a third son by Maria Qabtiyyah 🕮. The first son was named Qâsim and the Prophet 🕮 came to be known as Abu Qâsim.[1] The second son, 'Abdullâh was also known as Tâhir (the pure) or Tayyab (the good). Both died in their childhood and the disbelievers were overjoyed that the Prophet had no heirs to carry on his noble mission. The third son, Ibrâhim was born by his wife, Maria Qabtiyyah 🕮. He also died in infancy. When he saw Ibrâhim dieing, he gently picked him up and said that he was helpless and could do nothing before the Will of Allâh 🕮.

> 'We know that death is inevitable and is a fact of life. We also know that those who are left behind will catch up with those who have gone ahead; if this were not so we would grieve even more for Ibrâhim. The heart mourns and the eye weeps, but it is not fitting that we utter words which might displease our *Rabb*, our Creator and Sustainer.'

On the day Ibrâhim passed away there was a solar eclipse. The Arabs of ancient times were superstitious and associated these phenomena of nature - lunar and solar eclipses - with a great man's death. Many Muslims even started associating the solar eclipse with Ibrâhim's death. But the Prophet 🕮 immediately went up to the pulpit and in his sermon said,

> 'Solar and lunar eclipses are signs of Allâh. They never occur because of the death of any human being. When you see any of these offer *Salât*.'

His enemies now started calling him *Abtar*, the one who had no descendants, whose lineage was cut off. But, Allâh 🕮 had more lasting bounties in store for him. He then revealed to him the beautiful Verses of *Surat Al-Kauthar*, the 108th *Surah* of the Noble Qur'ân.

> "Verily, We have granted you *Al-Kauthar*. Therefore turn in prayer to your Lord and sacrifice. For he who hates you, he will be cut off." (108:1-3)

---

[1] Abu or father of Qâsim

When the disbelievers saw that Islâm was attracting more and more followers in spite of all their tactics, they had a meeting to decide what steps should be taken to stop the spread of this new religion. They decided to declare an open and total political and economic boycott of the tribe of Banu Hâshim. This took place in the seventh year after the Prophet ﷺ declared himself the Messenger of Allâh ﷻ. This is also known in Islâmic history as the Shi'ab Abi Tâlib.

It was so severe that innocent children faced starvation and hunger, and adults survived eating the leaves of trees. Yet the firm followers of Muhammad ﷺ did not turn away from their true religion and they came out of the ordeal stronger and purer than before.

Khadijah ﷡ who had been brought up in luxury in her wealthy father's home now faced the economic hardships with patience and courage, which are a necessary part of any siege.

Khadijah's ﷡ nobility of character and conduct pleased Allâh ﷻ so much that He sent special greetings for her. This incident was narrated by Muhammad ﷺ to Abu Huraira ؓ and quoted in a *Hadith* of *Sahih Al-Bukhâri*.

Khadijah ﷡ was the ideal wife and mother. The Prophet ﷺ lived in her house which became a blessed place due to his presence and the fact that Jibril ؑ came often to visit him there with Qur'ânic revelations. It became the centre of Islâm, where the Companions and women Companions visited often to partake of the hospitality of Muhammad ﷺ and his wife.

After the Hijrah (migration) of the Prophet ﷺ to Al-Madinah, the house was occupied by the brother of 'Ali. Later Mu'âwiyah bin Abu Sufyân ؓ who transcribed some of the Divine Revelations purchased this house and built a mosque. Thus the site of the house of Khadijah ﷡ became a place of prayer and worship for all time. She had been used to praying two *Rak'aât* of *Salât* (prayer), mornings and evenings with the Prophet ﷺ, even before prayers were made compulsory by Allâh ﷻ. There is one incident recorded in history regarding this. After accepting Islâm she became more contemplative and inclined towards worship; she found a blessed feeling of peace in prayer. 'Afif Kindi relates that 'Abbâs bin 'Abdul Muttalib was a great friend of his and he used to visit him often in Yemen in connection with his business in perfumes. On one occasion when they were standing and chatting in Minâ, they saw a handsome young man approach. He carefully washed his hands and feet and then stood respectfully with his arms crossed on his breast. Soon a dignified lady of noble bearing and a young handsome young lad joined him. 'Afif asked 'Abbâs what they were doing and whether this was a new form of exercise. 'Abbâs replied that the youth was his brother 'Abdullâh's son, and the lady was his wife. She was a woman of great wealth and virtue, and an ideal wife and mother. The lad was his brother Abu Tâlib's son. Muhammad had announced that he was a Messenger of Allâh and had started preaching a new religion called Islâm. In due course 'Afif accepted Islâm, but he always regretted the fact that he had not joined the Muhammad ﷺ and his Companions in their prayers and supplication on that memorable day in Minâ, when he had first heard of Islâm.

Khadijah ﷺ passed away just three years before the Hijrah, or the Prophet's ﷺ migration to Al-Madinah. She died at the age of sixty-five, having given almost twenty-five years to Muhammad ﷺ and the cause of Islâm. When Muhammad ﷺ saw her in the throes of death he consoled her saying, Allâh ﷻ had so ordained it, and that the thing she was dreading, would prove favorable for her. Her eyes lit up and as she gazed at her beloved husband, and her soul left its earthly body. Her grave was prepared at a place called Hujjoon, near Makkah. Muhammad ﷺ stepped into it to see that everything was as it should be, and with his own hands lowered her gently into it. Thus passed away the 'Mother' of all Muslims, the one who had sacrificed her all for Islâm.

The same year the Prophet's ﷺ greatest supporter and protector from among his family, his uncle Abu Tâlib passed away. Thus within the space of a few months two of his closest companions, supporters and benefactors had passed away. Besides his personal sense of loss and bereavement, Muhammad ﷺ was deeply disturbed by the fact that his work of spreading the word of Allâh ﷻ was faced with problems and obstacles. His uncle had protected him at critical moments with his influence and authority; his wealthy wife gave her all generously to the cause, and also provided great moral and emotional support. Her house was a haven of peace for him as she took upon herself all of the responsibilities of running the household and bringing up four young daughters. Whenever he was abused by the disbelievers she provided moral support and unflagging faith.

One of the ladies of the Quraish, Khawlah bint Hakim, visited the Prophet 變 to console him, and saw his state of depression and grief and remarked on it. He replied it was only natural that he should be touched by her absence, as she had been a loving mother to his now neglected children; she had been a loyal and sympathetic wife who shared his secrets. It was only human and natural that he should feel her loss as she was there for him during his most difficult times.

A Companion of the Prophet 變 narrates that whenever any gift was brought to him he would immediately send it to some lady who had been a friend of Khadijah 變. 'Aishah 變, a favourite wife of Muhammad 變 says that whenever a goat was slaughtered the Prophet 變 would send some meat to Khadijah's friends; when she remarked about this on one occasion he told her,

> 'I have great regard for her friends, as she has a special place in my heart.'

'Aishah رضى الله عنها said she never experienced such a feeling of natural feminine jealousy for any other wife of the Prophet 變 as she did for Khadijah 變.

She also narrates that whenever Muhammad 變 spoke of her he would talk at great length and praise her qualities, and pray for her forgiveness.

As Allâh 變 says in *Surah Al-Fajr* in the Noble Qur'ân that it will be said to the pious – believers.

> "O the one in complete rest and satisfaction! Come back to your Lord – well-pleased (yourself) and well-pleasing (unto Him)! Enter you then among My (honored) servants, and enter you My Paradise." (89:27-30)

Saudah bint Zam'ah رضي الله عنها

> The prophet ﷺ said:
>
> "Allâh has commanded me to marry only with the women of Paradise."
>
> 'Aishah رضي الله عنها said:
>
> "I did not wish seeing any women except Saudah bint Zam'ah رضي الله عنها if I could be in her skeleton."

Saudah bint Zam'ah رضي الله عنها

The first lady to enter the household of the Prophet ﷺ after the passing away of Khadijah ﷺ was Saudah ﷺ - who was obedient and generose, and loyal with a sense of sacrifice. 'Aishah ﷺ was very impressed by her simple and selfless nature. She was among the first to accept Islâm, and also had the distinction of emigrating twice, first to Abyssiniah and then to Al-Madinah. Her life is a beacon for all Muslim women.

Her mother, Shammoos was from the tribe of Bannu Najjâr, a branch of the Quraish; her father was also from a branch of the Quraish, Banu 'Âmer bin Loii. She was married to her cousin, Sakran bin Amar, and then married the Prophet ﷺ on his death. All her husband's brothers, Sohail, Sahel, Hâtib and Saleet had the honor of being Companions of the Prophet ﷺ. Both she and her husband accepted Islâm in its earliest days and they both had the distinction of migrating to Abyssiniah for the cause of Allâh, joining the second band of migrants. They were blessed with a lovely boy whom they named 'Abdur-Rahmân. They stayed in Abyssiniah for a considerable period of time before returning to Makkah.

One day Saudah ﷺ dreamt that the Prophet ﷺ entered her house and caught hold of her by the nape of her neck. When she told her husband about her dream, he interpreted it to mean that after his death she would marry Muhammad ﷺ. Some time later she had another dream; she saw the moon descending into her lap. She told Sakran about this dream as well; again he interpreted it for her. His death was imminent he said, and she would marry the Prophet 鑫. A few days later he fell ill, and passed away. She was left lonely and it seemed as if there was no purpose to life.

One of her friends was Khawlah bint Hakim, the wife of Uthmân bin Madh'aon. One day she visited the Prophet 鑫 and remarked that he was leading a very lonely and sad life with the responsibility of bringing up his four daughters, and was missing his wife Khadijah 鑫. He replied that she was right and that Khadijah 鑫 had been a remarkable and great lady. She suggested to him that he should get married. He asked who he could possibly marry, who would be willing to take on the responsibility of his household and daughters.

She replied that she had in mind a certain lady and if he agreed she would approach that person. On learning the identity of the lady the Prophet 鑫 agreed. Khawlah 鑫 was very happy that her suggestion was accepted and immediately went to see Saudah 鑫. She told her that she had great news for her. When she heard of the proposal, she was overcome by the honor being bestowed on her. But she said Khawlah should also discuss this matter with her elderly father who was going blind. Of course her father was only too happy that his widowed daughter had been chosen to be the companion and wife of the Prophet 鑫.

Khawlah then visited Muhammad 鑫 with the good news. Soon the marriage took place and Zam'ah performed the ceremony. The Prophet 鑫 gave a *Mahr*[1] of 400 *Dirhams* to his wife Saudah 鑫 on the occasion. Her brother 'Abdullâh had not yet converted to Islâm and was very upset and saddened by the news; he expressed his grief in a barbaric and uncivilized manner by throwing dust on his head. Later when he converted to Islâm, he realized his mistake and how disgracefully he had received the greatest honor possible to himself and his family.

鑫鑫鑫鑫鑫

Saudah 鑫 was of course very happy, having moved into the house of Khadijah 鑫 where Prophet Muhammad 鑫 lived with his daughters,

---

[1] Marriage dowry either payable at the time of marriage or at a mutually agreed time.

Umm Kulthoom and Fâtimah رضـي الله عـــهـما. She felt she was very fortunate that now her future was assured. She would often relate her memorable experiences in Abyssiniah, and talk especially about his daughter Ruqayyah 🌼 and her husband, Uthmân bin Affân and the Prophet 🕋 would listen with great interest.

On one occasion Ruqayyah 🌼 visited Makkah. The sisters received her with mixed emotions of joy and sorrow, joy on seeing her after so many years and sorrow because they were meeting each other for the first time after the death of their mother. Saudah 🌼 stepped forward and embraced Ruqayyah. Ruqayyah and Saudah رضي الله عـهـما never expected that they would be meeting again after their days in Abyssiniah, now as mother and stepdaughter. But it was a very cordial relationship and the Prophet 🕋 was extremely happy to meet his daughter and son-in-law.

He got news of the latest developments, of how the refugee *Sahâbah* were fareing, and of the position of the ruler of Najâshi. The social conditions in Makkah continued to be bad, the Muslims were cruelly treated and oppressed; and the disbelievers were not prepared to change their policy. Everyday brought fresh stories of torture and harsh treatment of the Muslims, and the only alternative appeared to be migration. The Prophet 🕋, keeping all these circumstances in view, now decided his followers should migrate to Al-Madinah. A few days later Allâh 🕋 ordered him to migrate as well. So the Prophet 🕋 set out on his sacred journey in the company of his most trusted Companion, Abu Bakr Siddique 🕋. On reaching Al-Madinah they stayed over at the house of Abu Ayyub Ansâri. Once he was settled he sent Zaid bin Harithah and Abu Rafi'a to Makkah with some camels and 500 Dirhams to bring all the members of his family. These two trusted Companions reached there and immediately left for Al-Madinah with Saudah, Ruqayyah, Umm Kulthoom, Fâtimah رضي الله عـهم. Umm Aiman 🌼 the wife of Zaid bin Harithah and his son Osamah also were part of the caravan, which was put up at the house of Hârithah bin No`amân Ansâri 🕋 on reaching Al-Madinah. During his stay in Makkah, the Prophet 🕋 had married 'Aishah 🌼, who now came to live with him in his household.

Later at different stages in his life the Prophet 🕋 married Hafsah bint 'Umar, Zainab bint Hajash, Umm Salmah رضي الله عـهم and others who had the good fortune to be associated with him. It was an age when the desert of Al-Madinah bloomed into a garden whose heady perfumes seemed to have enchanted the world. The pebbled streets of Al-Madinah became the focal point for all believing Muslims, and the axis on which the whole Islâmic world revolved. The bustling activity and the liveliness as a new city-state evolved were magnified by the charismatic presence of Muhammad ﷺ. Even the angels seemed envious of these early Muslims and the role they were playing in spreading Islâm across the world, and the Angel Jibril ﷺ visited this glorious city many times.

❀❀❀❀❀

When Saudah bint Zam'ah ﷺ became old she feared that Muhammad ﷺ would divorce her and a settlement be made. Her desire was to be raised on the Day of Judgment with the other members of the Prophet's wives, so she said she would entrust 'Aishah ﷺ the time allotted to her. It was at this point of time that *Âyah* of *Surat An-Nisâ'* was revealed to the Prophet ﷺ.

> "And if a woman fears cruelty or desertion on her husband's part, there is no sin on them both if they make terms of peace between themselves; and making peace is better." (4:128)

'Aishah ﷺ was very touched by her gesture and they became even closer than before. Her heart was so pure that it was totally free of jealousy or malice.

Saudah ﷺ was a tall, healthy woman with a sense of humor. Ibn Sa'ad mentions how once she was offering voluntary night prayers, standing behind the Prophet ﷺ. The next morning she told him how his very long prayer made her fear that her nasal vein would burst and her nose would bleed! So she said that while in the bowing position, she held on to her nose! This comical image that she presented of herself made the Prophet ﷺ burst into laughter. She was a very warm and simple person.

She had a slow lumbering walk because of her build and when she went with the Prophet ﷺ on *Hajj* she took special permission to leave for Muzdalifah earlier as to avoid the crowds. 'Aishah ﷺ who was also part of the group, later wished she had also left with her since she really enjoyed her company and missed her liveliness.

When Saudah 🏵️ first heard about the Dajjâl[1] from the Prophet 🕌 she was terrified. Being the simple person that she was, it became a hobby for the others to talk about it and frighten her and then laugh at her. On one occasion 'Aishah 🏵️ and the Mother of the Believers Hafsah 🏵️ started talking about it in front of her. She was so scared that she immediately ran into a dark room full of cobwebs to hide from the monster. When Muhammad 🕌 walked in he found the two enjoying the joke. He asked them what was so amusing. On being told what had happened he called out to Saudah 🏵️ to come out as there was no monster around. She came out sheepishly laughing at herself.

On one occasion, the Prophet 🕌, 'Aishah and Saudah رضي الله عنهما were sitting together and chatting. The former cooked a special dish and offered it to the latter. But she declined. 'Aishah 🏵️ was a lively young person, and threatened to force feed Saudah 🏵️ And when she continued to remain serious, she actually splashed it all over her face! So this lighthearted gaiety and spirit of comaraderie was very much part of the Prophet's household. There was no malice and jealousy in this pure atmosphere. It was reflective of the pleasant ambiance in the household of the Prophet 🕌 where there was always a loving concern and affection for all. But when the call to prayer, or *Athân* was given by the *Mu'aththin*, Muhammad 🕌 would immediately rise and leave for the mosque as if he did not even know the family members gathered around him.

The History of At-Tabari, *Kâmil* of Ibn Atheer, and the *Seerah* of Ibn Hâshim have recorded an incident that occurred after the victory in the Battle of Badr. The triumphant Muslim army was on its way back to Madinah with many prisoners; among them was Sohail bin Amr, the brother of Sakrân bin Amr, the first husband of Saudah 🏵️. He was under the care of Mâlik bin Dakhtham.

On the way he told his captor that he wished to relieve himself, and managed to escape. When the Prophet 🕌 was informed, he asked the army to stop and ordered that the escaped prisoner should be

---

[1] A one-eyed man, the anti-Christ who will appear just before the Day of Judgment.

captured or shot where found. The *Mujahideen*[1] fanned out to search and soon found him, hiding behind a tree. His hands were bound together and tied to his neck; in this state he entered the city.

When Saudah ﷺ saw him, she involuntarily exclaimed that he should have died a noble death, rather than live to see such a shameful day. She did not realize that the Prophet ﷺ had heard her. He told her that she was stirring up the prisoner against Allâh ﷻ and his Prophet ﷺ; how could the death of one fighting against the forces of Allâh ﷻ be noble? She was very ashamed at this and immediately apologized, saying that she just could not take what she had seen and blurted out what first came to her mind. She said she was really loyal and obedient to the Will of Allâh ﷻ and his Prophet ﷺ, and was sorry if she was offensive in any way. The Prophet ﷺ relented with a smile, and announced that the captors should treat all prisoners with consideration. The result was that the *Mujahideen* first fed the prisoners in their charge and then ate themselves. And ultimately, because of this kind treatment many disbelievers, among them Sohail bin 'Amr and his brothers, converted to Islâm.

❀❀❀❀❀

After the Prophet's ﷺ Farewell *Hajj*, he told his wives that they should remain in their homes as it was the Will of Allâh ﷻ,

"And stay in your homes." (33:33)

Thus, Saudah and Zainab bint Jahash رضي الله عنهما did not travel after the death of Prophet Muhammad ﷺ, and they stayed in their homes in Al-Madinah, saying that they performed *Hajj* and *'Umrah* in the company of the Prophet ﷺ and would follow the command of Allâh ﷻ.

Saudah ﷺ was extremely generous. During his rule 'Umar bin Khattâb ﷺ, sent her a bag full of Dirhams. She asked what it was, and on learning that it was money she was very surprised and said this was like dates being packed in a bag! She then distributed the money among the poor and needy.

---

[1] Those fighting the *Jihâd*.

There are five authentic *Ahâdith* attributed to her, according to Imam
Thahbi. She narrated how when one of their goats died they used the
skin until it got worn out. Thus it is proved that it is permissible to use
the skin of a dead animal. Similarly in the *Musnad* of Imâm Ahmad
the following *Hadith* is attributed to Saudah 🌸. A man came to the
Prophet 🌸 and asked if it was possible to perform *Hajj* for his aged
father, who could no longer undergo its rigors. The Prophet 🌸 asked if
he would pay his father's debts if he had any, and if this would be
acceptable. The man replied that it would. Then Muhammad 🌸 told
him that Allâh 🌸 was Oft-Forgiving and Most Merciful and he should
perform the *Hajj* on behalf of his father.

The Caliphs who succeeded after the Prophet's death thought it a
great honor to look after the welfare of the Mothers of the Believers,
and diligently did their duty by them.[1] Saudah 🌸 lived to the ripe old
age of eighty. She passed away during the caliphate of 'Umar bin
Khattâb 🌸 and was buried in *Jannatul-Baqi'*.

As Allâh 🌸 says in *Surah Al-Fajr* in the Noble Qur'ân that it will be
said to the pious – believers:

> "O the one in complete rest and satisfaction! Come back to your
> Lord – well-pleased (yourself) and well-pleasing (unto Him)!
> Enter you then among My (honored) servants, and enter you
> My Paradise." (89:27-30)

---

[1] Thus, *Ummul Momineen* Saudah 🌸 with her maturity, simplicity and
amiable nature came at an opportune moment into the Prophet's household
providing support for her husband, motherly love for the girls and a
carefree and pleasant atmosphere in the home. (*Translator's note*)

'Aishah bint Abu Bakr رضي الله عنها

'Aishah رضي الله عنها said:

Angel Jibril عليه السلام brought my picture wrapped in the cover of green silk in his dream and said:

"She is your wife in this world and hereafter."
(*Tirmithi* in the chapter of *Fadhâ'il*)

'Aishah bint Abu Bkar رضي الله عنها

A'ishah 🌸 was the favourite daughter of one of the closest friends, Companion and associates of the Prophet 🌼, Abu Bakr Siddique. Several *Âyât* of the Noble Qur'ân which were revealed were associated with her, and she was justifiably proud of this honor. She was in an enviable position among the Mothers of the believers in that she was considered the foremost among them. Allâh had chosen her Himself in the heavens as a bride for Muhammad 🌼; a portrait of hers, wrapped in silk, was brought to him in his dream by the Angel Jibril 🕊. He told him that he was to marry her, and she would be his consort in the life hereafter as well.

She had a brilliant mind and a remarkable memory; and the distinction of being the source of the most *Ahâdith* because of her long association with Muhammad 🌼. Her knowledge of the many branches of religion like *Fiqh* and *Shari'ah*, her wisdom in interpretation, her mastery of the teachings of the Prophet 🌼, her trustworthiness and integrity - all these qualities made her one of the most remarkable personalities of the time. She was very tender-hearted and no needy person left her house empty-handed. The Angel Jibril 🕊 personally greeted her. During her lifetime the Prophet 🌼 gave her the wonderful news that she earned a place for herself in Paradise. It was while resting in her lap that the Prophet 🌼 passed away, and it was her apartment that became his final resting-place. Angels surrounded her apartment even during her lifetime and for all time the blessings of Allâh 🌼 will be showered on it, since as it is in the centre of the sanctuary at Al-Madinah.

She said that there were nine blessings of Allâh ﷻ which distinguished her from all other women in the world except Maryam bint 'Imrân, the mother of 'Isa ﷺ.

1. The Angel Jibril ﷺ had presented her portrait wraped in green silk to Muhammad ﷺ and told him that this was the picture of the lady chosen by Allâh ﷻ to be his consort both in this world and the next.

2. She was the only virgin to have become the wife of the Prophet ﷺ.

3. When the Prophet ﷺ passed away, he was resting in her lap and was buried in her apartment.

4. Many times angels encircled her apartment with love and respect.

5. Very often divine revelation would come to Muhammad ﷺ when they were lying together resting in peace and tranquillity.

6. She was the daughter of the loyal and true friend of the Prophet ﷺ, Abu Bakr Siddique ﷺ.

7. *Âyât* acquitting her of any wrongdoing had descended from the heavens from Allâh ﷻ, proving her innocence.

8. She was born a Muslim and had been brought up in pure a environment, and spent her formative years with the purest and best of creatures, the Prophet ﷺ.

9. Allâh, the Lord, the Sustainer of the Universe promised her Divine Forgiveness and abundant bounties.

❀❀❀❀❀

'Aishah ﷺ had claims to noble birth from both sides of the family. Her mother was Umm Român ﷺ and her father was Abu Bakr Siddique ﷺ. Umm Român earlier married 'Abdullâh Azdi and had a son by him named 'Abdur-Rahman. 'Aishah ﷺ was born in 614 CE. Her father Abu Bakr Siddique ﷺ is mentioned in the Noble Qur'ân in glowing terms. He was a pure God fearing man, the foremost and staunchest supporter of the Prophet ﷺ, whom he loved dearly, even more than his life, and thus 'Aishah's cradle was the cradle of Islâm. Abu Bakr Siddique ﷺ had the honor of being buried next to his beloved leader and Prophet ﷺ, in the sanctuary of Al-Madinah. He will enter Paradise in the company of the Prophet 🕮.

'Aishah's favorite pastimes as a girl were swinging and playing with dolls. Once on a visit to her father, Muhammad 🕮 saw her playing with a winged horse; she was barely five years old at the time. He asked her what it was; she replied it was a horse. He smiled and answered that horses did not have wings! She promptly retorted that the Prophet Sulaimân 🕮 had winged horses! This incident reveals several things about her - she was intelligent, quick-witted, well-informed on religious and historical matters - and at such a tender age! She had a memory like a computer, which never seemed to fail her. She hardly ever forgot something once she heard it. At the time of Hijrah, (migration) of the Prophet 🕮 to Al-Madinah, she was barely eight years old, yet she remembered years later even minor details about that historic and momentous move, when the first Islâmic state was on the rise.

She was barely nine years of age when she joined the household of the Prophet 🕮. This was the time when he was grief stricken by the loss of his loving and supportive wife Khadijah 🕮. Both she and his uncle Abu Tâlib, had protected him against the most powerful chieftains of the two foremost tribes of Arabia. With their deaths he felt lonely and isolated. Then, he and his faithful followers faced the cruelest religious prosecution seen in history.

When 'Aishah 🕮 joined his household in Al-Madinah, she did not find herself in a royal mansion. A number of small rooms were constructed in the locality of Bani Najjâr, around the Prophet's Mosque, and she occupied one of these, located on the eastern side of the Mosque. It was about six feet wide, had earthen walls and the roof was of leaves and twigs. To prevent the rain water from seeping in the roof was covered with a blanket. The roof was so low that a person standing upright could touch the roof. There was a single shuttered door, which was never closed; a blanket served as a curtain. Close to the room, on a slightly higher level was another small room, which Muhammad 🕮 occupied on the one occasion when he had boycotted the Mothers of the believers. A mat, a thin mattress, a pillow filled with the bark of trees, a leather water bag, a small plate for dates and a glass for drinking water were all the things in the room. There were none of the signs of worldly wealth and pomp, but this little room was filled with spiritual treasures.

The Prophet 🌸 liked the lack of riches and material comforts; he often prayed that he should live and die in poverty, and be reborn on the Day of Judgment in the company of the poor and the needy.

Bilâl ⚬ was incharge of the arrangements and provided for the needs of the families of the Prophet 🌸. It was he who used to distribute the annual supply of grain. At times it became necessary to even borrow money in order to fulfill their needs. When the whole of Arabia was under the authority of Islâm, huge quantities of grain and cash flowed into the central treasurey. But on the day that Muhammad 🌸 passed away, there was not even food for a single day in his household. 'Aishah 🌸 maintained this tradition of generosity and liberality right up to her last days. During the days of prosperity, abundant riches arrived daily, but she always distributed them among the needy by the time evening fell. The most outstanding trait of her character was her innate magnanimity and benevolence. Her generosity was now well-known, and no beggar left her door empty-handed.

'Abdullâh bin Zubair ⚬ mentioned that 'Aishah 🌸 and her sister, Asmâ' 🌸 were both very large-hearted and benevolent. They spent all that they would receive in the Name of Allâh 🌸. The only difference between them was that 'Aishah 🌸 would collect a sizable amount gradually and then give it away in charity; Asmâ' 🌸 on the other hand, would give what ever she had in hand. In fact she would even fall into debt to help someone in need. When asked why she took on debts unhesitatingly, she replied that if a person had every intention of repaying the debt, Allâh 🌸 would help him or her. She added she was looking for His Mercy and Help.

On one occasion, at one sitting, 'Aishah 🌸 gave away 70,000 Dirhams in charity for Allâh 🌸 and got up showing her empty handkerchief to the people seated there. One evening she received Dirhams 1,00,000 from Amir Mu'âwiyah ⚬ who was in Syria and by nightfall the entire sum had gone to charity. Her maid reminded her that she was fasting and she should have kept something for herself. She asked her why she had not reminded her earlier. On another occasion, 'Abdullâh bin Zubair ⚬ sent her 1,00,000 Dirhams, and similarly they were also given away as early as possible.

One day she was fasting and a beggar came to her apartment and asked for some food. She told her maid to give the lady the piece of bread they had. The maid answered that there was nothing else with which she could break her fast. 'Aishah 🍃 answered curtly that she should help the hungry woman and the evening would take care of itself. By the evening someone sent her a dish of cooked meat; she said to the maid that Allâh 🍃 had provided her with something even better than what she had given away. She owned a house which she sold to Mu'âwiyah 🍃 and gave away all the money in charity.

She loved her sister's son, 'Abdullâh bin Zubair 🍃, very deeply. He in turn loved her very much and always looked after her needs. On one occasion he remarked that her generosity needed to be restrained. 'Aishah 🍃 was very upset and angry when she heard this; she swore she would never to talk to him. She asked who on earth thought that he could stop her from spending in the way of Allâh 🍃. She asked how he could even dare to say such a thing. And finally, when she calmed down and made up with him, she freed several slaves as penance for breaking her oath.

'Aishah 🍃 was very tender-hearted, and broke into tears easily. On one occasion when a beggar woman carrying two small children came to her door; she had only three dates in the house. These she gave her; the woman gave one each to the children and started eating one herself. One of the children ate his share quickly and started looking longingly at his mother eating her date. The woman could not bear her child's hunger and took the date from her mouth, broke it into two halves, and gave a piece to each of the children. When 'Aishah 🍃 saw this heartrending scene she could not control her tears.

🍃🍃🍃🍃🍃

'Aishah 🍃 was a modest, pure, and pious lady, yet she could not escape the slanderous and malicious plotting of the hypocrites. In the month of Sha'abân[1] in year 5th of the Hijrah, Muhammad 🍃, led the Muslim army towards Qadeed, and a minor battle ensued between

---

[1] The 8th month of the Hjirah calendar.

them and the tribe of Banu Mustalaq. Several hypocrites were also part of the army during this particular battle. A few people were killed, but most were captured. The army was camped on the banks of a stream named Marisa'.

'Aishah 🌼, a very slim and petite fourteen-year old had also accompanied the Prophet 🌟 on this expedition. She had borrowed a delicate necklace from her sister Asmâ' 🌼. On the way back when the army had camped in the desert, she went far into the desert to relieve herself. Suddenly she realized that the necklace had fallen somewhere along the way. She retraced her footsteps looking for it and luckily found it, but after a very long search. By the time she reached the camping site, the caravan left. Now the normal procedure was that the ladies, who were segregated from the men folk, would get into their litter[1] and draw the curtains. Then the camel drivers would place the litter on the camel's back. Since 'Aishah 🌼 was very light no one realized her absence. When she came back after her search to the camping site, she found the caravan had left. Fearless as she was she just lay down, waiting for her companions to return for her when they found her missing.

Safwân bin Mu'attal had the responsibility of checking the camp site for things which might have been left behind inadvertently after the departure of the caravan; at daybreak he arrived to find a figure lying down wrapped in an *Jilbâb*.[2] When he saw it was a lady, he moved away after alighting from the camel, so she could get on to it. When 'Aishah 🌼 heard him she woke up, and got on to the camel. He then walked leading the camel by the bridle.

In the afternoon when the caravan had just reached the next camp site to rest, they saw 'Aishah 🌼 arriving with Safwân bin Mu'attal. She got off the camel in front of all the people assembled there. This incident became the material for a scandal for the hypocrites, led by 'Abdullâh bin Ubayy bin Salool. His intrinsic nature, his natural propensity for

---

[1] A litter was like a palanquin or howdah, but with curtains, and placed on camels for the ladies.

[2] A cloak that covers the entire body.

foul and wicked suspicions, made him indulge in slanderous gossip. The whole of Al-Madinah was flooded by this filthy talk that 'Aishah 🌺 was a loose woman and her character was suspect. Hasân bin Thâbit, Hamnah bint Jahash, and Mastah bin Athâthah also joined the hypocrites in this mud-slinging. The Prophet 🌺 was naturally extremely disturbed when he heard this talk about a member of his household, and his favorite wife; but 'Aishah 🌺 was blissfully ignorant of all this gossip going the rounds about her and Safwân bin Mu'attal.

One night when she went out with the aged mother of Mastah bin Aththâthah. The old lady tripped and started cursing her son. 'Aishah 🌺 was surprised; remonstrating with her and said that he was a Companion of the Prophet 🌺 who fought courageously in the Battle of Badr and deserved respect. The old lady retorted that 'Aishah 🌺 was ignorant of the fact that he was involved in an awful and frightening plot; then she revealed what had been taking place behind her back to her. 'Aishah 🌺 was appalled at the depths to which sheer willful malice can make a person fall. After returning home, she took the permission of Muhammad 🌺, and went to visit her parents. They also corroborated the story she had heard. She was heartbroken and started weeping. Her sympathetic and loving mother tried to console her, but she failed to stem the flood of tears. She told her that since she was the favorite of Muhammad 🌺, the people jealous of her position had deliberately hatched this plot. She advised her to be patient and everything would be cleared up. Her father also tried to soothe her and calm her down. But this living image purity and integrity could not accept the fact that people could descend to such cruel depths, and life could be such a mental torture. After two days and nights of continuous weeping she fell ill. On the third morning her parents were sitting with her and trying to comfort her, when the Prophet 🌺 came to see her. He told her very gently that if she erred she should ask Allâh for His forgiveness. At this her tears dried up and, and she asked her mother to answer him. But her mother remained silent, sorrowful and tearful. When she saw that her mother was speechless she appealed to her father, Abu Bakr Siddique 🌺 to speak to Muhammad 🌺, but he too did not say anything. Finally she spoke to her husband and said that if she denied she was guilty, nobody would believe her; but she was innocent and only Allâh 🌺 knew it. The best answer to these accusations was to quote the answer of the father of Yusuf ,

> "So (for me) patience is most fitting. And it is Allâh Whose help
> can be sought against that (lie) which you describe." (12:18)

She was so disturbed that even though she tried very hard, she just
could not remember the name of Ya'aqub 🕮, the father of Yusuf 🕮.
At precisely this moment, the *Âyât* of announcing her innocence were
revealed to the Prophet 鑾.

When the revelation was over his brow was full of beads of
perspiration from the exertion; he then turned to 'Aishah with a smile
and started reciting the *Âyât*,

> "Verily, those who brought forth the slander are a group among
> you. Consider it not a bad thing for you. Nay, it is good for you.
> Unto every man among them will be paid that which he earned
> of the sin, and as for him among them who had the greater
> share therein, his will be a great torment. Why then, did not the
> believers, men and women, when you heard it (the slander),
> think good of their own people and say: "This (charge) is an
> obvious lie?" Why did they not produce four witnesses? Since
> they (the slanderers) have not produced witnesses! Then with
> Allâh they are the liars. Had it not been for the Grace of Allâh
> and His Mercy unto you in this world and in the Hereafter, a
> great torment would have touched you for that whereof you
> had spoken. When you were propagating it with your tongues,
> and uttering with your mouths that whereof you had no
> knowledge, you counted it a little thing, while with Allâh it was
> very great. And why did you not, when you heard it, say: "It is
> not right for us to speak of this. Glory be to You (O Allâh)! This
> is a great lie." Allâh forbids you from it and warns you not to
> repeat the like of it forever, if you are believers. And Allâh
> makes the *Âyât* (proofs) plain to you, and Allâh is All-Knowing,
> All-Wise. Verily, those who like that (the crime of) illegal sexual
> intercourse should be propagated among those who believe,
> they will have a painful torment in this world and in the
> Hereafter. And Allâh knows and you know not. And had it not
> been for the Grace of Allâh and His Mercy on you, (Allâh
> would have hastened the punishment upon you). And that

Allâh is full of kindness, Most Merciful. O you who believe! Follow not the footsteps of *Shaitân*. And whosoever follows the footsteps of *Shaitân*, then, verily, he commands *Al-Fahshâ'* (illegal sexual intercourse), and *Al-Munkar* (evil and wicked deeds). And had it not been for the Grace of Allâh and His Mercy on you, not one of you would ever have been pure from sins. But Allâh purifies (guides to Islâm) whom He wills, and Allâh is All-Hearer, All-Knower." (24:11-21)

Her parents were overpowered by a proud sense of relief; pride that their daughter had been honored with a Qur'ânic revelation, and relief that she was acquitted of any wrongdoing. They asked their daughter to rise and thank her husband, but 'Aishah ﷻ promptly replied that she was grateful to her Allâh ﷻ for He had revealed Qur'ânic *Âyât* in her honor. And these would be recited until the Day of Judgment. This episode is known in Islâmic History as the Event of *Ufuk*.

❀❀❀❀❀

After this incident the Prophet's respect for 'Aishah ﷻ increased even more. 'Amr bin 'Aas once asked Muhammad ﷺ who he loved most in this world, and he replied that he loved 'Aishah ﷻ more than anyone else. Then he asked him about the men folk. And the Prophet ﷺ answered that he loved Abu Bakr Siddique ﷺ the most. On one occasion 'Umar ﷺ told his daughter Hafsah not to try and compete with 'Aishah ﷻ as Muhammad ﷺ respected her and valued her very highly. One of the reasons for this was her mastery and knowledge of the decrees and articles of faith as well as her brilliant interpretation of Islâmic law.

The Prophet ﷺ loved to listen to 'Aishah ﷻ talking and always smiled when she spoke. He always tried to please her. On one *'Eid* day there were some Africans displaying their skill with spears; 'Aishah ﷻ wanted to watch this sport, so the Prophet ﷺ stood in front of her so she could enjoy herself and not be seen. And he did not move until she tired of it. Often just to entertain themselves they would narrate stories to each other. The Prophet ﷺ told her the story of a man called Kharâfah whom the *Jinn* had taken away. 'Aishah ﷻ narrated a detailed story about eleven ladies who were friends and how each of them described her husband. The Prophet ﷺ listened intently as she spoke.

The eleven women agreed that they would be frank and not conceal anything about their husbands. The first one said that her husband was like a piece of camel meat placed on top of a mountain - there was no means by which one could reach it; and in any case it was not anyone's to take.

The second one said there was so much to say about her husband that if she started she didn't know what she would leave out; it was really better not to start.

The third friend said that her husband had such a foul temper that if she spoke against him he would immediately divorce her, and if she didn't that would be another problem. It was as if she was married, yet not married.

Now it was the turn of the fourth friend. She said her husband was like the nights of Hijâz, neither too cold nor too warm, he had a very balanced temperament.

The fifth lady said her husband was like a cheetah in the house and lion outside; if he gave his word he never broke it, and did not even need to be reminded about it.

The sixth lady said her husband never followed the middle path in anything. When he started eating he ate up everything that was set before him; the same with any drink that was there. Even when he slept, he would pull the whole sheet to cover himself. He would not even ask how his wife was managing.

The seventh one said her husband was a useless man who had a vile temper. In his rage he could break a person's head or crush his bones.

The eighth lady said her husband was as soft and delicate as a bunny rabbit to the touch, and he smelt like the sweet-smelling jasmine.

The ninth wife was very happy describing her husband; she said that he was tall, lived in a huge mansion, and was a very open-hearted and generous man.

The tenth friend said her husband was better than all those described, he was a very wealthy man who owned many camels. He was so hospitable that he entertained frequently, and took pleasure in slaughtering his camels for his guests.

The eleventh lady was very proud of her husband, Abu Zara'a, because he was rich and had loaded her with gifts of jewelry. His smiling and pleasant face kept her happy. He first saw her when she was just a shepherd's daughter, but he brought her into a home, which was rich in grains, and had plenty of livestock, camels and horses. There was plenty on all sides, and a pleasant atmosphere; even if she slept late in the morning he would never disturb her. His mother was a very great lady and also very well to do. She had lots of clothes and a large house. His son took up very little space and ate only the best of delicacies, which was goat's meat. His favorite daughter was well mannered and obedient to her parents. Abu Zara'a's maidservant was a loyal woman who did not carry tales about the happenings in the house; she was very faithful and hones and kept the house clean and tidy. And so the story went on and on.

The Prophet listened to 'Aishah 🌸, totally engrossed and then told her that he was as good a husband for her as Abu Zara'a was for Umm Zara'a. But all this pleasant entertainment could not distract Muhammad 🌸 from his duty to Allâh 🌸. Just at the moment when he was enjoying himself, the *Mu'aththin's* call to prayer would be heard, and immediately he would rise and prepare to go the mosque. 'Aishah 🌸 said that it seemed as if he did not even know his family or friends; the love for Allâh 🌸 had priority over all other affections and interests.

"How perfect Allâh is and I praise Him. How perfect Allâh is, the Supreme."

Another incident which brought the blessings of revelation occurred on a journey when 'Aishah 🌸 was travelling with the Prophet 🌸. Her father and many Companions had accompanied them. They camped at a place in the desert and once again 'Aishah's 🌸 necklace fell off. Some of the companions were sent to search for it, but it could not be found. The Prophet 🌸 was resting in his tent, when the call for morning prayers was given. But there was no water for their ablutions. The Companions were worried about the morning prayers, and they said that 'Aishah 🌸 was responsible for this predicament. Abu Bakr Siddique 🌸 curtly rebuked his daughter for creating a situation, which might lead to the *Fajr* prayers being missed. Exactly at this moment this *Âyât* was revealed to the Prophet 🌸,

"And if you are ill, or on a journey, or one of you comes after
answering the call of nature, or you have been in contact with
women (by sexual relations) and you find no water, perform
Tayammum[1] with clean earth and rub therewith your face and
hands. Truly, Allâh is Ever Oft-Pardoning, Oft-Forgiving." (4:43)

Immediately the very same people who had been criticizing and
complaining about 'Aishah ﷺ started praising her and expressed their
appreciation and thanks for such a great favor Allâh ﷻ granted
because of her. The noted Companion, Aseed bin Hudhair ﷺ, said that
the family of Abu Bak Siddique ﷺ had often been responsible for the
many favors and blessings bestowed by Allâh ﷻ. Abu Bakr Siddique
ﷺ himself who just a few minutes earlier had been rebuking his
daughter, now was full of smiles. He said he had not realized until
that moment how pleased Allâh ﷻ was with her, that he had revealed
such *Âyât* which would be a source of blessings for the Muslim
Ummah until the Day of Judgment. He prayed for a long and happy
life for her, as she had been a source of great ease and comfort for all
followers of Islâm. After the prayer when the camels were ready for
departure, the necklace was found under one of them.

❁❁❁❁❁

By the ninth year after Hijrah, the might of Islâm had spread over
most of the Arabian Peninsula. The newly founded centre of Islâm,
Al-Madinah, had become a flourishing city-state. Some of the wives of
the Prophet ﷺ had been used to a luxurious life style before marriage,
and when they saw that there were riches and comforts to be had,
they presented a request for their allowances to be suitably reviewed
and increased. This desire of his wives for worldly comforts disturbed
the Prophet ﷺ. He declared that for one month he would separate
himself from his wives, and he went into seclusion in the little room
above the apartment of 'Aishah. During this period he was suffering
from an injury after having fallen from his horse. Naturally this
caused a furor among the households. After 29 days he came down to

---

[1] Striking your hand on earth and passing the palm of each on the back of the
other and then blowing off dust from them and then wiping your face with
them; this is called *Tayammum*. (*Editor's note*)

'Aishah's apartment, and told her that she could make her choice after consulting her parents; either she could choose him and a life of hardship and near starvation, or she could leave him and lead a life of comfort and ease. 'Aishah 🌸 had no doubt whatsoever in her mind; she immediately answered that both she and her parents would willingly sacrifice their lives for him if the need arose. She said there was no need to consult her parents and she would prefer life with him to the world and its attractions and temptations. A beautiful smile lit up his face. And then Allâh 🌸 revealed the following *Âyât*,

> "O Prophet (🌸)! Say to your wives: 'If you desire the life of this world, and its glitter, them come! I will make a provision for you and set you free in a handsome manner (divorce). But if you desire Allâh And His Messenger, and the Home of the hereafter, then verily, Allâh has prepared for the good-doers among you an enormous reward.'" (33:28-29)

After telling him what she felt about the matter, 'Aishah 🌸 very naively asked him to keep it a secret as she wanted to see what the others would say, uninfluenced by her decision. He told her, smiling very gently, that he had been sent as a teacher and not as a dictator or oppressor by Allâh 🌸. Finally, all the wives took the same decision as 'Aishah 🌸, and the wave of tension which had had Al-Madinah in its grip changed; and the same era of joy, peace and tranquillity returned.

There are two recorded incidents when 'Aishah 🌸 herself saw the Angel Jibril 🌸 personally.

🌸🌸🌸🌸🌸

On one occasion, 'Aishah 🌸 saw the Prophet 🌸 with his hands on the mane of a horse talking to the rider. She asked him who he was; the Prophet 🌸 sounded rather surprised and asked if she had seen him. Then he told her that it was the Angel Jibril 🌸 in vision of a human and he requested that his greetings be conveyed to her. She prayed spontaneously that Allâh 🌸 should give a good reward to the honored guest and to his noble host.

🌸🌸🌸🌸🌸

Anas 🕯 narrates how once the Prophet 🕯 was praying in 'Aishah's apartment, when she saw a stranger standing outside the door. She informed him, and he finished his prayers and stepped out. Who should he see but the Angel Jibril 🕯. Muhammad 🕯 requested him to enter, but the Angel replied that they did not enter places where there were dogs or pictures. When the Prophet 🕯 looked around he saw a puppy in a corner of the room; when he was chased out, the Angel Jibril 🕯 entered.

'Aishah 🕯 attained a lofty status because of the knowledge and wisdom with which she had been blessed. She was consulted by the other Companions and women Companions on the finer points of religion. Many of the traditions and authentic *Ahâdith* originate from her. From among the many Companions associated with the Prophet 🕯, there are only seven noble ones to whom thousands of *Ahâdith* are attributed. Among these are-

1. Abu Hurairah 'Abdur-Rahman bin Sakhar Dosi 🕯 - (5374 *Ahâdith*)

2. 'Abdullâh bin 'Umar bin Khattâb 🕯 - (2630 *Ahâdith*)

3. 'Aishah 🕯 - (2210 *Ahâdith*)

4. 'Abdullâh bin 'Abbâs 🕯 - (1660 *Ahâdith*)

5. Jâbir bin 'Abdullâh Ansâri 🕯 - (1540 *Ahâdith*)

6. Sa'ad bin Mâlik Abu Saeed Khudri 🕯 - (1540 *Ahâdith*)

7. Anas bin Mâlik 🕯 - (2286 *Ahâdith*)

Imâm Thahbi wrote that 'Aishah 🕯 was superior to all other women in her knowledge and wisdom. She was a theologian of the highest order. And he was just in his evaluation; after all she was born and nurtured under the tutelage of a father liked Abu Bakr Siddique 🕯, spent her married life with the Prophet 🕯 from a very tender age. She imbibed divinely inspired knowledge and wisdom from the very fountainhead of Prophethood; she was an eyewitness to the problems and questions that the divine revelations answered. Her apartment was the centre where *Âyât* were revealed by the divine Mercy of Allâh 🕯. Thus she was given the title of 'Horizon of the Ladies of Islâm'.

During the caliphate of the *Khulfâ-u-Râshideen*,[1] her *Fatwâ*[2] was accepted. Once someone asked Masrooq if 'Aishah 🕮 had mastery over the *Shari'ah* laws regarding inheritance. He swore that he had personally seen revered Companions asking her questions about the finer points of the laws of inheritance. 'Urwah bin Zubair 🕮, her sister's son often visited her to discuss religious issues with her. Other Companions envied him as he could freely approach her at any time to clear his doubts as he was the son of her sister Asmâ' 🕮, and thus her *Mahram*.[3]

🌸🌸🌸🌸🌸

The Prophet 🕮 loved deeply and respected her because of her command over religious matters and other praiseworthy qualities. On one occasion when the Prophet 🕮 was ill, 'Aishah 🕮 also was not feeling well. The Prophet 🕮 said that if she died before him he would personally bathe her and shroud her and lower her into her grave and pray for her. She lightheartedly replied that it seemed as if he would celebrate her death; and she told him that in case she died before him, he should bring a new wife into her apartment. The Prophet 🕮 smiled at this; but it was during this illness that he left this world to join his Lord.

🌸🌸🌸🌸🌸

'Aishah 🕮 narrated that she was proud that when it was her turn, in her apartment, in her lap, the Prophet 🕮 passed away. Her brother, 'Abdur-Rahmân came in during his last moments with a *Miswak*[4] in his hand; the Prophet 🕮 looked longingly at it. 'Aishah 🕮 understood what he wanted, and asked him if she could offer one to him. When he nodded, she took it from her brother; since it was hard she softened it with her teeth and offered it to him. He cleaned his teeth; and dipping his hand frequently into a bowl of water kept near him, he

---

[1] The first four caliphs after the Prophet; Abu Bakr Siddique, 'Umar bin Khattab, 'Uthmân bin Affân, Ali bin Abi Tâlib رضي الله عنهم.

[2] A judicial decree or verdict.

[3] Certain relatives with whom marriage is forbidden

[4] Twig of a tree used to clean the teeth and mouth.

kept wiping his face again and again, repeating the words,

"There is none worthy of worship but Allâh. Verily, death has pains."

Then he pointed upward with his hand and said,

"Toward the best friend".

Thus the soul soared up from the prison of the body.

Previously 'Aishah 🌺 had a dream that three moons descended into her apartment. When the Prophet 🌺 passed away he was buried in her apartment. Then her father told her that part of her dream come true that day - the first moon irradiated her apartment. Later, her father was buried next to the Prophet 🌺, and still later 'Umar Farooq ⚭. Thus, the prophecy of her dream was fulfilled.

Imam Thahbi quoted a saying of the Prophet 🌺 that a Prophet's soul leaves its body in the place that he likes the best. Thus it is proven he died in his favorite place, the apartment of 'Aishah 🌺.

❀❀❀❀❀

She left this earthly existence for Paradise in the year 58 *Hijirah* on the 17th of Ramadhân at the age of 66,

"To Allâh we belong and to Allâh we return."

She was buried in the graveyard at Al-Madinah, *Jannatul Baqi'*. Abu Hurairah ⚭ led the funeral prayers. 'Abdullâh bin Muhammad bin 'Abdur-Rahmân bin Abu Bakr Siddique and 'Abdullâh bin 'Abdur-Rahmân bin Abu Bakr Siddique رضي الله عنهم placed her gently into her grave.

> "O the one in complete rest and satisfaction! Come back to your Lord – well-pleased (yourself) and well-pleasing (unto Him)! Enter you then among My (honored) servants, and enter you My Paradise." (89:27-30)

Hafsah bint 'Umar رضي الله عنها

One day the Angel Jibril عليه السلام visited the Prophet ﷺ and narrated about Hafasah رضي الله عنها :

"She is often fasting and worshiping lady and she will be your wife in Paradise too."

(Mustadrak Hakim 4/15)

Hafsah bint 'Umar رضي الله عنها

Hafsah ﷺ was the daughter of 'Umar Farooq ﷺ, and the niece of another famous *Sahâbi* (Companion), 'Uthmân bin Maz'oon ﷺ who was fortunate to have the Prophet ﷺ lead the funeral prayer and bury him himself in *Jannatul Baqi'*- the first *Sahâbi* to be buried there. Her uncle from the paternal side, a martyr and a General of the Muslim army was Zaid bin Khattâb. 'Umar Farooq ﷺ acknowledged the superiority of his brother when he said that Zaid ﷺ accepted Islâm before him and attained martyrdom before him. 'Abdullâh bin 'Umar رضي الله عنهما, who was declared by the Prophet ﷺ to be an excellent man, was her brother.

Hafsah ﷺ was an extremely religious lady who used to spend her time in prayer and fasting. An excellent writer and orator, an ardent follower of Islâm, She could number seven of her family members among the warriors at Badr: her father 'Umar bin Khattâb, her paternal uncle Zaid bin Khattâb, her husband Khanees bin Hathâfah, three of her mother's brothers, 'Uthmân bin Maz'oon, Qudâmah bin Maz'oon, and 'Abdullâh bin Maz'oon, and Sâ'ib bin 'Abdullâh bin Maz'oon رضي الله عنهم. All of them had taken part in the Battle of Badr and fought so courageously in the cause of Islâm that the Prophet ﷺ said that they would surely enter Paradise.

Hafsah ﷺ had such noble qualities and such an amiable nature that 'Aishah ﷺ remarked that among wives of the Prophet ﷺ only she could compare with her. Her life is exemplary, brought up as she was by a Companion of the caliber of 'Umar bin Khattâb ﷺ.

❀❀❀❀❀

Five years before the Prophet ﷺ was chosen to be the Messenger of Allâh the renovation of the Ka'bah took place. When it came to the point when the Black Stone had to be re-installed in the walls of the Ka'bah, an argument erupted. This argument could very well have turned into a lengthy series of battles among the tribes, each of whom wanted to have the honor of installing it into the wall of the Ka'bah. Finally it was decided that the matter would be left to chance! Whoever entered the House of Allâh first in the morning would install the Black Stone.

Though Muhammad ﷺ had not yet attained the status of a Prophet, from his early years, he was well known for his honesty, integrity and wisdom. So when he entered first, the tribal chiefs were happy, and agreed that he would have the honor. But he was too wise to accept a spur of the moment decision that might have set off serious complications and rivalries in the future. He stunned the people by asking for a large sheet; picking up the Black Stone, he placed it in the centre of the sheet. Then he asked each of the chiefs to hold the edges of the sheet and raise it. Picking up the Black Stone, he placed it in the niche in the wall. Thus, a thorny issue was very simply yet brilliantly resolved. Word of the wise yet simple decision taken by Muhammad ﷺ became the subject of conversation everywhere. It was during this period that a baby girl, Hafsah ﮩ, was born in the family of a great warrior and wrestler, 'Umar bin Khattâb ﷺ who was well known for his martial skills. In her growing years she was brought up in a completely Islâmic environment, both her parents and her aunts and uncles having already converted to the new religion. When she was old enough, she was married to Khanees bin Hazafah Sehmi. He was influenced by the teaching of Abu Bakr Siddique ﷺ and had accepted Islâm.

When the leaders of the Quraish first heard about Khanees bin Hazafah Sehmi ﷺ becoming a Muslim they were enraged, and he also was subjected to the worst cruelty and oppression possible. He therefore joined the caravan of the persecuted migrants leaving for Abyssina. It is said this was around the time when the Prophet ﷺ had not yet started educating the new converts. But Khanees bin Hazafah Sehmi ﷺ was very homesick there and just could not settle down. He sorely missed Makkah where he spent his childhood and youth and decided to return. Again he faced the sufferings that were inflicted on the followers of the new religion. After some time the call was given by the Prophet ﷺ to migrate to Al-Madinah.

Khanees ﷺ answered the call, thus becoming one of the few faithful followers who went through the rigors of migrating twice in obedience to the Prophet's call. This time around he was with his wife Hafsah ﷺ. Here he was welcomed by Rafâ'h bin 'Abdul Manzar ﷺ and stayed in his house as his guest. After practically all the Muslims had reached Al-Madinah, the Prophet ﷺ also undertook the journey. He entrusted all the things that the people left with him to 'Ali ﷺ for safekeeping. Escaping the watchful eyes of the enemy who had surrounded his house, he reached the house of Abu Bakr Siddique ﷺ; accompanied by him he set out on his historic journey. The first stop they made was for three days in the cave of Thour; then they continued on the second lap of the journey. The disbelievers tried their very best to track him, but they failed. Abu Jahl, one of his greatest enemies set a very large reward on his head - a hundred camels - but met with no success. If Allâh Almighty wills to protect someone, no earthly enemy can cause him any harm.

On reaching Al-Madinah, the Prophet ﷺ strengthened the bonds of brotherhood between the migrants and their hosts, the *Ansâr*. For instance, Abu 'Abbâs bin Jaber Ansâi and Khanees bin Hazafah Sehmi رضي الله عنهما were declared brothers in Islâm. Both were students, as it, in the best school of all - the school of the Prophet ﷺ - and both were accomplished horse riders in the battlefield.

Both Khanees and Hafsah رضي الله عنهما loved the new life in Al-Madinah. Hafsah ﷺ made special arrangements to memorize the *Âyât* of the Qur'ân as and when they were revealed. Then she would give deep thought and attention to the meaning and interpretation of the *Âyât*. Her husband meanwhile was enthusiastically preparing himself for *Jihâd* and improving his martial skills. He was constantly alert to the movements of the enemy and was ever ready to meet them head on.

News came that the Quraish of Makkah – after making elaborate preparations for a war to wipe out the Muslims – were marching towards Al-Madinah. Abu Jahl had sworn to reach the plains of Badr, camp there for three days, slaughter camels and have an orgy of dance and music before attacking the small band of Muslim soldiers. He believed that once people heard of his huge forces, no Arab tribe would have the courage to face them. Even if the puny Muslim army dared to confront him, he would teach them a lesson they would never forget.

The heavily armed forces of Abu Jahl set out; the Muslims under the leadership of the Prophet, practically unarmed, reached Badr and set up camp taking control of the only source of water. All they had with them was their strong faith in the Allâh. When the army of Abu Jahl was sighted, the Prophet ﷺ prayed to the Almighty that if this small band of the faithful were destroyed there would be no one left on the face of the earth to pray to Him.

Khanees bin Hazafah, 'Umar Farooq رضي الله عنهما, and the maternal and paternal uncles of Hafsah ﴿ and her cousin were all part of this courageous band. Her husband was determined to win the battle for Allâh and bring to dust the pomp and grandeur of Abu Jahl's forces. Finally the forces met and Khanees bin Hazafah ﴾ went tearing through the ranks of the enemy. He was seriously wounded, but most of the leaders of the disbelievers were killed, and Islâm triumphed. It is one of the greatest battles fought in history where a handful of unarmed and outnumbered men routed a powerful and well-equipped army.

The Prophet ﷺ stayed at Badr for three days, while the injured were attended to; then he led the victorious and jubilant Muslim forces back to Al-Madinah. When Hafsah ﴿ heard of her husband's heroic deeds she was very happy, and praised his valour in battle; but she also realized that in his condition he would need the best care possible. She immediately recited the *Âyah* of *Surat Al-Anfâl* which were revealed in connection with the Battle of Badr,

> "Allâh made it only as glad tidings, as that your hearts be at
> rest therewith. And there is no victory except from Allâh.
> Verily, Allâh is All-Mighty, All-Wise." (8:10)

These Words of the Allâh Almighty promising victory inspired her and she happily turned to the task of nursing her husband back to health. But it was not to be, for he was to be blessed with an exalted position. A few days later he succumbed to his injuries and joined the ranks of those who are blessed with eternal life. When the Prophet ﷺ heard of his passing away he arranged for him to be buried in *Jannatul Baqi*, next to the uncle of Hafsah ﴿; he personally led the funeral prayers. Hafsah ﴿ was, naturally, grief stricken, but being a true believer she respectfully submitted to the Will of Allâh. She turned towards her Maker and courageously gave herself even more than before to prayer and meditation. She was at this time barely twenty-one years old.

🏵🏵🏵🏵🏵

For her father it was very painful to see his daughter in this state. Her silent courage under these circumstances, her patient prayers and her study of the Qur'ân irradiated her countenance with a spiritual beauty and innocence, but there was also a sadness because of the harsh loneliness that had become part of her life. After deep thought 'Umar Farooq 📿 decided to approach 'Uthmân bin Affân 📿, whose wife Ruqayyah 📿 the Prophet's daughter, had passed away. He thought that sharing a common bond would help to alleviate their sorrow in losing worthy spouses. So, having taken this decision he went direct to 'Uthmân 📿. After the formal greeting and expression of condolences on his wife's death he broached the topic closest to his heart. 'Uthmân 📿 lowered his eyes and then after a few moments pause, he said he needed time to think it over.

'Umar Farooq 📿 met him again after a few days and asked him if he had thought over the proposal. 'Uthmân 📿 answered that he was not presently planning on marriage. From there he went to Abu Bakr Siddique 📿 and offered him his daughter in marriage. He too lowered his gaze and did not answer him. Imâm Bukhâri in his book of *Hadith*, *As-Sahih Al-Bukhâri*, has given a whole chapter to the topic of an honorable man offering his sister or daughter in marriage.

'Umar Farooq 📿 was very upset because both the men he approached had either avoided or refused marriage to his daughter. He was confident of a willing and joyful acceptance but things turned out otherwise. He was very upset and worried at the turn of events; in a sense it was an affront to him and his position as a sincere defender of the faith. People, he thought, would consider it an honor to have an alliance by marriage with him. With this grievance he went to the Prophet 📿 and explained to him the position he found himself in. The Prophet 📿 smilingly answered that he should neither grieve nor worry, and Allâh willing he would find a man better than 'Uthmân 📿 for Hafsah 📿, and 'Uthmân 📿 in turn, would find for himself a better woman than Hafsah 📿.

'Umar Farooq 📿 was pleased on hearing this from the Prophet 📿 himself, but also a little perplexed over who such a man could be? A few days later the Prophet 📿 married his daughter, Umm Kulthom 📿 to

'Uthmân ﷺ. 'Umar Farooq ﷺ realized that one part of the prediction had come true, but he continued to puzzle over the second half of the statement. Who could possibly be a better man than 'Uthmân ﷺ? One day the Prophet ﷺ proposed marriage to Hafsah ﷺ. 'Umar Farooq ﷺ could not believe his ears; his daughter would have the honor of joining the select band of women who were known as the Mothers of the believers! 'Aishah and Saudah رضي الله عنهما were already part of the Prophet's household. It seemed too good to be true. Thus Hafsah ﷺ was joined in marriage to the Prophet ﷺ in the 3rd year after Hijrah, before the Battle of Uhud. She was about twenty-two years old at the time. On seeing off his daughter to her husband's house, 'Umar Farooq ﷺ told her that she should never try to compete with 'Aishah ﷺ, who was the Prophet's favourite and better than her in many respects. He said she should respect her sincerely and live happily as a member of the first and foremost family.

Sa'eed bin Musayyab, a learned scholar, states that the Prophet's prediction that he was a better husband for Hafsah ﷺ than 'Uthmân ﷺ was proved right, as was his statement that Umm Kulthom ﷺ was a better wife for 'Uthmân ﷺ than Hafsah ﷺ. After the marriage Abu Bakr Siddique ﷺ met with 'Umar Farooq ﷺ and told him the truth was that the Prophet ﷺ had mentioned to him that he planned to marry Hafsah ﷺ. That was the reason he had remained silent, as it would not have been proper to betray his confidence. If matters were different he would have been only too happy to accept her hand in marriage. 'Umar Farooq ﷺ expressed his happiness by quoting the following *Âyah,*

> "This is by the Grace of my Lord – to test me whether I am grateful or ungrateful! And whoever is grateful, truly, his gratitude is for himself; and whoever is ungrateful, (it is for the loss of only himself). Certainly my Lord is Rich, Bountiful." (27:40)

✿✿✿✿✿

After attaining the position of the Mother of the Believers, Hafsah ﷺ became even more absorbed in studying the finer points of religion. She memorized the different *Âyât* as and when they were revealed. She would store in her mind conversations of Muhammad ﷺ which would to a better understanding of Islâm. Often she would discuss any points

that arose in her mind about the *Shari'ah*. Jaber bin 'Abdullâh Ansâri رضي
narrates an incident which was related to him by Umm Mubasher رضي الله
عنها. She and Hafsah رضي الله عنهما, and the Prophet 🕮 were sitting and
chatting together. He said that all the people who had given the pledged
of allegiance at Hudaybiyah under the tree would go to Paradise, and
not to Hell. She asked how that was possible. The Prophet 🕮 got annoyed,
but Hafsah 🕮 did not give up and quoted an *Âyah* from *Surah Maryam*.

"There is not one of you but will pass over it (Hell)." (19:71)

In reply he quoted the very next *Âyah*, also from *Surah Maryam*.

"Then We shall save those who use to fear Allâh and were
dutiful to Him. And We shall leave the wrongdoers therein to
there knees (in Hell)." (19:72)

This news of Hafsah 🕮 disputing with the Prophet 🕮 spread in Al-
Madinah. On that day the Prophet 🕮 was very disturbed; and when
'Umar Farooq ⚜ heard about it he chided his daughter. She replied
that 'Aishah 🕮 too spoke in the same manner to him. Her father again
cautioned her not to compete with 'Aishah 🕮 and maintain a certain
decorum, or else she would bring trouble on herself.

Among the Mothers of the believers, 'Aishah, Umm Habibah, Saudah
and Hafsah رضي الله عنهن all belonged to the tribe of Quraish. The others
came from various other tribes. Everyday after the *'Asr* prayer, the
Prophet 🕮 would visit them all for a little while to see if they needed
anything; the time of the visits was routine and each would wait eagerly
for his arrival. On several occasions, it so happened that he spent more
time with Zainab 🕮. This upset 'Aishah 🕮 and she spoke about it to
Hafsah and Saudah رضي الله عنهما. They got together and found out that a
certain relative had sent Zainab 🕮 a special kind of honey and she used
to offer it to the Prophet 🕮 everyday. This was his favourite and he used
to be delayed in her apartment, enjoying it. 'Aishah 🕮 was so fond of
the Prophet 🕮 that she could not bear for him to be late coming to her
apartment. Because of her regard for him she could not object directly.
So she consulted with the other two – Hafsah and Saudah رضي الله عنهما –
and they decided that when he came to each of them by turn, they
would all say that there was a strange smell emanating from his
mouth. When he heard the same thing from all three of them he

thought it was due to the honey he had, and decided to give it up for good. If this had been an incident in the life of an ordinary person it would have been of no consequence. But this was with the last Prophet of Allâh ﷺ, and his every word and every action would become the law or *Shari'ah* for all Muslims for all time to come. Thus it had a special significance.

So Allâh ﷻ rebuked him in *Âyah* of *Surat At-Tahreem*.

"O Prophet! Why do you forbid (for yourself) that which Allâh has allowed to you, seeking to please your wives? And Allâh is Oft-Forgiving, Most Merciful." (66:1)

It was around the same time that the Prophet ﷺ confided a secret matter to Hafsah ﻬ, and warned her not to speak to anyone about it. But she told 'Aishah ﻬ. Allâh then revealed to the Prophet ﷺ what happened. Allâh revealed this in the following *Âyah* of *Surat At-Tahreem*,

"And when the Prophet disclosed a matter in confidence to one of his wife, then she told it. And Allâh made it known to him; he informed part thereof and left a part. Then when he told her thereof, she said: "Who told you this?" He said: "The All-Knower, the All-Aware has told me." (66:3)

By the year 9th after Hijrah, most of the Peninsula was under the Islâmic government at Al-Madinah; the granaries were full and all the riches were reaching the centre from the different regions of Arabia. Many of the ladies in the household of the Prophet ﷺ had been brought up in the lap of luxury; so when they saw this reign of prosperity, they too put forward demands for an increase in their household allowances. When 'Umar Farooq ﻬ heard of this he was very upset; he told his daughter Hafsah ﻬ that she should ask her father if she needed anything and not make any demands on the Prophet ﷺ. He also advised all the Mothers of the Believers not to make any demands. Umm Salamah ﻬ did not quite like this and felt that he had the habit of interfering in every matter. She told him frankly that he should refrain from meddling in the affairs of the Prophet's wives.

It was at this time that the Prophet ﷺ had fallen from his horse and been injured; keeping all these things in view he decided to go into seclusion and moved to an upper room adjacent to the apartment of

'Aishah 🙵. The whole city was buzzing with the gossip the hypocrites spread saying that he divorced his wives. But actually no such thing happened. All the Companions were disturbed by this situation, but no one had the courage to approach the Prophet 🙵 and talk to him directly. Finally 'Umar Farooq 🙵 known for his forthrightness went to him and asked him if the rumor was true. When he denied it he was delighted. Then he asked if he could announce this good news to the rest of the Muslims. When he received permission, he joyfully informed the community that everything was fine with the Prophet's household. The whole city was relieved that the Messenger of Allâh 🙵 had not been offended in any way. On the twenty-ninth day he came down into the apartment of 'Aishah 🙵. She asked him smilingly why he came down before the month was over. He replied that often the lunar month did consist of only twenty-nine days. Hafsah 🙵 promised her father that she would never ever ask for a raise in her allowance and she stood by her word to the end of her life.

🙵🙵🙵🙵🙵

Hafsah 🙵 died in the year 41ᵗʰ after Hijrah aged fifty-nine. At the time of death she was fasting. The funeral prayers were led by the governor of Al-Madinah, Marwan bin Hakam. Abu Hurairah and Abu Sa'eed Khudri رضى الله عنهما, the eminent Companion of the Prophet 🙵 were among those who carried the shroud to *Jannatul Baqi'*. Her two brothers, 'Abdullâh bin 'Umar and 'Asim bin 'Umar رضى الله عنهما placed her gently into her final resting place. Sâlem bin 'Abdullâh, 'Abdur-Rahman bin 'Abdullâh and Hamza bin 'Abdullâh, all the sons of 'Abdullâh bin 'Umar رضى الله عنهم also attended funeral.

So a righteous and learned writer and reciter of the Noble Qur'ân who devoted herself from her youth to prayer, fasting and meditation passed into history.

These *Âyât* from *Surat Al-Qamar* express an apt tribute to this great Mother of the Believers.

"Verily, the pious will be in the midst of Gradens and Rivers (Paradise). In a seat of truth, near the Omnipotent King." (54:54-55)

Zainab bint Khazeemah رضي الله عنها

The Prophet ﷺ said:

"Allâh has commanded me to marry with the women of Paradise only."

She is the lady who was known as 'The Mother of distressed and needy' because she would give charity to deserving people.

Zainab bint Khazeemah رضي الله عنها

The Prophet ﷺ said that Allâh had ordained that he could marry only those women deserving of Paradise. And Zainab ﷺ was a lady who was known as 'The Mother of the poor and needy because she was the most generous among the ladies of the household.

She was born thirteen years before Muhammad ﷺ was chosen as the Messenger of Allâh. When he declared himself as the chosen Prophet of the Allâh he caused a furor in Makkah. Even those who loved and respected him, those who called him 'Truthful' and 'Trustworthy', turned into enemies who wanted to kill him. But there were some who were fortunate enough to have the sense to answer his call immediately with the pledge of allegiance to Allâh and to him. They called out that they believed and that he was truthful in his claim. Among the righteous band of people who first proclaimed his truthfulness was Zainab bint Khazeemah ﷺ. She had been married to 'Abdullâh bin Jahash ﷺ. This highly respected Companion attained martyrdom during the Battle of Uhud. The widows and orphaned children of the martyred Companion found security with the other Companion who married the widows and took the children under their protection. Thus Zainab bint Khazeemah ﷺ who was heafter the death of her husband attained the enviable position of becoming a wife of the Prophet ﷺ.

The husband of Hamnah bint Jahash ﷺ was also martyred during the Battle of Uhud and she was also grief stricken. Seeing this the Prophet ﷺ said:

"The place a husband held in his wife's heart could not be taken
by any other."

Hamnah told him sighing deeply that it was the thought of the
orphaned children that troubled her most and she asked him to pray
that Allâh ﷺ should give her patience and strength. The Prophet's
prayers for her were accepted and she married the noble Companion
Talhah bin 'Abdullâh ﷺ. He was an ideal husband and a loving father
for the orphaned children of her first husband.

Zainab ﷺ was in the same plight as Hamnah ﷺ, but she did not
appeal to any human being. She entrusted her affairs entirely to Allâh
and devoted herself to prayer and meditation. So when she received a
proposal from the best man possible, the Prophet ﷺ, she was
overjoyed with the good fortune that Allâh had bestowed on her.

The Prophet ﷺ married her with a dowry of four hundred *Dirhams*, and
a apartment was constructed for her near those of Hafsah and 'Aishah
رضي الله عنهما. Thus she joined the selected band of pure and virtuous ladies
of the Prophet's household. Allâh in the Noble Qur'ân speaks of these
ladies of his Prophet's household,

"Allâh wishes only to remove evil deed from you, O member
of the family (of the Prophet), and to purify you with a
thorough purification." (33:33)

And also,

"O wives of the Prophet, You are not like any other women."
(33:32)

Zainab bint Khazeemah ﷺ, even before the advent of Islâm was
known as 'Mother of the distressed and needy'. This was because she
could not bear to see a person hungry or in dire need. She was
eulogized in verse by some of the famous poets of the time.

Ibn Katheer wrote that she earned the title because of her deeds of
charity and generosity.

Qastalâni writes that she was known by this name even during
pre-Islâmic times.

This great quality of generosity became even more pronounced and intense when she converted to Islâm, which has always strongly advocated giving in charity.

The two ladies who were already part of the household – 'Aishah and Hafsah رضي الله عنهما – welcomed this new friend and tried their best to give her their sincere sympathetic companionship. They knew that the Prophet 🌸 married Zainab 🌸 because she was deeply affected by the death of her first husband. Because of the kind behavior of these two noble ladies, her grief was lightened and she felt more at peace. Yet she lived barely eight months after her marriage to the Prophet 🌸. She was just thirty years old when she passed away. The Prophet led the funeral prayers and she was buried in *Jannatul Baqi'*. Khadijah 🌸 was the first wife to have passed away in the lifetime of Muhammad 🌸, and Zainab 🌸 was the second.

Allâh will be pleased with them and they with Him.

Umm Salamah bint Abu Umayyah رضي الله عنها

The Prophet ﷺ said:

"Allâh has commanded me to marry only with the women of Paradise."

Umm Salamah ﷺ participated in Rizwân pledge, therefore, she deserved the Paradise.

Umm Salamah bint Abu Umayyah رضي الله عنها

Her real name was Hind bint Abu Umayyah who became famous by the name Umm Salamah. She was noble by birth, intelligent, learned, wise and skillful. She was first married to 'Abdullâh bin 'Abdul Asad Makhzumi know as Abu Salamah. He was the son of the Prophet's paternal aunt Barrah bint Abdul Muttalib. He too belonged to the select band of people who were the first to accept Islâm. He was known for his integrity, valour, generosity, tolerance and patience. He was the eleventh person to come into the fold of Islâm. He was also the foster brother of the Prophet 鐚 by suckling.

Umm Salamah 鐚 was also one of the earliest converts to Islâm. Her mother was 'Atikah bint 'Amer bin Rabee'ah bin Mâlik bin Khazeemah. Her father Abu Ummayyah bin 'Abdullâh bin 'Amr bin Makhzoom was a very wealthy man and famous throughout the Arab world for his public service and charity. People who traveled with him did not have to carry food and necessities for the journey because they were always treated as his guests, and he bore all the expenses. Umm Salamah 鐚 seemed to have inherited this trait from her father. She was always amiable and kind to her neighbors. When she married the handsome and brave son of the equally wealthy family of Makhzoom, she carried a friendly demeanor of pleasant serenity into her new household. There was an atmosphere of gaiety and love in the home of the newly married couple.

But things changed radically when the couple embraced Islâm. The whole family turned against them; mischievous and wicked elements like Walid bin Mughairah Makhzoomi started creating problems for them. Finally, when matters nearly at their worst, the Prophet ﷺ advised his staunch followers to migrate to Abyssiniah where the Christian King was more tolerant of the new religion. Sixteen people set out on that historic first migration of the followers of Islâm - twelve men and four women.

These were the people who had that honor.

1. 'Uthmân bin 'Affân ؓ

2. Abu Huthaifah bin 'Utbah ؓ

3. Abu Salamah 'Abdullâh bin 'Abdul-Asad Makhzumi ؓ

4. 'Amir bin Rabee'ah ؓ

5. Zubair bin 'Awâm ؓ

6. Mus'ab bin 'Umair ؓ

7. 'Abdur-Rahmân bin 'Auf ؓ

8. 'Uthmân bin 'Auf ؓ

9. Abu Sibrah bin Abi Raham ؓ

10. Hâtib bin 'Amr ؓ

11. Sohail bin Wahab ؓ

12. 'Abdullâh bin Mas'ood ؓ

The following four noble ladies were also part of this migrant group.

1. Ruqiyyah ؓ bint Muhammad ﷺ, wife of 'Uthmân bin 'Affân ؓ

2. Sehlah bint Sohail ؓ, wife of Abu Huzifah bin 'Utbah ؓ

3. Umm Salamah ؓ, wife of Abu Salamah ؓ

4. Lailah bint Abi Hashmah ؓ, wife of 'Amer bin Rabee'ah ؓ

When this caravan reached the shores of the ocean two trading vessels were waiting for departure. They got on board and set sail for Abyssiniah. The next group of immigrants that left for Abyssiniah consisted of eighty-three men and nineteen ladies. Ja'far bin Abi Tâlib ؓ was among them.

Umm Salamah 🌸 narrated that life was very peaceful in Abyssiniah, free of all religious persecution. She first gave birth to a daughter, whom they named Zainab. Then she had a son Salamah, hence her name and her husband's name.

The next child was also a son, 'Umar. Finally they had another daughter who they named Durrah. So life was very smooth and time passed uneventfully, in peace and happiness. The ruler of Abyssiniah, Najâshi, was very kind to the migrants. When the leaders of the disbelievers heard this news they were enraged and thought that the Muslims were becoming a real source of danger for them. They decided to take strong measures to stem the riding tide of Islâm.

After a great deal of thought they evolved a plan of action. They sent the leading politician of the Arab world, 'Amr bin 'Aas and 'Abdullâh bin Abi Rabee'ah with expensive gifts for Najâshi, in order to persuade him to hand over the Muslim migrants to their custody. Before meeting the ruler personally, they met the important advisers and ministers laden with gifts for them as well. This was to lay the ground for the final talks with Najâshi, himself. They presented their viewpoint and arguments for demanding custody of the migrants very strongly, and appealed to them for help in persuading the ruler. The ministers assured them of full cooperation and help.

Finally, they presented themselves before Najâshi, and after offering their gifts and respectful salutations, they proceeded to present their case. The refugee Muslims who were persecuted for their religious beliefs they called crazy rebels, who were sowing discord within families and tribes because of their 'heretic' views. Fathers were opposed to sons and brother was fighting brother. They were breaking away from the traditions and beliefs of their forefathers, and were following some weird new faith. They had been allowed to live peacefully because of the generosity and liberal views of Najâshi, but they were not to be trusted. They could cause trouble in his country as well, since they did not believe in the Christian faith either. The best solution would be to hand them over to the Quraish, who knew best how to deal with them.

Najâshi looked towards his courtiers for their opinion. They agreed with the viewpoint of the Quraish that this was an internal dispute and the political refugees should be handed over to the representatives of the Quraish. Najâshi was a fair minded, far-sighted and frank man. So he called for the leader of the refugees to present their case. The delegation chose Ja'far bin Abi Tâlib ﷺ as their leader.

When the delegation reached the court of Najâshi, they wished him and took their seats. 'Amr bin 'Aas immediately found fault with them, saying they were too arrogant; they should have followed the formal protocol of the court and prostrated themselves before the ruler. Najâshi asked them why they had not observed the decorum of the royal court. Ja'far ﷺ replied that they believed that they should prostrate only before the Creator and not before any of the Almighty's creations. This would amount to worship of a being other than Allâh.

Najâshi replied that he heard that they adopted a strange new religion. Ja'far ﷺ explained to him eloquently the tenets of Islâm.

He said,

"Your Royal Highness, we were an uncivilized people who used to worship idols, eat dead carcasses, and have drinking orgies. Internal and tribal feuds were common with us and these could go on for a hundred years. We did not maintain good relations with our own kith and kin; we forgot that our neighbors had rights upon us. The law of the jungle prevailed, and might was right. In short we lived like animals. Then Allâh sent a Messenger to guide us to the right path. He was one of our own from a tribe and a family known to us. We all acknowledged that he was an exceptional man of integrity, honesty and modesty. He invited us to worship Allâh, to always speak the truth and be honest in our dealings and keep our promises. He taught us what is lawful and to abstain from what is not lawful. He said the orphans, the poor, the distressed and women – all had rights in society, and it was wrong to usurp these rights. He taught us the values of chastity and virtue, and asked us to abstain from slander and backbiting. He said we should remember Allâh in prayer and fasting; we should pay our poor dues so that there could be equitable distribution of money. And soon it was as if we became a new people. Lawlessness, crime, debauchery and constant feuding –

all were forgotten. The same people now became a caring community; each wanted for his brother what he wanted for himself.

The nation turned against us because of our virtuous behavior and started torturing us. But we were not ready to sink into that morass of evil again, and when persecution reached its peak, we decided to flee and come to you, as we had heard that your rule was just, and you were tolerant, sympathetic and hospitable to refugees."

Najâshi then answered that he had heard their Prophet received revelations from his Allâh, and that he would like to hear to some of these.

Ja'far ﷺ took advantage of the opportunity to recite *Surah Maryam* in such a heartrending manner that Najâshi started shaking, tears started coursing down his cheeks and his beard. The courtiers were speechless. Finally, gaining control, Najâshi said that it seemed these *Âyât* and those in the Bible had the same Divine origin. The people in his court were stunned and they thought to themselves that the same magic that Muhammad ﷺ had used to bewitch and entrance people in Makkah was now working on their ruler as well. Najâshi then told the emissaries of the Quraish that these were people of good character and could continue to live in Abyssiniah as long as they wished. Further, he would continue to give every kind of protection necessary, and the delegation from Makkah could leave carrying back their gifts. If someone gave him even a mountain of gold in exchange for these righteous people he would not surrender them. 'Amr bin 'Aas and 'Abdullâh bin Abi Rabee'ah felt really small after this open snub, and started looking at each other. How would they face their leaders after the failure of their mission?

All their plotting came to nothing. They then left, but not for home; they could not give up so easily and started discussing alternative strategies to gain their ends.

Finally, 'Amr came up with an idea. He said he would tell Najâshi something that would really enrage him. He felt confident that this scheme could not fail. 'Abdullâh asked him what he would tell the king.

'Amr said that the Muslims looked upon 'Isa ﷺ as a human being and the servant of Allâh, but the Christians called him the son of God. This new revelation, they thought, would certainly change the attitude of Najâshi. He said the whole court would be mesmerized by this new revelation.

After reaching Najâshi's court the next morning, they greeted him and plunged in with the information, they said they had forgotten to bring to his attention. These Muslims were so insolent that they refused to acknowledge 'Isa ﷺ as the son of God and claimed that he was an ordinary mortal and servant of Allâh. They requested the king to call the Muslims and ask them what their opinion about 'Isa ﷺ was.

The Muslims were summoned to the court and questioned about the status of 'Isa ﷺ. Ja'far ؓ replied that their Prophet ﷺ told them that he was the servant and Messenger of Allâh; and he was also the spirit and Word of Allâh. Najâshi was so happy to hear this complete answer that he beat his palm on the floor, and exclaimed that what he had heard was exactly right and there was absolutely no difference between this statement and what 'Isa ﷺ had stated about himself. Then he told the migrant Muslims that they could live with peace and goodwill in his country; no one could dare to harm them in even the smallest degree. Then he turned to the representatives of the Quraish and said they could return to their country with their gifts; by the grace of Allâh he and his people had enough and more.

The embarrassed delegates returned empty-handed, mission unfulfilled! Umm Salamah ؓ has written about this memorable first migration of the Muslims, and described the greatness of Najâshi in such a moving manner that it has become an integral and important part of Islâmic history.

❀❀❀❀❀

Umm Salamah ؓ narrates that their life in Abyssiniah was very peaceful and Najâshi was very kind, but all the same they were homesick for Makkah. They continued longing for the time when peace would finally prevail so they could return to their beloved country. One day news reached that 'Umar bin Khattâb ؓ accepted Islâm and that the conditions in Makkah had changed completely. It was said that because of the authority and influence of 'Umar the persecution of Muslims came to an end. They were all so excited at this good news, writes Umm Salamah 🌸 that they decided to set out for their homes. 'Uthmân bin 'Affân 🌸 also set out with them with his family. On reaching Makkah they realized it had been just a rumor and things were much worse than before. Muslims were the targets of worse crimes and persecution. But it was too late.

An accepted tradition states what had actually happened. The disbelievers heard the Prophet 🌺 reciting *Âyât* from the Noble Qur'ân, and prostrated involuntarily at one *Âyah* with him. Like all rumors this too ballooned into news that the Quraish had converted to Islâm. In reality this was not so.

Weary of the constant problems they faced, they decided to leave for Abyssiniah again. It was at this time that the Prophet 🌺 ordered staunch Muslims to migrate to Al-Madinah. The delegation from there had brought the news that those who swore allegiance to Allâh and His Prophet 🌺 at 'Aqabah had invited Muslims to settle there, and he accepted. The Ansâr of Al-Madinah, (as they came to be called), had said they would look after their migrant brethren.

Abu Salamah 🌸 with his family left on camels for Al-Madinah. When members of her family saw this they caught the bridle of the camel and told him that he could go where he wanted but he would have to leave behind their daughter. They said it seemed like a joke - he was always off somewhere or the other, Abyssiniah, then Al-Madinah! He never seemed to give her a peaceful settled life.

Abu Salamah's family heard this they were enraged. They came and took her sons away, saying she could not take them with her; they were their flesh and blood and they would bring them up. So, in a moment the whole family was split up in three different places. Abu Salamah 🌸 left for Al-Madinah, his wife was left with her parents and the sons were with the grandparents. It was such a shock – this being torn apart from husband and sons – that she just could not stop weeping. Every day she used to visit the spot from where the husband and children had been torn away from her and weep for her loved ones. One day one of the members of her tribe passed that way and saw her grieving and asked her what happened. She told him about her plight. He then went and gave a piece of his mind to the elders of both families, rebuking them for their cruel behavior towards a noble and helpless lady. His emotional and blunt outburst made them realize how unjust they were and they relented. They gave back her sons to her, and her family too gave her permission to proceed to Al-Madinah.

But how could she travel alone? No one was willing to accompany her. Finally, gaining courage and solace from the fact that she now had her sons with her, she set out for Al-Madinah. When she reached Tan'eem she met 'Uthmân bin Talhah 'Abdari, who had not up to that time converted to Islâm. He asked her where she was travelling all alone. She replied that she was going to join her husband. He was surprised that not a single member of the family accompanied her. She said no one agreed to go with her and she was totally dependent on Allâh Almighty who was her Defender and Protector; only He would protect her. 'Uthmân bin Talhah 'Abdari took the bridle of the camel and said he would help her in reaching destination.

Umm Salamah 🌸 said that such a decent, pure-hearted man, with not a trace of evil in him would be difficult to find. Whenever they reached a camping site he would tie the camel to a tree and move far away to lie down and rest. So she also had some privacy and could rest at ease, relaxed with her children. When it was time to resume the journey he would bring the camel and make it sit down. Once she got on the camel's back with her children, he would take the bridle in his hand and start walking. After several days they reached Qubâ which is in the environs of Al-Madinah. Banu 'Amr bin 'Auf were settled there; he said that since Abu Salamah 🌸 was also there he could leave her and return. Umm Salamah 🌸 says in her book that his gentlemanly behavior and his goodness affected her deeply. When she finally saw her family after so long her joy knew no bounds. So this divided family once again was at peace and the children had the benefit of a good upbringing that only united and happy parents can provide.

Abu Salamah 🌸 took part in the Battle of Badr and once again had the honor of fighting for Islâm in the Battle of Uhud. But in this last mentioned battle Abu Osâmah Jashmi wounded him seriously in the side with his spear. He underwent treatment for a month but to no avail. The wound apparently healed, but that was only on the surface, and it continued to fester inside. Barely two months after the battle of Uhud the Prophet 紫 received news that Banu Asad was planning to attack the Muslims. He ordered his men to prepare for battle, and made Abu Salamah عنه the Commander of the Islâmic forces. This, inspite of the fact that worthy and experienced heroes like Abu 'Ubaidah bin Al-Jarrah and Sa'd bin Abi Waqas رضــى الله عــهما were present. When the Prophet 紫 gave the army flag to Abu Salamah عنه he outlined the strategy to be adopted. He told him to reach the territory of Banu Asad and camp there, then attack them before they had a chance to do so. Abu Salamah عنه obeyed the Prophet's orders and with his band of a hundred and fifty men he suddenly swooped down on the Banu Asad immediately after crossing their border. The clang of swords and the battle cries of the warring *Mujâhideen*, who had sworn to win or die in the attempt, challenged Banu Asad who had been taken unaware. This was a very crucial battle for Islâm, as it would be a compensation for the defeat at Uhud. A decisive victory was essential to impress the tribes in the surrounding territories. So every *Mujâhid* played on his life to fight and win. Abu Salamah عنه forgot his grievously wounded side and fought valiantly; he moved like lightening and the enemies fell under his sword. But his wound had only healed on the surface and it started bleeding. The battle was won, and Banu Asad was crushed. The Muslims got the rich spoils of a war well fought. After twenty-nine days on the 8th of *Safar* in the year 4th after Hijrah, the army re-entered Al-Madinah. But Abu Salamah عنه was totally spent. When Umm Salamah عنها saw his grievous injuries she became extremely worried.

Abu Salamah عنه was lying in a very serious condition when the Prophet 紫 came to visit him. He realized that he was approaching death, and patting his hand consoled him. The Prophet 紫 prayed for him and Abu Salamah عنه also prayed and asked Allâh to give his family a protector and provider like him. And he also asked Him to give Umm Salamah عنها a husband who would give her neither sorrow nor hardship.

After this prayer he passed away. The Prophet 紫 closed his eyes with his hands. Umm Salamah عنها often thought of her husband's last prayer for her and wondered who could possibly be better than Abu Salamah عنه. She asked the Prophet 紫 what she should ask Allâh for herself. He taught her to pray for forgiveness both for herself and for Abu Salamah 🕮 and ask Allâh to give her a better future.

Umm Salamah 🕮 says that she prayed thus and Allâh 🕮 granted her prayer. When she finished the prescribed period of waiting, Abu Bakr Siddique 🕮 sent a proposal of marriage to her, but she refused. Then 'Umar bin Khattâb 🕮 proposed and she refused him as well. Then the Prophet 🕮 proposed. She told him that she had three reservations regarding his proposal. She was hot-headed and had a temper; she felt she might be rude to the Prophet of Allâh 🕮, and thus lose the reward for all her good deeds. Secondly, she was an elderly lady; thirdly, she had many children. The Prophet answered that he would pray to Allâh, and Allâh 🕮 willing, her temper would subside. As far as age was concerned, he was also an elderly man. Thirdly, as far as her children were concerned – that was the precise reason for proposing to her – he wished to be their guardian and share the responsibility. She writes that this answer gave her great happiness and thus she attained the honor of becoming part of the Prophet's household. Thus Allâh granted both hers and Abu Salamah's prayer, and she married the Prophet 🕮 in the month of Shawâl, in the 4th year after Hijrah.

🌸🌸🌸🌸🌸

'Aishah 🕮 narrated that it was the habit of the Prophet 🕮 to visit each of his wives in turn after the *'Asr* prayers. He would inquire about their welfare and if they needed anything. He would start from the apartment of Umm Salamah 🕮 because she was the eldest among them, and finish his rounds at the apartment of 'Aishah 🕮 .

Umm Salamah 🕮, because of her beauty, knowledge and wisdom held an eminent position. After the truce of Hudaibiah, the Prophet 🕮 ordered his Companions to sacrifice the animals they brought along for the purpose, and shave their heads. But they all seemed reluctant and did not rise to obey his command. When Umm Salamah 🕮 saw the situation she suggested that he should not speak about the subject to anyone, but just go out from the tent and offer the sacrifice and shave his head. Then he could see the effect of his action. And what she expected happened - all the Companions followed suit.

Umm Salamah 🕮 was a very astute and wise lady. She was educated and was very devoted to the welfare of the destitute and needy.

Several of the *Âyât* of the Noble Qur'ân were revealed to the Prophet 🙰 when he was in her apartment. For instance, *Âyât* in *Surat Al-Ahzâb*,

> "And Allâh only wishes to remove evil deeds from you, O members of the family (of the Prophet), and to purify you with a through purification." (33:33)

Also some of the *Âyât* of *Surat At-Taubah* were revealed while he was with her.

> "And (there are) others who have acknowledged their sins, they have mixed a deed that was righteous with another that was evil. Perhaps Allâh will turn unto them in forgiveness. Surely, Allâh is Oft-Forgiving, Most Merciful." (9:102)

He also said:

> "And (He forgave) the three who did not join till for them the earth, vast as it is, was straitened and their ownselves were straitened to them, and they perceived that there is no fleeing from Allâh, and no refuge but with Him. Then He forgave them that they might beg for His pardon. Verily, Allâh is the One Who forgives and accepts repentance, Most Merciful." (9:118)

This *Âyah* refers to the turning towards Allâh 🙰 of Ka'b bin Mâlik, Hilâl bin Umayyah and Mararah bin Ar-Rabi' in sincere repentance. These three Companions, without any valid reason, avoided joining the Muslim army in the Battle of Tabuk. They were therefore ostracized by the Prophet and the rest of the Companions. They were so stricken by guilt that they kept praying for Divine Forgiveness, until finally Allâh 🙰 granted it to them. The Prophet 🙰 was sleeping in the apartment of Umm Salamah 🙐 when this last *Âyah* was revealed to him. He woke up in the late hours of the night and told her that the supplications for forgiveness of these three Companions had been accepted. She asked him if this good news should be conveyed to them immediately. He said they should not be disturbed so late at night; after the *Fajr* prayers he sent for them and congratulated them. They were overjoyed and so were all the other Companions.

🙰🙰🙰🙰🙰

Umm Salamah ﷺ also had the distinction of taking part in many battles of significance in the history of Islâm. She was with the Prophet ﷺ during the Battles Bani Mustalaq, Tâ'if, Khaibar, Hunain and the conquest of Makkah. She was present at the signing of the historic treaty of Hudaibiah or *Ridhwân* the oath of allegiance taken place.

Salmân Fârsi ﷺ narrates that someone mentioned to him that the Angel Jibril had come down from the Heavens and was in conversation with the Prophet ﷺ. When he went there he saw that the person with the Prophet was Dahiyyah Kalbi, and that Umm Salamah ﷺ was also present. When conversation ended, the Prophet ﷺ asked if they knew who that gentleman was. She said he was one of his most faithful followers, Dahiyyah Kalbi. Thereupon the Prophet told her, smiling, that it was actually the Angel Jibril in human guise.

Umm Salamah ﷺ was very learned in religious matters. She knew three hundred and eighty-seven *Ahâdith* of the Prophet ﷺ by heart. She knew very well the finer points of Islâmic law about foster-relations through suckling and divorce. 'Abdullâh bin 'Abbâs رضي الله عنه used to consult with her for many points of *Shari'ah*, (Islâmic law). Leading the list of names of Companions whose judgments on points of law were regarded as valid is the name of Umm Salamah ﷺ.

The following is the list of Companions who were known for their ability to give legal verdicts:

1. Umm Salamah ﷺ
2. Anas bin Mâlik ﷺ
3. Abu Sa'eed Khudri ﷺ
4. Abu Hurairah ﷺ
5. 'Uthmân bin 'Affân ﷺ
6. 'Abdullâh bin 'Amr bin 'Aas ﷺ
7. 'Abdullâh bin Zubair ﷺ
8. Abu Musâ Ash'ari ﷺ
9. Sa'd bin Abi waqâs ﷺ
10. Salmân Fârsi ﷺ
11. Jâbir bin 'Abdullâh ﷺ

12. Mu'âth bin Jabal ﷺ

13. Abu Bakr Siddique ﷺ

14. Talhah bin 'Obaidullâh ﷺ

15. Zubair bin 'Awâm ﷺ

16. 'Abdur-Rahmân bin 'Auf ﷺ

17. 'Imrân bin Husain ﷺ

18. 'Obâdah bin Sâmit ﷺ

19. Mu'âwiyah bin Abi Sufyân ﷺ

Umm Salamah ﷺ had hardly any equal in mastery over language. When she spoke her words and phrases were well chosen and exactly appropriate for the expression of ideas. Her written language was suited for literary expression. Many Comapnions and followers have noted down traditions attributed to her.

❀❀❀❀❀

She lived to the ripe old age of eighty-four and died in the year 62nd after Hijrah. She lived to see the rule *Khulafâ' Ar- Râshideen.* Zainab bint Jahash ﷺ was the first among the Mothers of the Believers to pass away and Umm Salamah ﷺ the last. This was during the rule of Yazid bin Mu'âwiyah and she was laid to rest beside the other wives of the Prophet in *Jannatul Baqi'.*

"O the one in (complete) rest and satisfaction! Come back to your Lord – well pleased and well pleasing. Enter you then among My (honored) servants, and enter you My Paradise."

Zainab bint Jahash رضي الله عنها

One day Allâh's Messenger ﷺ said to the mother of the believers,

"Among you she would meet me first in Hereafter whose hands would be long."

Amongst the mother of the believers,

"Zainab ﷺ was the first lady who died first, and she became the guest of Paradise."

Zainab ﷺ would often give charity. Generosity is referred to long hands.

ty

Zainab bint Jahash رضي الله عنها

S he was the daughter of Umaimah bint 'Abdul Muttalib bin
Hâshim, who was the Messenger of Allâh's paternal aunt. Her
brother was the distinguished general, 'Abdullâh bin Jahash ﷺ.
Another brother was a noted author of religious poetry, Abu Ahmad
bin Jahash ﷺ. Her sister was another famous women Companion,
Hamnah bint Jahash ﷺ. Her mother was Umaimah bint 'Abdul
Muttalib bin Hâshim ﷺ. Her paternal uncles were the 'Leader of the
Martyrs' Hamzah bin 'Abdul Muttalib ﷺ, and 'Abbâs bin 'Abdul
Muttalib ﷺ, who was renowned for his works of charity. Her paternal
aunt was Safiyyah bint 'Abdul Muttalib bin Hâshim ﷺ.

Known for her generosity and sympathy for the needy, sobriety and
abstinence and devotion in prayer, she was first married to Zaid bin
Hârithah, the adopted son of the Prophet ﷺ. After her divorce she was
married to the Prophet ﷺ at the express command of Allâh ﷺ, in order
to destroy the barbaric custom of giving the same status to adopted
children as to their own flesh and blood. At the banquet given at her
wedding the Âyah of Hijâb was revealed.

She was an innately good woman who used to devote a great deal of
her time to prayer and fasting. On her death she left a house which
was bought by Waleed bin 'Abdul Malik for fifty thousand Dirhams
and included by him in the precincts of the Prophet's Mosque at Al-
Madinah. The Prophet ﷺ told 'Umar bin Khattâb ﷺ that she was a
God fearing woman, hospitable, modest. She was so generous and
soft-hearted that the poor and distressed of the city broke into tears

when they heard they lost their benefactress and patron. She was also one of the fortunate who the Prophet 鑫 said would go to Paradise.

❀❀❀❀❀

She was born about thirty years before the Hijrah of the Prophet 鑫 She was influenced by the teachings of her brother, 'Abdullâh ﷺ bin Jahash, to convert to Islâm. Beautiful, intelligent, wise and of noble birth she was the envy of many.

The increasing popularity and influence of Islâm roused a towering rage among the Quraish; the new converts faced indescribable tortures. Some were made to lie on beds of coal, while others some were dragged naked across the burning desert sands. Still others were wrapped up in straw mats and strung over smoke, to suffocate them and stop them from breathing. Everyday saw new methods of the art of torturing these people who had sworn allegiance to the Allâh. The sole purpose was that they should give up the belief and practices of Islâm. Makkah became too small to hold both them and the Quraish. The Prophet 鑫 exhorted his followers and friends to be patient and brave, but finally he gave them orders to migrate; first to Abyssiniah and then to Al-Madinah. Under the leadership of 'Abdullâh bin Jahash ﷺ the Jahash family set out. The caravan included the blind poet Ahmad bin Jahash ﷺ, who was admired for his liguistic mastery. He wrote an epic poem depicting in detail the tortures inflicted by the Quraish, the reasons for migration and the heroic deeds of the Muslims. This poem is considered to be a masterpiece of Arabic literature.

Muhammad bin 'Abdullâh bin Jahash, Zainab bint Jahash, Hamnah bint Jahash who was the wife of Mus'ab bin 'Omair and Umm Habibah bint Jahash, wife of 'Abdur-Rahmân bin 'Auf رضي الله عنهم, were all companions on this journey. Since all the members of the family left, their house was lying vacant. Taking advantage of this opportunity, Abu Sufyân, the leader of the Quraish occupied it. The very house in which people used to pray to Allâh and read the Noble Qur'ân, was now in the possession of idolaters.

'Abdullâh bin Jahash ﷺ, was upset to hear this and on the occasion of the conquest of Makkah, he spoke to the Prophet 鑫. When he saw this ardent follower in such distress, he asked him if he would not prefer to have a far better house in Paradise. Of course, 'Abdullâh 🌿 replied, he would much rather have a house in Paradise. Upon which the Prophet 🌺 consoled him saying he did, indeed, have a better home there.

❋❋❋❋❋

Time passed peacefully in Al-Madinah, and the ties between the immigrants and the Ansâr, the original inhabitants created an atmosphere of brotherly love and affection. It seemed they were members of one united family. The best individual in the society was neither master nor slave, neither man nor woman, neither rich nor poor, but a God-fearing person of good character and morals.

In the context of such an ideal society the Prophet 🌺 suggested to his cousin Zainab 🌿 that he had decided to get her engaged to Zaid bin Hârithah 🌿, his adopted son and a freed slave. When Zainab 🌿 heard this she was stunned; she told him that she was from a noble family and she was neither keen nor willing to marry a freed slave. She was doubtful if they could get along with each other. He answered that he had chosen Zaid 🌿 for her and she should accept him. Before Zainab 🌿 could answer him, an *Âyah* was revealed to the Prophet 🌺. This was *Âyah* of *Surat Al-Ahzâb*,

> "It is not for a believer, man or woman, when Allâh and His Messenger have decreed a matter that they should have any option in their decision. And whoever disbelieves Allâh and His Messenger, he has indeed strayed into a plane error." (33:36)

Thus Zainab 🌿 and Zaid 🌿 were married, but separated as they were by totally different social backgrounds they were never happy, and their marital life was far from peaceful.

❋❋❋❋❋

Zainab 🌿 was biased and from the very beginning the relations were always strained. Zaid 🌿 felt that the respect and importance that a husband should get from his wife was never given to him. Disappointed in his marriage, he went to the Prophet 🌺 and told him that he was very upset as he and Zainab 🌿 seemed totally incompatible. The advice that he received from his mentor, Allâh has incorporated in the Noble Qur'ân,

"Keep your wife to yourself, and fear Allâh." (33:37)

But in spite of all the best efforts the marriage did not work out, and finally he divorced Zainab 🕮.

❀❀❀❀❀

Arabs thought it was wrong for a man to marry the widow or divorcee of his adopted son. Allâh wanted to abolish this uncivilized custom, so He sent the Angel Jibril to tell the Prophet 🕮 in secret that Zainab 🕮 would one day be his wife. He was very distressed as it was against the accepted norm of behavior. He feared social censure and was very ashamed and embarrassed at the implications. But the decision had been made in the heavens by Allâh 🕮, and soon he received the revelation ,

"And (remember) when you said to him (Zaid bin Hârithah 🕮) on whom Allâh has bestowed grace (by guiding him to Islâm) and you have done favour (by manumitting him): "Keep your wife to yourself, and fear Allâh." But you hid in yourself that which Allâh will make manifest, you did fear the people (i.e., their saying that Muhammad 🕮 married the divorced wife of his manumitted slave) whereas Allâh had a better right that you should fear Him. So when Zaid had accomplished his desire from her (i.e. divorced her), We gave her to you in marriage, so that there may be no difficulty to the believers in respect of (the marriage of) the wives of their adopted sons when the latter have no desire to keep them. And Allâh's Command must be fulfilled." (33:37)

When Zainab 🕮 completed her period of waiting, the Prophet 🕮 sent her a proposal through Zaid bin Hârithah 🕮. When he went to her, she was kneading dough; keeping his back turned to her, he gave her the Prophet's message, that he wanted her to join the select group of the Mothers of the believers. She said she could not answer immediately, but would have to consult her Maker. She began praying to Allâh for guidance. She was still in the middle of her prayer, when the Prophet 🕮 received a revelation that the marriage had already been performed in the Heavens by Allâh 🕮 Himself. After this Heavenly order, the Prophet 🕮 immediately went to Zainab 🕮, without observing any of the formalities that were observed with acquaintances and friends. He did not inform her in advance nor did ask for permission. There are some exceptional points to be noted regarding this marriage.

- Only the order of the Qur'ân was based as a guardian or a witness.

- It abolished a barbaric custom that equated a blood relationship with an adoptive one; in which the father could not marry an adopted son's ex-wife or widow.

- Zainab 🕮 used to say very proudly to the other Mother of the Believers that her marriage had been performed not by her family but by Allâh above the Heavens with His beloved Prophet.

- When the hypocrites criticized the Prophet 🕮 for this marriage, Allâh 🕮 replied,

  "There is no blame on the Prophet in that which Allâh has made legal for him. That has been Allâh's way with those who have passed away of (the Prophets of) old. And the Command of Allâh is a decree determined. Those who convey the Message of Allâh and fear Him, and fear none save Allâh. And Sufficient is Allâh as a Reckoner." (33:38-39)

And to clarify the finer points still further he revealed *Âyât* which again are part of *Surat Al-Ahzâb,*

  "Muhammad is not the father of any of your men, but he is the Messenger of Allâh and the last of the Prophets. And Allâh is Ever All-Aware of everything." (33:40)

On this occasion Allâh revealed the order clarifying the position of adopted sons as,

  "Nor has he made your adopted sons your real sons. That is but your saying with your mouths. But Allâh says the truth, and He guides to the (Right) Way. Call them (the adopted sons) by (the names of) their fathers, that is more just with Allâh." (33:4-5)

On the occasion of this wedding Allâh revealed revelation regarding *Hijâb* and also made it clear that no man could marry any of the Mothers of the Believers after the Prophet ﷺ. These two commands were revealed in *Âyât* of the same *Surat*,

> "O you who believe! Enter not the Prophet's houses, unless permission is given to you for a meal, (and then) not (so early as) to wait for its preparation. But when you are invited, enter, and when you have taken your meal, disperse without sitting for a talk. Verily, such (behaviour) annoys the Prophet, and he is shy of (asking) you (to go); but Allâh is not shy of (telling you) the truth. And when you ask (his wives) for anything you want, ask them from behind a screen that is purer for your hearts and for their hearts. And it is not (right) for you that you should annoy Allâh's Messenger, nor that you should ever marry his wives after him (his death). Verily, with Allâh that shall be an enormity." (33:53)

❀❀❀❀❀

'Aishah ﷺ says that in terms of values and position, Zainab ﷺ was her equal. She said she had never seen any other person who was so eager to get closer to Allâh ﷻ. To gain nearness to Him she was more charitable than most, and her generous behavior with relatives was impeccable. When 'Aishah ﷺ was wrongfully accused, the whole of Al-Madinah was polluted with taunts and filthy talk; in fact even the Prophet ﷺ was disturbed. The Prophet ﷺ asked Zainab ﷺ what her opinion was of 'Aishah ﷺ. The noble character of this lady is revealed in her answer; she promptly said she did not wish to be involved, and did not want to defile and taint her ears, her eyes and her tongue with such terrible accusations. Swearing by Allâh she said, she found 'Aishah ﷺ to be a truly God-fearing lady of exemplary character. She found in her the most wonderful traits of integrity, sincerity and honesty. She said she had not seen in her anything but goodness and virtue. 'Aishah ﷺ narrated that Zainab ﷺ very easily have taken advantage of the situation and passed derogatory remarks about her, for after all, in a sense they were rivals. 'Aishah ﷺ says she never forgot the fact that she stood by her at the worst time in her life when almost the whole world had turned against her.

On one occasion Zainab called Safiyyah a Jewess and this deeply distressed the Prophet . In fact he was so upset that he stopped talking to her. Zainab felt guilty and realized that she committed a grave mistake and offended the Prophet . Finally she requested 'Aishah to advocate her case with him and tell him that she was sincerely repentant; she was the only one who could talk to him in such a direct manner. When the Prophet visited 'Aishah she looked for an opportune moment and brought up the subject, pleading the case for Zainab . The Prophet forgave and family life returned to normal in the household.

When Zainab passed away 'Aishah recalled an occasion when the Prophet said that among the Mother of the Believers, she would meet him first who had the longest arms. Zainab was short compared to the others and naturally her arms were also shorter. All the ladies took this statement literally and started measuring their arms. It was only upon the death of Zainab that they realized what this meant. It really meant that the person with the longest arms was the most generous or liberal person, who only thought of how she could benefit others. There was an implicit prophesy in this statement, which became clear when Zainab passed away. It meant she would meet him in Paradise before the others. And she passed away before any of the other wives of the Prophet . 'Aishah says Zainab worked with her own hands, and what she thus earned she spent on works of charity. She says she was a God-fearing, straight-forward lady who practiced abstinence. All her actions were aimed at pleasing Allâh . Sometimes she could lose her temper, but then she was quick to repent and ask for forgiveness. She was very pure at heart and never carried resentments and grudges.

The Prophet had a very organized routine. After the *'Asr* prayers he would visit the different apartments to inquire about the well being of the ladies of his household. He was always very just in the attention he paid to them and the amount of time he spent with each one of them. Once Zainab received some special honey from a relative, and it so happened that this was the Prophet's favourite. Whenever she offered it to him he would spend some time longer in her apartment, as it took time to really flavor and enjoy it. The other wives felt impatient and restless waiting for their turn with him. So 'Aishah, Saudah, and Hafsah رضي الله عنهم, worked out a plan. Each of them would tell him that there was a peculiar smell in his mouth. And if all of them said the same thing he would certainly believe them and realize that the only thing which could have given him bad breath would have been the honey he just had. Since he was very concerned about personal hygiene, he would definitely stop eating the honey. Of course the three Mothers of the Believers did what they did, not out of spite, but because they loved him and wanted him to come to them sooner. In fact Allâh ﷻ has Himself spoken of them in the highest terms of respect in the Qur'ân.

"O wives of the Prophet (ﷺ)! you are not like any other women." (33:32)

And it happened as they planned; the Prophet ﷺ developed a distaste for honey and decided he would never eat it again. In the case of an ordinary human being this may not have been a problem. But the Prophet ﷺ was swearing not to have something that actually was not forbidden by Allâh ﷻ; this could lead to any follower of his also forswearing something not forbidden by Allâh.

So Allâh rebuked him,

"O Prophet! Why do you forbid (for yourself) that which Allâh has allowed to you, seeking to please your wives? And Allâh is Oft-Forgiving, Most Merciful." (66:1)

As a result the Prophet ﷺ broke the oath he had taken and performed the penance for this in accordance with the injunctions of Allâh.

✿✿✿✿✿

Zainab ﷺ made a little mosque in a corner of her house and used to spend a lot of time there in prayer and meditation. The Prophet ﷺ would also pray there sometimes. She believed strongly in asking Allâh for counsel through prayer and supplication, before taking any action. All her life's major decisions were made in this way. In fact even when the Prophet ﷺ proposed she turned to prayer for guidance.

This righteous lady died during the caliphate of 'Umar Farooq ؓ at the age of fifty-three. When she realized she was about to meet her Maker, she told the people around her that she already prepared a shroud for herself. If 'Umar Farooq 邏 sent one for her, one should be used and the other given away in charity. She was such a modest lady that a curtain was drawn in front of her dead body, even though it was wrapped in a shroud.

'Umar Farooq 邏 led the funeral prayers and all her close relatives – Osamah bin Zaid, Muhammad bin 'Abdullâh bin Jahash, 'Abdullâh bin Abi Ahmad bin Jahash and Muhammad bin Talhah bin 'Abdullâh رضي الله عنهم – got down into the grave to lower her gently into her final resting place in *Jannatul Baqi'*.

> "O the one in (complete) rest and satisfaction! Come back to your Lord – well pleased and well pleasing. Enter you then among My (honored) servants, and enter you My Paradise."

Juveriah bint Hârith رضي الله عنها

The Prophet ﷺ said:

"Allâh has commanded me to marry with the women of Paradise only."

'Aishah رضي الله عنها said:

"I did not see any lady except Juveriah ﷺ who became a source of blessing for her tribesmen more than Juveriah ﷺ because hundreds of her tribesmen liberated from the slavery by her action."

Juvriah bint Hârith رضي الله عنها

Islâm had begun to spread rapidly and a major portion of the Arabian Peninsula was under the influence of Islâm by the year 5th after Hijrah. Al-Madinah had by now become the centre of a stable and rapidly expanding Islâmic state. The Islâmic forces were on a triumphal march, inspired by spiritual strength.

The tribe of Banu Khuzâ'ah was sympathetic to the cause of Islâm and the Prophet ﷺ, except one of their branches, Banu Mustalaq, who planned to attack Madinah. The chieftain of this tribe was Hârith bin Abi Dharâr, who was an arrogant man drunk with his power and wealth. He had a beautiful daughter, Juveriah ﷺ, who had been born just before the advent of Islâm. She was brought up in the lap of luxury, and had all the refinements and graces of a princess. Intelligent and wise, she mastered language and literary style. This was an accomplishment much prized by contemporary Arabs. She was happily married to one of the rising youths of the tribe of Banu Khuzâ'ah, Musâfa' bin Safwân.

❀❀❀❀❀

It was at this time that the Prophet ﷺ received news that Hârith bin Abi Dharâr was making elaborate preparations to attack the Muslim forces at Al-Madinah. So he sent one of his most trusted Companion, Buraidah bin Haseeb ﷺ, to survey the situation and get facts and information about the enemy in order to work out an appropriate strategy. Buraidah ﷺ met with Hârith and many other important people who were close to him. He noted that there was a lot of activity and that the young men were busy making preparations for war. There were many weapons to be seen, and from his discussions with people it was quite obvious that they were planning to go to war. Buraidah ؄ came back and informed the Prophet ﷺ of all that he had seen and heard. The Muslim forces were now alerted by their leader and they too started preparing for a battle. In no time at all an army of seven hundred was ready to leave, under their General, the Prophet ﷺ himself. 'Aishah ؅ accompanied him on this march.

The Marisa' was an important strategic point for the tribe of Banu Mustalaq as it was the source which provided water for drinking as well as for other purposes. The Muslim forces reached this important position and sent a message to the Banu Mustalaq to accept Islâm. If they did so they could continue to live in their lands in peace and security as before. But, of accepting Islâm they came out on to the plains and declared war. One of the soldiers of Banu Mustalaq, shot an arrow which lodged in the body of a *Mujâhid*. Wild fighting then broke out. The Prophet ﷺ ordered his troops to keep to their ranks and launch a united attack on the enemy, who were cornered and found no way of escape. Ten people were killed and about seven hundred captured. The husband of Juveriah ؅, Musâfâ' bin Safwân was among those who were killed. Among the captives there were women as well. The *Mujâhideen* also got two thousand camels and five thousand goats.

On reaching Madinah, the spoils of war were distributed among the *Mujâhideen*. According to the custom of those days, men and women were distributed as slaves. Juveriah bint Hârith ؅ was given to the famous companion of the Prophet ﷺ, Thâbit bin Qais Ansâri. All who saw Juveriah ؅ were stunned by her exceptional beauty. Brought up as she had been in one of the foremost families of the time, she was not only beautiful but graceful, elegant and eloquent. At the first opportunity she went into the presence of the Prophet ﷺ and pleaded her case with him. She told him that she was the daughter of a chieftain and used to command. Because of unfortunate circumstances she found herself in this helpless position. From a throne made of gold she had fallen into dust. She had been given to Thâbit bin Qais Ansâri for a ransom of gold; but from where could she get the gold to give in exchange for her freedom? How could she possibly live the life of a slave? She pleaded with the Prophet 🕮 to take notice of the pitiful and desperate condition in which she found herself.

The Prophet 🕮 was moved by her sorrowful plea and asked her if she would like to live as a free woman and be part of his household if he paid her ransom. She had never in her dreams expected this offer. Moved deeply by this unexpected elevation in her status, she exclaimed she would be more than happy to accept. She was freed, and swearing allegiance to Islâm, she married Prophet Muhammad 🕮.

When the *Mujâhideen* heard of her conversion and marriage to the Prophet 🕮 they too freed all the slaves of the tribe of Banu Mustalaq. So in this way not only did she become free, but she also became a Mother of the believers. This action of hers had the far-reaching result of liberating all her tribe from slavery. And thus Juveriah 🕮 became a source of blessings for her tribe.

❀❀❀❀❀

When 'Aishah 🕮 first saw Juveriah 🕮 she exclaimed that she was as beautiful as a fairy. On another occasion she said she had yet to see a lady who proved to be such a source of blessings for her people. Through her, Allâh blessed a hundred families of her tribe with freedom.

Before her marriage to the Prophet 🕮 her name was Barah, but Muhammad 🕮 changed it to Juveriah 🕮. Zainab bint Jahash, Zainab bint Umm Salamah and Maimoonah bint Hârith were also named Barah, but the Prophet 🕮 changed their names as well.

In his book, Dalâ'l An-Nabuwwah, Imâm Baihaqi has quoted Juveriah 🕮, as saying that, three days before the Prophet 🕮 arrived she saw the moon coming towards her from the direction of Al-Madinah and falling into her lap. She did not like to talk about it to anyone, but when they were conquered and she was made a prisoner she hoped that her dream would be realized. Then the Prophet 🕮 freed her and subsequently married her.

In his book 'Siyar A'lâm Nubalâ' Imam Thahabi quoted her as saying that when the Prophet 🕮 married her she was a girl of twenty. Imam

Thahabi adds that she was an extremely beautiful lady.

Some time later, her father and all the men who had been freed on the occasion of her marriage presented themselves before the Prophet 變 and accepted Islâm as their religion. Thus, Juveriah 變 was blessed with a twofold honor – first of freeing her countrymen from slavery, and then of bringing them into the fold of Islâm.

❀❀❀❀❀

Most of the time she would be found engrossed in prayer. On one occasion when the Prophet 變 left home he found her lost in meditation. On returning in the afternoon he still found her in the very same position of prayer and supplication. He asked her if she had been praying continuously since he had left. When she answered in the affirmative, he asked her if she would like to learn four small sentences that could earn her more reward from Allâh than the whole morning's prayers. Then he taught her the following sentence,

> 'How perfect Allâh is and I praise Him by the number of His creation and His pleasure, and by the weight of His Throne, and the extent of His Words.'

Both Muslim and Abu Dawood quote Juveriah 變 narrating an incident similar to the one above. She said the Prophet 變 told her that after leaving her in the morning he recited the above four sentences, three times each, and these earned him more reward from Allâh than her whole morning's prayers.

Ibn Sa'd recorded that from the lands taken after the Battle of Khaibar the Prophet 變 fixed for Juveriah 變 80 *Wasaq*[1] of dates and 20 *Wasaq* of barley.

After the Prophet 變 passed away the first Caliph, Abu Bakr Siddique 變 fixed an equal amount to be given to the Mother of the believers for their household expenses. 'Umar bin Khattâb 變, however, fixed the sum of twelve thousand Dirhams for the rest, but for Juveriah and Safiyyah رضــــي الله عـــهـما he fixed only six thousand Dirhams each. They

---

[1] One *Wasaq* is approximately equal to 124 kg.

naturally refused to accept this amount. He explained that the others got double the amount because of their migration. But they argued that he had given preference to the others. Then 'Aishah 卷 pointed out to him that the Prophet 卷 used to make no distinction and divide everything equally between his wives. So 'Umar bin Khattâb 卷 decided to revoke his decision and gave them all an equal stipend of twelve thousand Dirhams.

Juveriah 卷 died at the age of sixty-five in Rabi'ul-Awwal in the year 50th after Hijrah during the caliphate of Mu'âwiyah bin Abi Sufyân. The governor of Al-Madinah, Marwân bin Hakam led the funeral prayer and she was buried in *Jannatul Baqi'*.

"O the one in (complete) rest and satisfaction! Come back to your Lord – well pleased and well pleasing. Enter you then among My (honored) servants, and enter you My Paradise."

Safiyyah bint Huyayee رضي الله عنها

The Prophet ﷺ said:

"No doubt, you are the daughter of a Prophet, your uncle is a Prophet and you are the wife of a Prophet."

Safiyyah bint Huyayee رضي الله عنها

Safiyyah bint Huyayee was the favourite daughter of Huyayee bin Akhtab the chieftain of the tribe of Banu Nadheer. Her mother was Barah bint Shamwâl who was the sister of Rafâ'ah bin Shamwâl. She was married to Salâm bin Mashkam first, but they separated soon on grounds of incompatibility. Her second husband was Kanânah bin Rabi' bin Haqeeq who was killed in the Battle of Khaibar, she was taken as a prisoner of war. One of the Companion, Dahyah Kalbi ◈, asked the Prophet ﷺ for a slave girl, and he gave him the freedom to choose for himself. He chose Safiyyah ◈. The others suggested that since she was the chieftain's daughter he should keep her for himself and give some other slave to Dahyah Kalbi ◈. The Prophet ﷺ did as they suggested; then he decided to free her and married her.

There is another tradition too. Wahshi bin Harb ◈ narrates how the Prophet ﷺ asked for their opinion about Safiyyah ◈. They told him that she would be more suitable for him and better than any of the others. So he freed her and took her hand in marriage.

Seerat Ibn Hishâm, Dalâil An-Nabuwwah by Baihaqi and Dalâil An-Nabuwwah by Asbahâni - all recorded what Safiyyah ◈ had to say about her life before her marriage to the Prophet ﷺ. Her father and her paternal uncle, Abu Yâsir, loved her deeply and they used to live in Al-Madinah. When the Prophet ﷺ migrated and came there he first stayed in the valley of Banu 'Amr bin 'Auf, both her father and her uncle went to see him. On their return both looked tired, fed up and disappointed. They did not pay any attention to her, which was very unusual for her. She became anxious over what could possibly have happened. Her uncle asked her father if this was the same man. He swore by God that it was certainly the same man. Her uncle wanted to confirm again if it really was the same man, and if he had recognized him. Again her father replied in the affirmative. Then her uncle asked him for his sincere opinion about the stranger. Her father answered that he would always treat this man as a foe. Safiyyah ﷛ heard this cryptic conversation filled with malice and vindictiveness and was shocked.

Time passed and the Treaty of Hudaibiah was signed. When the Prophet ﷺ returned after that the Quraish prevented them from entering Makkah. The news spread like wildfire through the whole of the Arabian Peninsula that the Muslims had bowed down and accepted an unfair treaty. People thought they had weakened, were desperate and fast losing hope. When the Jews in Khaibar heard this news, they thought this was the appropriate moment to strike and started preparing to attack Al-Madinah. They invited all the Jews in the surrounding areas to join forces with them. When the Prophet ﷺ heard about the warlike preparations of the Jews of Khaibar, he took with him the very same fourteen hundred people who had set out with him to perform 'Umrah but had not been allowed within the precincts of Makkah after the treaty of Hudaibiah. Women also were part of this group of pilgrims. He had returned from Hudaibiah in the month of Dhul-Hajj, and left for Khaibar with his army in the early days of the month of Muharram. When he first sighted Khaibar he ordered his army from to stop right there, and lifted his hands in supplication to Allâh ﷻ. Whenever he travelled, it was his usual practice to recite this prayer whenever his eyes first fell on a city.

'O Allâh, Lord of the seven heavens and all that they envelop, Lord of the seven earths and all that they carry, Lord of the devils and all whom they misguide, Lord of the winds and all whom they whisk away. I ask You for the goodness of this village, the goodness of its inhabitants and for all the goodness found within it and I take refuge with You from the evil of this village, the evil of its inhabitants and from all the evil found within it.'

It was nightfall when they reached Khaibar. He camped with his forces on the plains just on the outskirts of the city. This again was a typical strategy of his; whenever he led his men to engage in battle, he planned to reach there by nightfall. But he was so principled that he would never attack the enemy at night in order to take them unawares.

The Muslim army was encamped just outside Khaibar, but the people of the city were quite unaware of this. When they woke up in the morning and started going about their usual chores, they were shocked to see a whole army encamped on their doorstep, as it were!

Soon after *Fajr* (early dawn) prayers, the Prophet 🌸 ordered the *Mujâhideen* to advance and attack. The Jews of Khaibar started scattering towards their homes. When the Prophet 🌸 saw them running he called out,

'Allâh is Great, Khaibar is deserted, Khaibar is broken, Khaibar is destroyed and ruined!'

By the Grace of Allâh Almighty the Muslims triumphed and all the forts of Khaibar were taken. The father of Safiyyah 🌸, Huyayee bin Akhthab was killed in the battle of Bani Quraidhah. Her husband Kanânah bin Rabi'ah bin Haqeeq was captured and killed for the crime of misgovernment. And Safiyyah 🌸 was made a prisoner of war.

Dahyah Kalbi 🌸 was given the option to choose a slave girl for himself, and he chose Safiyyah 🌸. One of the Companion suggested that it would be better if the Prophet 🌸 kept Safiyyah 🌸, the daughter of a leader and chieftain, for himself and gave some other slave girl to Dahyah Kalbi 🌸. So he chose the sister of Safiyyah's husband Kanâna bin Rabi'ah. The Prophet 🌸 then freed Safiyyah and married her. Her dowry was her liberty, writes Hafiz Ibn Qayyam.

On the return journey to Al-Madinah, the Prophet 🌸 camped with his army twelve miles away from the city. One of the *Sahâbiyât*, Umm Salim Ansâriah, dressed up Safiyyah 🌸 in her bridal finery.

In his book, Seerah A'lâm Nubalâ' Imam Thahabi describes the qualities and character of Safiyyah 🌸. He says she was noble both by birth as well as by nature; she was God-fearing, intelligent, beautiful,

patient, tolerant and dignified. When the Prophet ﷺ saw the mark of
an injury just above her eye, he asked her how she got hurt. She
answered that she had dreamt that the moon had fallen into her lap.
When she told her husband about her dream, he slapped her hard and
told her that it meant she was in love with the king of Yathrib. When
she married the Prophet ﷺ, Safiyyah ﷺ was just seventeen years old.

Safiyyah ﷺ traveled in the company of the Prophet ﷺ from Khaibar to
Al-Madinah. She says that she never came across a person who was
more refined and well-mannered than him. He was always pleasant
and behaved like a perfect gentleman. When the people of Al-
Madinah heard of his approach, they came out to greet him and his
victorious army. The faces of the Muslims were glowing with
pleasure, and those of the hypocrites were downcast and gloomy. All
the Mothers of the believers were waiting impatiently in their
apartments, longing to meet the Prophet ﷺ and congratulate him on
this great victory. When word came that he married the young and
beautiful daughter of the Jewish leader, 'Aishah ﷺ was disturbed by a
twinge of feminine jealousy, which was but natural. The Prophet ﷺ
also did not consider it proper to take his new bride to any of his
wives' houses. He went directly to the house of Hârithah bin Nu'mân
Ansâri and stayed there. The ladies of Al-Madinah came there to meet
Safiyyah ﷺ; and all of them were full of praise for her.

After resting for some time the Prophet ﷺ went to his daughter
Fâtimah ﷺ, and met his beloved grandchildren Hasan and Husain رضي
الله عنهما. After that he visited each of his wives and inquired about their
welfare. He found a certain strangeness and distance in the behavior
of 'Aishah ﷺ, but he thought it better to ignore it for the moment.
'Aishah ﷺ after some time decided to visit the new bride in the house
of Hârithah bin Nu'mân Ansâri. The Prophet ﷺ then asked her for her
opinion of Safiyyah ﷺ. 'Aishah ﷺ, still vexed by her feminine
jealousy replied dryly that she had seen the Jewess. The Prophet ﷺ
gently rebuked her, saying that Safiyyah ﷺ should no longer be
referred to as a Jewess as she had accepted Islâm.

'Aishah and Hafsah رضي الله عنهما were very close friends and the latter
was the only person in whom the former could safely confide.
Actually it was the intense love that 'Aishah ﷺ had for the Prophet ﷺ

that made her express her emotions in this manner.

🌸🌸🌸🌸🌸

Once Safiyyah 🌸 moved into her own place she displayed her noble upbringing by adopting a pleasant and friendly attitude with the other Mothers of the believers. She brought expensive gold jewellery with her from Khaibar, and she presented this to the other wives. She loved the Prophet's favourite daughter Fâtimah 🌸 and gave her gold earrings as a gift. She tried her best to win a place in the affections of 'Aishah and Hafsah رضى الله عنها because she realized the Prophet 🌸 held them in high esteem and loved them dearly. She narrated that on one occasion she mentioned to him that she heard that Hafsah 🌸 taunted her, calling her the daughter of a Jew.

> The Prophet 🌸 told her that she should have told Hafsah 🌸 that she could not be better than her; her husband was Muhammad 🌸, her father was Hâroon 🌸 and her uncle was Musâ 🌸.

On another occasion 'Aishah 🌸 spoke of Safiyyah 🌸 in very disparaging terms. Prophet 🌸 told her that if the expressions she had used were thrown into an ocean they could make the whole of it bitter.

🌸🌸🌸🌸🌸

An incident about Safiyyah 🌸 is mentioned in *Sahih Al-Bukhâri*. During the last ten days of Ramadhân when the Prophet 🌸 was in *Ah'takaf* (secluding himself in the mosque) she went to visit him. Afterwards, when she got up to leave he also rose and accompanied her outside. Two of the Ansâr saw him there talking to her, and greeted him.

He asked them to stop and explained to them that the lady was his wife and had come to visit him.

They said in praise of Allâh 🌸; "*Subhânallâh*, O Prophet of Allâh!" And they were upset that he should have felt the need to explain his actions.

He answered that Satan could become part of human beings to such an extent that he could course through the body with their blood. He added that he did not want Satan to sow evil suspicions in their hearts.

🌸🌸🌸🌸🌸

Safiyyah 🌸 gave a lot of time to the reading of the Noble Qur'ân, and its effect on her heart was so intense that because of the fear of Allâh, tears would course down her cheeks, and she would start sobbing.

In the Qur'ân, Allâh says that the true believer is he whose heart starts quaking when the Name of Allâh is taken before him. And when he listens to the Verses of the Noble Qur'ân being read his faith grows. If the Name of Allâh Almighty is taken and his heart does not quake with fear. If the Verses of the Noble Qur'ân are recited and he does not feel himself in the pleasure of listening to it, then it is high time he should start worrying about the status of his faith and belief in Allâh.

Abu Nu'aym Asbahâni wrote in his book *Hiliyyahul-Awliâ'* that once some Companions gathered in the apartment of the Mother of the Believers Safiyyah 🌸, they mentioned Allâh, recited the Noble Qur'ân and prayed voluntary prayer. Safiyyah 🌸 said to them that their voluntary prayer, recitation and rememrance of Allâh were all good, but they should weep too with the fear of Allâh.

In fact if the fear of Allâh is strongly rooted in one's heart, then involuntarily the tears will start flowing, and the truth is that it is these tears of penitence which clean and purify the heart; and they are invaluable in the eyes of Allâh Almighty. The eyes which shed these tears will go to Paradise as they are the proof of the intensity and the fervor of the love for Allâh.

❀ ❀ ❀ ❀ ❀

Safiyyah 🌸 was an extremely tolerant, patient, loving and kind-hearted woman. Imam Thahabi has narrated an incident from her life in his book, *Siyar A'lâm Nubalâ'*. He said Safiyyah 🌸 had a slave girl, who went and told the Caliph 'Umar Farooq ⚘ that in spite of the fact that her mistress had converted to Islâm, she still observed the Saturday Sabbath of the Jews; and she also kept good terms with the Jews. The Caliph met with Safiyyah 🌸 and questioned her regarding these two accusations. She answered that after Allâh had told Muslims about the sanctity and blessings of Friday she stopped giving importance to Saturday. As far as her terms with the Jews were concerned, they were her relatives and she was following the dictates of Allâh and His Messenger to maintain good relations with kindred.

As human beings too they deserved sympathetic and kind treatment from her.

She later discovered that it was her slave girl who had carried these tales to Caliph 'Umar Farooq 🕸. She asked her why she had done this. The girl very innocently and nervously answered that it was Satan who had incited her.

She immediately set the girl free. As Allâh says,

> "Who repress anger, and who pardon men; verily, Allâh loves the good-doers." (3:134)

She was extremely knowledgeable and spent most of her time in reciting the Noble Qur'ân, of which she knew by heart many more of the *Surahs*. After leading a very full life she passed away in the year 50th after Hijrah, during the caliphate of Mu'âwiyah 🕸, and was buried in *Jannatul Baqi'*. She left a hundred thousand Dirhams that were distributed as per her will.

> "O the one in (complete) rest and satisfaction! Come back to your Lord – well pleased and well pleasing. Enter you then among My (honored) servants, and enter you My Paradise."

Umm Habibah Ramlah bint Abi Sufyân رضي الله عنها

Pointing towards Amir Mu'âwiyah ☙ and Umm Habibah ☙, Allâh's Messenger ﷺ said:

"By Allâh, I wish by heart that she, you and I might drink the clean wine in Paradise together."

Umm Habibah Ramlah
bint Abi Sufyân رضي الله عنها

Waraqah bin Naufil, 'Uthmân bin Haweerath bin Asad, Zaid bin 'Amr bin Nafeel and 'Obaidullâh bin Jahash were four friends who were very disheartened by the plague of idol worship which was so widespread in Arabia. They often used to get together and discuss how this terrible evil could be eradicated from their people. They could not talk about it openly, so they used to have their sessions late at night when the entire world was silent and asleep.

They were upset that it was not only the common unenlightened and uneducated man on the street who was involved in this barbaric practice of idol worship, but even the noble tribe of the Quraish had lost their spiritual bearings. How could any rational man believe that the stones they themselves carved with their hands, who were deaf and incapable of moving even a finger, were all powerful and could help them? How could they prostrate themselves before these stones, worship them with all their hearts and souls and believe they could help them solve all life's problems? People used to sacrifice animals before these idols and eat the food and drink the blood of the animals sacrificed! They came to a decision one night that they should stop worrying about these irrational, uncivilized and shortsighted people and find a way out of this confusion for themselves. The Quraish, the leading tribe lost their way and these four friends decided they had to find the way to the pure and unsullied religion of Ibrâhim ﷺ for themselves. They had the strong belief that this was the straight and simple path of virtue and righteousness. The guidance given by their ancient Prophet Ibrâhim ﷺ. They knew, what was the way to salvation, but they had to keep their thoughts and intentions secret as the followers of the barbaric practices could make life really difficult for them.

They decided they had to set out and search for the truth whatever the cost. With this plan in mind they dispersed from the meeting moving in different directions. Their objective was to find the religion of the Prophet Ibrâhim ﷺ, in its pure form.

Waraqah bin Nofil had given up idol worship right from barbaric times and had given up eating the flesh of animals sacrificed in the name of idols. He knew the Torah and the Injil by heart.

His cousin Khadijah had taken the Prophet ﷺ to him on the occasion of the first revelation in the cave of Hirâ. The Angel Jibril ﷺ had embraced him tightly, and Muhammad ﷺ was terrified. His wife consoled him; recognizing the purity and virtuous qualities of her husband, she told him that a person such as he would surely be protected by Allâh Almighty. Waraqah then told her that the being he saw in the cave must have been the same Angel who delivered Messages from Allâh to earlier Prophets. He said that Muhammad must be the chosen Last Messenger, whose coming was foretold in both the Torah and the Injil. He would soon be elevated to that great position, the whole nation would turn against him and he would be forced to flee his motherland. Waraqah said that if he was alive at that time he would certainly help him and stand by him. But he passed away before Muhammad ﷺ openly declared himself the Last Messenger and Prophet of Allâh.

The second friend, 'Uthmân bin Haweerath bin Asad, traveled to Syria, and worked as a missionary to spread Christianity. He became a close friend of the Roman Emperor Caesar and was finally elevated to the papal position.

Zaid bin 'Amr bin Nafeel, the third of these companions, accepted neither Christianity nor Judaism. He stopped worshipping idols. He gave up eating dead animals and drinking their blood. He hated eating the flesh of the animals sacrificed and often talked of the pure religion of the Prophet Ibrâhim ﷺ. He too died before the proclamation of Muhammad as the Messenger of Allâh.

'Obaidullâh bin Jahash, the fourth friend, regrettably, fell into such doubts and perplexity that he vacillated between right and wrong, between what to do and what not to do. He married the beautiful, intelligent and well-educated daughter of the Quraishi chieftain, Abu Sufyân Sakhr bin Harb.

It was around this time that Makkah was shaken by the news that Muhammad 🕋 was rejecting all the idols and declared that they were not deserving of worship, he invited people to worship the Allâh 🕋 and proclaimed he was His Last Prophet and Messenger. The leaders of the Quraish were furious and the community was split into two factions. Some people pledged allegiance to Allâh 🕋 and His Prophet and became Muslims. The others challenged the validity of this new religion that went against the practices and beliefs of their forefathers. They became sworn enemies of the Muslims and were determined to persecute and torment them.

But the intelligent and wise daughter of Abu Sufyân, Ramlah, accepted Islâm and so did her husband 'Obaidullâh bin Jahash. His two brothers 'Abdullâh bin Jahash and Abu Ahmad bin Jahash had also become Muslims. The two sisters, Zainab bint Jahash and Hamnah bin Jahash too had come into the fold of Islâm. The former had joined the select group of the Mother of the Believers. Abu Ahmad bin Jahash was a very famous blind poet of those days and wrote about the history and exploits of the Muslim *Ummah* as it was happening. Hamnah was the wife of one of the most loyal Companions of the Prophet 🕋. The whole family was fortunate to have obeyed the call to Islâm, but while in Abyssiniah 'Obaidullâh had the misfortune to reject Islâm after having accepted it. He became an apostate and heretic and turned to Christianity. He started drinking and died on the same belief. However, his wife Ramlah remained faithful to Islâm; in fact her love and support for it grew stronger. And ultimately she joined the ranks of the Mother of the Believers. Her life is a study in loyalty and steadfastness, in her love for the truth.

🕋🕋🕋🕋🕋

Abu Sufyân Sakhr bin Harb was a chieftain of the Quraish, who led the disbelievers in many of their wars. Besides his daughter Ramlah, he had two sons, Yazid and Mu'âwiyah. Both of them were renowned for their services to Islâm. Ramlah accepted Islâm when the Muslims were facing a lot of opposition and were being cruelly persecuted. Abu Sufyân was a very powerful man, but he was helpless in the matter of his daughter Ramlah. The human mind is always free though the body can be captured or subdued. She was a helpless frail girl, but he could not stop her from accepting Islâm. She openly declared herself a Muslim, and the oppression of the Quraish could in no way deter her. What Allâh Wills no one can change, for surely He is All Powerful and can bring the dead to life.

In spite of all his best efforts Abu Sufyân could not make his daughter recant.

Meanwhile, after surveying the situation the Prophet ﷺ decided that the staunch supporters of Islâm had taken enough of the torture and oppression from the Quraish. They would have to migrate, and he ordered them to leave for Abyssiniah, where the ruler was known for his kindness and hospitality to refugees from tyrannical rule.

Ramlah bint Abu Sufyân and her husband 'Obaidullâh bin Jahash were among the second group of migrants who left for Abyssiniah. There Ramlah gave birth to a girl who they named Habibah; hence Ramlah was now known as Umm Habibah ﵂. So the days passed swiftly for her as she kept busy seeing to the upbringing of her little daughter; all her free time was spent in prayer and meditation.

One night she dreamt that her husband's face was mutilated. She woke up panic stricken, but was too nervous to talk about her dream to her husband. A few days later he told her that he originally had been a Christian and then converted to Islâm. But since coming to Abyssiniah he gave a great deal of careful consideration and thought to the matter. He finally had come to the conclusion that Christianity offered the best system of beliefs for the leading of a successful life. Hence he was recanting and going back to the fold of Christianity. He advised her to do the same and become a Christian.

Immediately it struck Ramlah that this was what her dream meant. The metamorphosis of her husband's face from a superior to a lower form and its mutilation meant that he had lost his identity as a Muslim. Then she told him about her dream, hoping that this at least would instill the fear of Allâh in his heart. But he was too far gone on the downward road; not only his face but his heart had been mutilated. 'Obaidullâh was not bothered; in fact he started drinking. He was so addicted that he was drunk for most of the time. Umm Habibah 🌺 was now growing desperate, worrying about the future of her daughter and herself. She prayed to Allâh to give her the strength to remain steadfast in her faith. After some time 'Obaidullâh died due to heavy drinking. Umm Habibah 🌺 was relieved, of course, but what was she to do now, how was she to survive? Only two activities kept her occupied – the upbringing of her daughter and her prayers. She would sometimes get together with the other Muslim ladies in Abyssiniah to talk of the latest developments. Ruqayyah 🌺, the daughter of the Prophet 🌺, Asmâ' bint 'Omais 🌺 and Lailâ bint Abi Hashmah 🌺 were the great ladies with whom she would spend her free time. But these ladies too soon returned home. Still, there were other ladies with whom she was friendly.

Years passed and the map of the Islâmic world changed, as did its history. Al-Madinah was attacked and battles continued to be fought. The Treaty of Hudaibiah was signed and the obsession of the Quraish for revenge was finally quenched. They, and many others like them, thought that this unequal treaty restrained the growing power and influence of Islâm.

One night while she was fast asleep she dreamt someone called out to her, "Mother of the Believers". When she woke up she felt a great sense of well-being and not just happiness, but ecstasy. During the time, the Prophet 🌺 had migrated to Al-Madinah, and the first Islâmic State had been established. Someone, while talking to him about the state of affairs in Abyssiniah, mentioned that Umm Habibah 🌺 was undergoing. The daughter of a wealthy and noble family was living from hand to mouth. After the husband had recanted and died, the daughter of a chieftain of the Quraish was living under tragic circumstances. When the Prophet 🌺 heard this, he sent 'Amr bin Omayyah Adhmri 🌺 to Najâshi with the message that if Umm Habibah 🌺 liked she could marry him.

When Najâshi got the message he sent his slave girl Abraha to Umm Habibah 🌺. Umm Habibah 🌺 was overjoyed when she heard of the proposal, and could not understand how she could possibly reward the bearer of the message. She was so happy that she rewarded Abraha with all the silver jewelery she was wearing - bangles, anklets and rings. Abraha also told her she should appoint someone as her representative for the ceremony. Umm Habibah ﷺ nominated her relative from the tribe of Quraish, Khâlid bin Sa'eed bin 'Aas ﷺ.

That very evening Najâshi sent a message to Ja'far bin Abi Tâlib ﷺ asking him to bring all his Muslim friends to his palace. When all the refugee Muslims were assembled in the court, he announced the news of Umm Habibah's marriage. After praising Almighty Allâh he said he had received a request from His Messenger to arrange for his marriage with Umm Habibah ﷺ, and he was giving her a dowery of four hundred Dinârs.

Then Umm Habibah's representative, Khâlid bin Sa'id bin 'Aas, read the marriage vows and said,

> 'All Praise is for Allâh, and I praise Him, seek His help and ask His forgiveness. I bear witness that None has the right to be worshipped but Allâh and Muhammad is His Servant and His Messenger, to whom He has sent with true Religion and a guidance to the Right Path to overpower His Religion over all the false religions though the polytheists will not like it. I have accepted the proposal of the Prophet ﷺ and married Umm Habibah bint Abu Sufyân to him. May Allâh bless this marriage and make it fruitful for Muhammad ﷺ.'

Najâshi then gave four hundred Dinârs to Khâlid bin Sa'id. When all the guests rose to leave, Najâshi asked them to stay on for a dinner he arranged in celebration of the marriage.

Umm Habibah ﷺ was so grateful to Allâh for the honor bestowed on her by making her one of the Mothers of the Believers that she sent for Abraha and gave her a sum of fifty Dinârs. She said by the Grace of Allâh she now had plenty, and apologized for not having rewarded her earlier in a suitable manner, as she had that time nothing but the little pieces of jewelry she had given her. She asked Abraha to make clothes and jewelry for herself. Abraha respectfully presented her with a little bag. It contained some very expensive perfumes which Najâshi had asked his wives to send for Umm Habibah 🌸. And Abraha presented her with the same jewelry she had received earlier from her, apologizing for her lack of resources. She also sent a message for the Prophet 🌸, saying she had embraced Islâm, but had kept it a secret. She said when Umm Habibah 🌸 met the Prophet 🌸, beloved of all Muslims, she should convey her greetings without fail and this would be the greatest favor she could for a poor woman.

🌸🌸🌸🌸🌸

When Umm Habibah 🌸 reached Al-Madinah she told the Prophet 🌸 about the happenings in Abyssiniah and about the goodness of Najâshi and how the wedding had been organized. She also told him about the slave girl Abraha and the respectful greetings she had sent him. The Prophet 🌸 was very pleased with her message; returning her greetings, he prayed that Allâh 🌸 should bless her with plenitude. Abu Sufyân heard about his daughter's marriage and he expressed happiness in spite of the fact that he had not yet accepted Islâm. He said the Prophet 🌸 was the youth who would never lose face, and always be honored.

When the Quraish broke the Treaty of Hudaibiah, he came to Al-Madinah to renew the treaty. He visited his daughter; just as he was about to sit down Umm Habibah 🌸 quickly stepped forward and rolled up the light mattress which was spread out. He was surprised and asked her if he was not worthy of the mattress, or the mattress was not worthy of him. She replied that actually it was a mattress used by a very pure and clean Prophet, and no idol worshipper could sit on it, as he was unclean. She had therefore rolled it up and put it out of his way. Abu Sufyân was very embarrassed and said she had forgotten her manners since moving away from him. She answered that the manners of Islâm had taught her different values and cleanliness had a different meaning for her now. Since he was not familiar with these concepts he was offended. She said I was thankful that Allâh 🌸 guided me to the path of Islâm. I was surprised that her father, in spite of being an important chieftain of one of the leading tribes of the Quraish, had not yet accepted Islâm. He was in a lofty position by worldly standards, but as far as the norms of a rational religion were concerned, he was really backward. How could he possibly worship a piece of stone that was both blind and deaf, could neither respond to his prayers nor reject them. Abu Sufyân was not happy with what his daughter told him. He asked her how he could possibly, at this stage, turn his back on a religion his forefathers had followed from generations and left his doughter's house.

❀❀❀❀❀

It was the earnest desire of Umm Habibah 🙵 that her father and brother should come into the fold of Islâm and earn the reward of a blessed Paradise. She did not want them to pass away from this world in a state of disbelief like Abu Jahl, Waleed bin Mughairah, 'Aas bin Wâ'il, 'Utbah bin Rabi'h and Shaibah bin Rabi'h. On the occasion of the conquest of Makkah, when Abu Sufyân and Mu'âwiyah pledged allegiance to Allâh and His Prophet, her joy knew no bounds. The following *Âyah* was revealed,

> "Perhaps Allâh will made friendship between you and those whom you hold as enemies. And Allâh has power (over all things), and Allâh is Oft-Forgiving, Most Merciful." (60:7)

'Abdullâh bin 'Abbâs ⚘ says that this particular Verse was revealed on the occasion of Umm Habibah's marriage to the Prophet 鄕. This marriage influenced important chieftains and prominent leaders like Abu Sufyân, Mu'âwiyah and Yazid bin Abu Sufyân to understand Islâm and join the ranks of the Prophet 鄕.

Abu Al-Qâsim bin Asâkar quoting Hasan ⚘ says once Mu'âwiyah was visiting the Prophet 鄕, while he was seated with Umm Habibah 🙵 beside him. When he turned to leave, Prophet 鄕 called out to him and invited him to sit with them.

The Prophet 鄕 then told him that he sincerely wished that they three should sit together and have the pure drink of Paradise there.

These words imply that they will all three, Allâh Willing, be in Paradise. In a similar manner the glad tidings of Paradise for Umm Habibah 🙵 are implied in a very famous statement of the Prophet 鄕 that he has been commanded by Allâh 鄕 to marry only ladies who were deserving of Paradise.

So this means that in this very earthly existence all the Mothers of the Believers had been given the joyous news that they would go to Paradise in the Hereafter.

❀❀❀❀❀

The name of Najâshi, the ruler of Abyssiniah, was actually Ashamah, meaning 'gift'. Since he was a very generous man who was always giving gifts to the distressed and needy. His name was very appropriate. He was a very kind and sympathetic ruler. He became a Muslim after he saw the Islâmic way of life of the refugees from Makkah. He was very kind to them. He not only promptly solemnized the marriage of Umm Habibah 🙏 to the Prophet 🙏, but he also hosted a wedding banquet and provided boats for the journey back. The Angel Jibril 🙏 informed the Prophet 🙏 when he passed away due to natural causes. The Prophet 🙏 prayed to Allâh for the forgiveness of his sins. All the refugees – the Companions and women Companions – who found peace and freedom of religious worship in his kingdom, were very grieved when they received the news of his death. All of them remembered his sympathy, his kindness, his cooperation and the protection he provided them in difficult times. They prayed that his sins be forgiven and he be given a place in Paradise.

❋❋❋❋❋

Umm Habibah 🙏, due to her knowledge, mastery over *Hadith* and eloquence was ranked third among the Mothers of the Believers. The first in rank was 'Aishah 🙏 and the second was Umm Salamah 🙏. There are sixty-five *Ahâdith* narrated by her. Some of them are quoted by men like Mu'âwiyah, 'Abdullâh bin 'Uthbah bin Abu Sufyân, 'Urwah bin Zubair, Sâlem bin Shawâl bin Maki, Abu Al-Jarâh Qurshi. The ladies - Zainab bint Umm Salamah Makhzoomiah and Safiyyah bint Shaiba 'Abdariah رضي الله عنهم quoted others.

In *Sahih Al-Bukhâri* it is mentioned that three days after receiving news of her father's death Umm Habibah 🙏 applied perfume. She then said there was no need for her to apply perfume that day, but the Prophet 🙏 had said,

> 'It is not permissible for a Muslim lady who believes in Allâh and the Last day of Judgment to mourn for more than three days for a dead person, except for her husband. Then she should observe mourning for four months and ten days.'

There is another *Hadith* associated with Umm Habibah 🙏 quoted by Abul Jarrâh Qurshi in *Musnad Abu Ya'lâ* regarding *Miswâk*. She says, the Prophet 🙏 said,

'If it had not been so difficult, I would have liked my *Ummah* (followers) to clean their teeth with *Miswâk* before every prayer just as they perform the ablution before every prayer.'

Another *Hadith* she narrated is quoted in *Musnad Abu Ya'lâ, Musnad Abu Ahmad* and by several other authoritative sources of *Ahâdith* like Abu Dawood, An-Nasâ'i, At-Tirmithi and Ibn Mâjah. This relates to the noon prayer. The Prophet ﷺ said,

'Whoever prays four voluntary *Rak'âh* (units) of prayer before and after the compulsory noon prayer Allâh will make Hell-fire forbidden for him.'

When someone conveyed the message that 'Uthmân bin 'Affân ﷺ was martyred in his house after being besieged, she was so upset that she prayed the killer's hands should be cut off and that he should be disgraced and shamed in public. And Allâh fulfilled her prayer. A man entered the murderer's house and attacked him with a sword; and when the murderer tried to protect himself with his right hand, it got cut off. Then he tried to flee from him and ran into the street, holding his sheet with his teeth. But he could not manage it, the sheet fell, and he was left standing naked in front of all the people on the street.

During her brother Mu'âwiyah's rule she visited Damascus, and it was during his caliphate that she passed away in Al-Madinah in the year 44th after Hijrah. Before her death Umm Habibah ﷺ sent messages to 'Aishah and Umm Salamah رضي الله عنهما apologizing for any offense she might have caused them when disagreements or differences had occurred. Both 'Aishah and Umm Salamah رضي الله عنهما were very touched by this gesture.

"O the one in (complete) rest and satisfaction! Come back to your Lord – well pleased and well pleasing. Enter you then among My (honored) servants, and enter you My Paradise." (89:30)

Maimoonah bint Hârith Al-Hilâliah رضي الله عنها

The Prophet ﷺ said:

"Allâh has commanded me to marry only with the women of Paradise."

'Aishah رضي الله عنها said:

"By Allâh, Maimoonah was the most Allâh-Fearing and nurtured the ties of kinship."

Maimoonah bint Hârith
Al-Hilâliah رضي الله عنها

Abu Hurairah and 'Abdullâh bin 'Abbâs رضي الله عنهم narrated that the original name of Maimoonah 🌸 was Barah, and was changed by the Prophet 🌸. Her father was Hârith bin Hazan, and he belonged to the tribe of Banu Halâl. Her mother's name was Hind bint 'Auf. Umm Al-Fadhal Labâbah Kubrâ and Lababah Sughrâ, Asmâ' and 'Uzzah were her sisters. Umm Al-Fadhal Labâbah Kubrâ was married to 'Abbâs bin 'Abdul Muttalib, and she had the honor of being the second lady to accept Islâm after Khadijah 🌸. Lababah Sughrâ married Waleed bin Mughairah; their son was Khâlid bin Waleed one of the greatest Generals of Islâm. Asmâ' bint Hârith married Ubay bin Khalaf and 'Uzzah married Ziyâd bin 'Abdullâh bin Mâlik. Asmâ' bint 'Omais, Salamah bint 'Omais and Salâmah bint 'Omais were her sisters from her mother's side.

Asmâ' bint 'Omais was first married to Ja'far bin Abi Tâlib 🌸. She had three sons by him – 'Abdullâh, 'Awn and Muhammad. When he was martyred she married Abu Bakr Siddique 🌸. She bore him a son, Muhammad bin Abi Bakr. When Abu Bakr Siddique 🌸 died, she married for the third time. Her third husband was 'Ali bin Abi Tâlib, and they had a son named Yahyâ. Salamah bint 'Omais married Hamzah bin 'Abdul Muttalib. And her third sister Salâma bint 'Omais married 'Abdullâh bin Ka'b.

Thus Hind bint 'Auf had the unique distinction of being the only woman who was the mother-in-law of the Prophet 🌸 , the first Caliph

Abu Bakr Siddique, Hamzah bin 'Abdul Muttalib, 'Abbâs bin 'Abdul Muttalib, Ja'far bin Abi Tâlib and 'Ali bin Abi Tâlib رضي الله عهم.

One of her grandsons was 'Abdullâh bin 'Abbâs, who was the greatest standard bearer of the Muslim army. He was a learned commentator on the Noble Qur'ân and well versed in *Hadith* and *Fiqh*. Another grandson was the greatest General mentioned above, Labâbah Sughrâ's son, Khâild bin Waleed. So, Maimoonah 🙺 came from a very illustrious family of martyrs, warriors and intellectuals.

❀❀❀❀❀

She was first married to Mas'ood bin 'Amr bin 'Omair Thaqafi, but they soon separated on grounds of incompatibility. Her second husband was Abu Raham bin 'Abdul 'Uzzah 'Amri Quraishi. He died shortly after their marriage and Maimoonah 🙺 was widowed at a very early age.

In the year 7th after Hijrah the Prophet 🙵 went with his Companions to Makkah to perform 'Umrah. It is said that Maimoonah 🙺 wished to marry him and become one of the honorable Mothers of the Believers. Soon this wish became an absorbing desire. She even mentioned it to her sisters.

She felt her tribe, Banu Hilâl should also be connected to the Prophet 🙵 in the same way that the other tribes like Banu Teem, Banu 'Adi, Banu Umayyah, Banu Makhzoom, Banu Asad and Banu Mustalaq were connected – by marriage. Lababah Kubrâ who was married to 'Abbâs bin 'Abdul Muttalib mentioned her sister's wish to her husband, saying that since he was the uncle and very highly respected by the Prophet 🙵 if he requested him, her sister's wish could be fulfilled.

When 'Abbâs ♣ spoke to the Prophet 🙵, he requested Ja'far bin Abi Tâlib ♣ to make the arrangements for the marriage. The Prophet 🙵 had finished his 'Umrah and was free, and Maimoonah 🙺 was on a camel. When she saw him, she involuntarily exclaimed that the camel and its rider were bequeathed to Allâh's Messenger. Thus, she gifted herself to the Prophet 🙵, and he accepted her very gracefully.

But a more popular tradition says that when he arrived in Makkah for his *'Umrah,* he sent Ja'far bin Abi Tâlib ♣ with his proposal of marriage to Maimoonah 🙺. She asked her brother-in-law, 'Abbâs bin 'Abdul Muttalib ♣ to handle matters. When the Prophet 🙵 finished his

'Umrah, 'Abbâs 🌸 arranged the ceremony.

Allâh said,

> "O Prophet! Verily, We have made lawful to you your wives, to
> whom you have paid their *Mahr*, and those (slaves) whom your
> right hand possesses — whom Allâh has given to you, and the
> daughters of your paternal uncles and the daughters of your
> paternal aunts and the daughters of your maternal uncles and
> the daughters of your maternal aunts who migrated with you,
> and a believing woman if she offers herself to the Prophet, and
> the Prophet wishes to marry her, a privilege for you only, not for
> the (rest of) the believers. Indeed We know what We have
> enjoined upon them about their wives and those whom their
> right hands possess, in order that there should be no difficulty on
> you. And Allâh is Ever Oft-Forgiving, Most Merciful." (33:50)

After his *Umrah* the Prophet 🌸 stayed in Makkah for three days. Then,
on the fourth morning Hawaitab bin 'Abdul 'Uzzâ came with some of
the polytheists and told him that since he had finished his *'Umrah*, he
ought to leave, according to the terms of the Treaty of Hudaibah. The
Prophet 🌸 requested that they be allowed to stay for a few more days,
and he invited them to attend the dinner he had arranged to celebrate
the marriage. Hawaitab answered that they were not interested in any
dinner; they just wanted him to go.

The Prophet 🌸 left and pitched camp at a place called Saraf, about nine
miles from Makkah, and here he celebrated the marriage. His slave, Abu
Râfi' brought Maimoonah 🌸 on a camel to Saraf. It was here that her
name was changed from Barah to Maimoonah 🌸. Both had completed
the rites of *'Umrah*; they changed their garments of *Ihrâm* and the
marriage could take place according to *Shari'ah*.

Maimoonah 🌸 was the last lady that Muhammad 🌸 married. She was
twenty-six years old at the time. When they reached Al-Madinah an
apartment, which was built next to the Prophet's mosque, was given to
her. The other wives of the Prophet 🌸 warmly welcomed her. She used
to pray in the Prophet's mosque because she heard him saying that one
prayer in it was the equivalent to a thousand prayers in all other
mosques, except in Masjid Harâm at Makkah. One prayer in Masjid
Harâm was equal to a hundred thousand prayers in any other mosques.

One year several delegations came to Al-Madinah; one of them was from the tribe Banu Halâl. One of the members of this delegation was the son of the sister of Maimoonah 🌸, Ziyâd bin 'Abdullâh bin Mâlik 'Amri. He visited his aunt in her apartment when the Prophet 🌸 happened to be out on some task. When he came and saw a stranger seated with her he was not pleased. Maimoonah 🌸, sensitive as she was, sensed his displeasure and immediately introduced him as her sister's son and a member of the visiting delegation. He expressed his pleasure and prayed for Allâh Almighty's blessings for him.

Maimoonah 🌸 was valued highly for her traits like God-Fearing and nurturing good relations with all members of the family. And this tribute was paid to her when she passed away by 'Aishah 🌸 in the words 'By Allâh! Maimoonah 🌸 has passed away, she was the most Allâh-Fearing and nurtured the ties of kinship.'

🌸🌸🌸🌸🌸

Maimoonah 🌸 had an excellent memory, and knew by heart many of the *Ahâdith* of Prophet 🌸. The most *Ahâdith* - two thousand two hundred and ten are attributed to 'Aishah 🌸. Next came Umm Salamah with three hundred and seventy-eight *Ahâdith*. Next came Maimoonah 🌸 – seventy-six *Ahâdith* were attributed to her. 'Abdullâh bin 'Abbâs, 'Abdullâh bin Shaddâd, 'Obaid bin Sabâq, Yazid bin Asam, 'Abdur-Rahmân Sâ'ib Al-Hilâli, 'Obaidullâh Khaulâni, Sulaiman bin Yasâr and 'Atâ' bin Yasâr رضي الله عنهم have quoted her.

In *Sahih Al-Bukhâri* a *Hadith* is narrated from 'Abdullâh bin 'Abbâs رضي الله عنهما and attributed to Maimoonah 🌸. Someone asked the Prophet 🌸 regarding a mouse that had fallen into some clarified butter. He said the mouse and what surrounds it should be thrown out and the rest could be eaten.

Musnad Abu Ya'lâ, Muslim, Abu Dawood and Nisâ'i have quoted another *Hadith* from Maimoonah 🌸. This was narrated by the wife of 'Abdullâh bin 'Abbâs 🌸.

One morning the Prophet 🌸 looked very worried and he seemed to be in the same mood in the evening. The next day the same mood continued. Maimoonah 🌸 asked him what was troubling him. He said the Angel Jibril 🌸 promised to come and visit him, but he had not turned up. Such a thing never happened before. Then the family noticed there was a puppy sitting under a bed. He was chased out and that part of the floor was washed on the directions of the Prophet 🌸. Soon after that the Angel Jibril 🌸 came. Then the Prophet 🌸 asked him why he had not come earlier as promised, and he said that this had never happened before. Then the Angel told him that angels do not enter places where there are dogs or pictures.

Maimoonah 🌸 sometimes used to take loans. Once a member of her family remarked on this and asked her why she did this. She did not quite like this question and replied that the Prophet 🌸 used to say if a Muslim borrowed money and he sincerely believed that Allâh 🌸 would help him to repay the loan, then Allâh 🌸 would surely arrange things in an unexpected manner.

'Aishah 🌸 relates that the last fatal illness of the Prophet 🌸 started while he was in the apartment of Maimoonah 🌸. He asked permission of his other wives to spend those days in the apartment of 'Aishah 🌸. They all readily agreed. When he passed away he was pleased with all his wives. When his pure soul left his body he was in the apartment of his favourite wife 'Aishah 🌸 resting his head in her lap. And he was buried in his favourite place, her apartment. Nine of his wives were alive at the time. They were 'Aishah, Maimoonah, Safiyyah, Juveriah, Saudah, Zainab, Ramlah, Hind, and Hafsah رضي الله عنهن.

It was during the caliphate of Mu'âwiyah 🌸, in the year 51th after Hijrah, that Maimoonah 🌸 died. She was in Makkah and she fell ill there. She was very restless and wanted to be taken some place else. Her relatives took her to Saraf, the same place where she had got married to the Prophet 🌸. After reaching the exact spot where she spent her wedding night, she passed away. 'Abdullâh bin 'Abbâs 🌸 conducted the funeral prayers, and she was buried with great honor.

"O the one in (complete) rest and satisfaction! Come back to your Lord – well pleased and well pleasing. Enter you then among My (honored) servants, and enter you My Paradise." (89:30)

Women Companions
Who were given the News of Paradise

Fâtimah رضي الله عنها bint Prophet Muhammad ﷺ

Prophet ﷺ told his daughter Fâtimah ﵂ :

"Would you like to be the leader of the women of Paradise?"

Allâh's Messenger ﷺ said:

"One day Angel came and told me the glad tiding that Fâtimah ﵂ will be the leader of women of Paradise."

'Aishah ﵂ narrated;

"She bore a remarkable resemblance to Allâh's Messenger ﷺ. Her way of speaking, sitting, standing and walking — in other words all her manners and gestures were exactly like his."

Fâtimah رضي الله عـنها bint
Prophet Muhammad ﷺ

She was the youngest daughter of the Prophet ﷺ and his favourite. She married his cousin 'Ali bin Abi Tâlib ﷺ and was the mother of the great martyrs of Islâm, Hasan and Husain رضي الله عنهما. She was born in Makkah a few years before her father was granted Prophethood. Though both Muhammad ﷺ and Khadijah ﷺ already had three daughters before her they expressed great happiness at her birth. Going against the accepted custom, her mother did not send her beloved youngest daughter away to be breast fed in any of the surrounding villages, but kept her with her and nursed her herself. She loved her too much to entrust her to anyone else's care. Some years later her father was declared by Allâh ﷻ to be His Prophet ﷺ and last Messenger.

She and her mother and her three elder sisters – Zainab, Ruqayyah, and Umm Kulthoom رضي الله عنهن – accepted Islâm and believed in their father as Allâh's Messenger from the very beginning. She spent her early years under the loving and tender care of her parents. Zeal for the defense of what is sacred and love of the righteous was ingrained in her. She would protect her father and the cause of Allâh ﷻ against all odds and at all times, with courage and conviction. At the very tender age of ten she had gone through the siege of Shi'b Abi Tâlib. And it was by no means a short siege; it lasted for three long years. It was a total social and economic boycott, where children sobbed with the pains of hunger, and mothers and sisters were tormented by the sight of loved ones suffering. During this period she showed exemplary courage, but this terrible time left an effect on her health which lasted till the end of her life. Just the everyday chores like grinding wheat for bread, fetching water and cooking left her exhausted. When she asked her father for a slave girl from the prisoners of war to help her, he said he would give her something better. And then he taught her some special prayers exalting and glorifying Allâh that would help to dispel her weariness.

'Aishah 🕮 said that she never saw anyone more devoted to the truth than Fâtimah 🕮. She stood shoulder to shoulder with the other *Muhâjir* and *Ansâr* women of Makkah and Al-Madinah tending to the injured and the dying in the Battle of Uhud. When she saw her injured and bleeding father, the Prophet 🕮 in the battlefield at Uhud she just could not take it. She helped to stop the bleeding and bandaged his wounds.

Before Muhammad proclaimed himself the Last Prophet of Allâh Almighty, he was the most popular, loved and respected man among the Quraish. The most important decisions that had to be made were referred to his wise judgment. If people needed some valuable goods to be left in the care and trust of a reliable person, he was the man they turned to. He was such an eminent and successful trader even in his youth, that experienced businessmen were amazed at his shrewdness and insight. And when he married Khadijah 🕮, the wealthiest businesswoman, exporter and importer of her time, people were amazed. And he became even more sought after and popular. But once he announced himself to be the Allâh's Prophet and Messenger, his whole life seemed to turn around. The entire city seemed to be shaken by an earthquake, as it were. He became the most unpopular and reviled man in Makkah and was the centre of a storm of objections and accusations. Those who wanted him to recant and give up his claims started using all kind of tactics – persuasion and torture. The streets he previously frequented were strewn with thorns and filth and garbage was thrown on him from balconies and rooftops. Elaborate plans were made to murder him. Naturally, all these trials and tribulations could not but leave a mark on his home life. Fâtimah 🕮 was passing the impressionable years of her childhood in the shadow of these events. Yet, her maturity was such that she faced all this with remarkable patience and determination.

She fought like a courageous little tigress to defend her father and protect him. She would stand in front of him to shield him from the attacks of devilish men like Abu Jahl, 'Utbah and Shaibah.

On one occasion, the Prophet 🐝 went into the sanctuary of Makkah with some of his Companions and started to pray, the disbelievers had just then sacrificed a camel. The filth and bowels of the camel were lying there, when a horrible idea came to Abu Jahl. He asked who among his friends would like to lift all that filth and pile it on the back of Muhammad 🐝. 'Oqbah bin Abi Mu'eet, the lowest of the low among his friends, got up shruggihis shoulders with satanic glee, and said he would perform the task. And he lifted up the bloody filthy mess and piled it on the Prophet's back while he was in the act of prostrating before Allâh 🐝. All of them then broke into peals of uncontrollable devilish laughter. When news of this dastardly act reached Fâtimah 🐝 in her house, she rushed to the sanctuary. Removing with her pure little hands all the filth she threw it into the distance. She then cleaned her father's back. And furious at the brutal treatment given to her beloved father, she scolded the disbelievers. When the Prophet 🐝 finished his prayers, he lifted his hands in supplication and appealed to Allâh 🐝 to hold these men – Abu Jahl bin Hishâm, Shaibah bin Rabee'ah, 'Oqbah bin Abi Mu'eet and Omayyah bin Khalaf, in His relentless grip. These devils became very nervous because they knew that any supplication made at the sanctuary in Makkah is never rejected by Allâh Almighty. And the Prophet's prayers were answered. All these men were killed in the Battle of Badr, except 'Oqbah bin Abi Mu'eet. He was taken prisoner and the Prophet 🐝 ordered him to be put to death. Trembling with fear, he asked what would be the lot of his children. Muhammad 🐝 said they would go to Hell. He asked if he would be put to death in spite of the fact that he was a member of the tribe of Quraish. The Prophet 🐝 answered in the affirmative. Then he looked up at his Companions and asked them if they knew what his crime was. Then he told them all this man's doings. Once when the Prophet 🐝 was prostrating before Allâh 🐝, this vile man placed his foot on his neck and pressed it so hard that his eyes almost popped out of their sockets. The next time again when he was in the same position of prostration, he put offal and filthy blood soaked intestines of a camel sacrificed in the name of one of the idols on his back. Then he narrated how his beloved Fâtimah 🌺 removed it and cleaned his back and his clothes.

Once Abu Jahl was sitting with the disbelievers in front of the Ka'bah planning how to eliminate this man for the 'crime' of rejecting the idols installed there as helpless stones which lacked movement. They hated him for propagating the Oneness of Allâh 🌟 and for proclaiming himself as His Last Prophet and Messenger. Fâtimah 🌺 happened to pass by and heard him. She was so terrified of what these cruel barbarians could do to her beloved father that she went running to tell him of their dastardly plot. As she wept she told him they had sworn in the names of their most famous idols – Lât, Manât, 'Uzzâ and Nâ'ilah – to kill him. All of them would get together and attack him the moment he stepped out of his house. She asked him innocently what would happen, as nothing could stop these men now. The Prophet 🌟 told her to have faith in Allâh 🌟, as He was her father's Protector. He then got up calmly, made the ablution for his prayers and went to the House of Allâh. When he passed Abu Jahl and his friends who were seated there, he looked up towards the Heavens, then turned his eyes downward. (Saying that Allâh Almighty would cover their faces with dust), he picked up a handful of mud threw it in their direction. These people were so taken aback and overcome that none of them could stir from their places or speak. It was as if the fear of the Almighty had struck them dumb.

Once Fâtimah 🌺 passed by Abu Jahl bin Hishâm on the street and he, for no reason, gave her a tight slap across the face. She went to Abu Sufyân, the leader of the Quraish, and complained to him about Abu Jahl's cruel and uncivilized behavior. Abu Sufyân took her with him to the place where the uncouth barbarian was still sitting and told her to slap him in exactly the same way as he had done. When she went home and narrated this incident to the Prophet 🌟 he was very pleased at Abu Sufyân's sense of justice and fair play. He then prayed that his heart should be enlightened, and that he should accept Islâm as the true religion. His supplications for Abu Sufyân were accepted and he finally swore allegiance to Allâh and His Prophet Muhammad 🐝.

Seven years had passed since Muhammad 🐝 declared himself to be Allâh's chosen Prophet. The whole might of the Quraish had not been able to silence him and his Message; the people who answered the call of Allâh 🐝 were persecuted and tortured in every way possible. They were made to lie on layers of burning coals, and dragged naked across the burning desert sands, but they continued to recite the word of Oneness of Allâh - 'None has the right to be worshipped but Allâh, and Muhammad is His Servant and His Messenger'. The numbers of the believers kept multiplying, regardless of the consequences they might face in this world.

When Hamzah bin 'Abdul Muttalib and 'Umar bin Khattâb رضي الله عنهما accepted Islâm the whole of Makkah was shaken by an earthquake, as it were. The people started pushing the leaders to take some action as otherwise they would lose their hold and all their power and their pomp would fall into the dust and become a story of the past. In the light of these new developments, Abu Jahl called a meeting of the richest and most influential people among the disbelievers. He asked them to suggest the best course of action to be taken against this new movement which was gathering strength against the religion of their forefathers. How could they stem this tide?

One of the devil's right hand men, a libertine and worthless fellow, Nadhar bin Hârith, was present at this meeting. He was an extremely cunning and devious man. His idea was to completely boycott these Muslims - socially and economically. No business, no trade no intermarriages - nothing should be allowed, he said. The tribes of Banu Hâshim and Banu 'Abdul Muttalib and the families who supported them and helped them should be ostracized as well. No food or water should reach them. A very alert and vigilant force should keep an eye on them to see that absolutely nothing reached them; in this way these people would perish and with them their new-born religion. This unusual plan appealed to all those present and was adopted unanimously. There were cries of acclaim from all sides and the Muslims went into a state of siege in Shi'ab Abi Tâlib.

This siege lasted for three years. Nothing could melt the hearts of the disbelievers. The screaming of hungry children, the sobbing of mothers and sisters, the helpless condition of the aged and the evil infirm – all this could not move their stony hearts. But every student of history was amazed to note that in spite of the worst siege in history being forced on the staunch followers of this new religion, not one – man, woman or child recanted and moved out. The truth and righteousness of their cause, the charismatic and magnetic personality of the Prophet ﷺ was their strength. This crucible of suffering burned out all the impure elements and their faith grew firmer and purer. The richest woman of Makkah, Khadijah ﷺ, her young daughters – the youngest Fâtimah ﷺ, barely ten years of age – stood like rocks by her father. They could give their lives for him. And in a sense little Fâtimah ﷺ did, because this mental and physical ordeal affected her health and physique for the rest of her life.

What is Divine Destiny? Who can fathom Allâh Almighty's will? Why did His loved ones who propagated His Faith have to suffer as if they had no one to help or assist them? Man's vision is very limited and he cannot account for the workings of the Divine plan.

Those who live for material benefits cannot understand the workings of the minds of those who do not care for the pleasures of this world. Their trials and tribulations give them a spiritual strength that gives immeasurable and incalculable satisfaction. Their tears seem to purify their souls, wash away the impurities and enlighten their hearts and minds. When the suffering soul of the God-fearing and righteous weeps while prostrating, he is closest to Allâh; perhaps this is why those beloved of Allâh Almighty are made to suffer to achieve nearness to Him. For this is sure; lovers of truth are more deserving reward in the Hereafter than the lovers of evil.

❊❊❊❊❊

Soon after the siege of Shi'b Bani Hâshim was lifted, the Prophet ﷺ and Fâtimah ﷺ and her sisters went through the trauma of losing their beloved Khadijah ﷺ. She had fallen ill during the siege. Ten years passed since Muhammad ﷺ declared himself to be the Messenger of Allâh ﷺ. It was at the same time that the Prophet ﷺ lost his greatest supporter and defender, his uncle Abi Tâlib. The disbelievers became bolder as they thought he was 'helpless.' Fâtimah, from a tender age, was facing all these troubles and experiencing them first hand side by side with her father. It was also at this time that the Prophet went to Tâ'if with the Message of Islâm. The people there were like the Makkans; they welcomed him with stones and he left Tâ'if injured and bleeding. But he did not curse these inhospitable and cruel people; on the other hand he prayed to Allâh to guide them to the right path. Umm Kulthoom and Fâtimah رضي الله عنهما were very upset and started weeping when they saw his condition. He affectionately wiped away their tears and consoled them. He said it was inevitable that Allâh would help to spread His religion and make it triumph against all odds. Easier times were bound to follow the hard and difficult days.

And sure enough Mus'ab bin 'Omair who was the Prophet's ambassador to Al-Madinah gave the good news that the people there were being drawn into the fold of Islâm. They invited Muhammad to settle in their city, and promised to help him in any way they could. The Prophet accepted their invitation and with the consent of Allâh Almighty decided to migrate to Al-Madinah. He commanded his followers to start the process of migration, and he followed later in the company of his most trusted Companion, Abu Bakr Siddique. He left his two daughters at home in Makkah, with Saudah bin Zam'ah, whom he had married after the death of Khadijah.

He sent for them later, and thus these three ladies also had the privilege of becoming migrants for the cause. But the disbelievers could not bear to see them all moving out either. Some mischievous elements caught hold of them on the outskirts of Makkah. One of them was the evil Quraishi youth, Hawairath bin Naqeeth. He started jabbing at the camel on which the Prophet's daughters were riding and the camel reared up in the air, and the two girls fell down. When he saw this he ran away. This little caravan continued on the journey borne by their spiritual faith and strength.

When they reached their destination, the Prophet received them. He was very happy to see them alive and well. Those whom Allâh Almighty protects, no one can harm them.

❀❀❀❀❀

In the year 2ⁿᵈ after Hijrah, the battle of Badr was fought and 'Ali ﷺ showed exemplary courage, valor skill at fighting. The Islâmic forces triumphed and archenemies like Abu Jahl and some other prominent leaders of the Quraish were killed in battle. Many of the disbelievers were captured as prisoners of war and brought to Al-Madinah. This victory lifted up the spirits of the Muslims as never before.

Fâtimah ﷺ was now eighteen years old and prominent personalities started proposing for her, but the Prophet ﷺ said he was waiting for a sign from Allâh ﷻ. One day 'Ali ﷺ came to see the Prophet ﷺ, but he was very shy and diffident and seemed to be holding something back. The Prophet ﷺ realized what was on his mind and asked him if he came to propose marriage to Fâtimah ﷺ. 'Ali ﷺ answered that he had. The Prophet ﷺ asked Fâtimah ﷺ what she thought of the proposal. She started to weep silently. He then told her that 'Ali ﷺ was a learned, kind-hearted and brave young man. Fâtimah ﷺ accepted her father's decision. He then asked 'Ali ﷺ if he had some money for the dowery. 'Ali ﷺ replied that the Prophet ﷺ had seen his life from the cradle and knew his financial position very well. Then the Prophet ﷺ asked him where his shield was, and said that would be the dowery for Fâtimah ﷺ. 'Ali ﷺ sent it to the market with his slave to be sold and got four hundred Dirhams for it. This he gave to the Prophet ﷺ, who asked him to keep the money and buy some things for the house and perfume for the wedding. Then he asked Anas bin Mâlik ﷺ to bring his Companions – Abu Bakr, 'Uthmân, 'Umar, Talhah, Zubair رضي الله عنهم, and other Ansâr and Mohâjir friends to attend the ceremony. When all these esteemed people assembled, he asked 'Ali ﷺ to read his own marriage speech. Then 'Ali ﷺ stood up and recited the words of the ceremony.

> 'All Praise is for Allâh. We are grateful to Him for His Bounties and His Blessings. I bear witness that None has the right to be worshipped but Allâh, vouching for Him so it will reach Him and gain His Favour. The Prophet ﷺ has married his daughter, Fâtimah ﷺ, to me and the *Mahr* has been fixed at four hundred Dirhams. Now all those present please listen to what the Prophet ﷺ has to say and bear witness.'

After that the Prophet ﷺ praised Allâh Almighty and recited the marriage ceremony, after asking Fâtimah 🌸 for her consent. He announced the *Mahr* and told all those present that Allâh 🌸 had commanded him to have Fâtimah 🌸 married to 'Ali 🌸. After that he prayed for a happy and blessed future for the bride and groom. Then dates were offered to the guests. All those present expressed their happiness and prayed that Allâh 🌸 should bless the newly married couple. The next day Hamzah bin 'Abdul Muttalib 🌸 slaughtered a camel to host a banquet to celebrate the wedding of his brother's son, 'Ali 🌸.

Some basic things were purchased for the house to which 'Ali 🌸 and Fâtimah 🌸 moved. A bed, a pillow filled with the leaves of dried date palm, a plate, a glass, a leather water bag and a grinding stone for grinding flour - these were the few things with which the daughter of the Prophet 🌸 set up her new home. The house that was available was quite a distance from the Prophet's Mosque. The Prophet 🌸 wished his daughter could live closer to him, so that he could see her daily. When one of the Companion Hârithah bin Nu'mân Ansâri 🌸, came to know of this he approached the Prophet 🌸 very respectfully, saying he had a number of houses close to the Prophet's Mosque and he was welcome to choose any one of them. This would make that particular house dearer to him. The Prophet 🌸 was very moved by this offer and chose one for Fâtimah 🌸, and prayed for increase and prosperity for his devoted follower. So, 'Ali 🌸 and Fâtimah 🌸 moved in and started the routine of daily life. It was usual for her to grind the wheat, fetch water from the well and cook their meals.

Since she was not very robust and healthy, the siege having left its mark on her, Fâtimah 🌸 used to get very tired with all this hard work. On one occasion after a battle, a lot of money, precious jewelery and prisoners of war, both men and women, were taken by the Muslim army. 'Ali 🌸 suggested that she should go to the Prophet 🌸 and ask him for a maid to help, since she used to get very tired with all the housework.

Fâtimah 🌸 went to see her father and request him for some help. He was not at home and she left a message with 'Aishah 🌸. At night, before going to sleep, her father came to visit her. He told her that he would give her something much better than a slave girl. And he taught her some phrases in praise of Almighty Allâh. These, he said, were better than any maid. And he taught her to recite thirty-three times *Subhânallâh* (Glory be to Allâh), thirty-three times *Alhamdulillâh* (All praise is for Allâh), thirty-three times *Allâh-u-Akbar* (Allâh is the greatest).

Fâtimah ﷺ spent her entire life as a God-fearing and pious servant of Allâh ﷻ. Always patient and grateful to her Maker, there was not a word of complaint from her, however difficult the circumstances. The world and its attractions held no charm for her. Her motto in life was always service for Islâm and its *Mujâhideen*. In the battles she was at the front nursing the woand the sick. When her father was injured in the battle of Uhud, it was she who burnt a part of a straw mat and used its ashes to stem the flow of blood. There is a narration in *Sahih Al-Bukhâri* that when the Prophet ﷺ was asked on one occasion whom he loved best in the world he named his youngest daughter, Fâtimah ﷺ.

'Aishah ﷺ, talking of her, says she bore a remarkable resemblance to her father. She not only looked like him, but her way of speaking, sitting, standing and walking – in other words all her mannerisms and gestures were exactly like his. Whenever her father visited her she would receive him and kiss his forehead with reverence and respect. They were exceptionally close to each other and whenever she visited her father, he would stand up and receive her. It was as if she left the sweet aura of her personality wherever she went. If he saw her troubled or sad he would also be grieved, and if he saw her happy he would also be pleased.

One day the Prophet ﷺ heard that there was some misunderstanding between 'Ali and Fâtimah رضي الله عنهما, so he went to meet them. On the way to their house he looked very troubled and sad, and when he left their house he seemed very much at peace. Some of his Companions noted that he was a different man while going to his daughter's house and a different man on the way back. He replied that he just settled some differences between his two children who were very dear to him. And his happiness made his face glow. On one occasion 'Ali made up his mind to marry Abu Jahl's daughter. Somehow Fâtimah ﷺ came to hear about it and told her father that 'Ali was planning to marry into Abu Jahl's family; the Prophet ﷺ was very disturbed when he heard this. He went to the mosque and gave a sermon, saying that Fâtimah ﷺ was a part of his heart and anything that made her unhappy displeased him. He said that the daughter of Allâh's Messenger and the daughter of His enemy could not be married to the same man. 'Ali ؏ changed his mind and apologized to Fâtimah ﷺ for any pain he might have caused her. And things went back to normal.

One day 'Ali ؏ asked the Prophet ﷺ who was dearer to him, himself or Fâtimah ﷺ? The Prophet ﷺ answered that he loved Fâtimah ﷺ more, but 'Ali was dearer to him than her. It was a masterly piece of diplomacy and yet it also was the truth, because he really did love both of them deeply.

❀❀❀❀❀

Their first son was born to 'Ali and Fâtimah رضي الله عنهما in Ramadhân of the year 3ʳᵈ after Hijrah. When the Prophet ﷺ heard the good news he was very happy and immediately went to see the child. He named him Hasan and recited the *Athân* for him. Then on the seventh day his head was shaved clean, and an amount of silver equivalent to the weight of the hair was distributed among the poor.

In Sha'bân of the year 4ᵗʰ after Hijrah, a second son was born. The Prophet ﷺ named him Husain, and in his ears too he recited the *Athân* himself. It is said a third son Mohsin was born but died in his infancy. The Prophet ﷺ loved these two grandchildren dearly. He used to say that they were like blossoms and would be the leaders of the youths of Paradise. Osâmah bin Zaid says that one day he saw the Prophet ﷺ carrying something wrapped in a sheet. He asked him what he was carrying. He opened the sheet and what should Osâmah ؏ see, but these two little boys all wrapped up in their grandfather's arms. He said that these were his daughter's sons and he would love all those who loved them.

In the year 5ᵗʰ after Hijrah a daughter was born to 'Ali and Fâtimah رضي الله عنهما; the Prophet ﷺ named her Zainab; in the year 7ᵗʰ after Hijrah another daughter was born and he named her Umm Kulthoom. When Zainab bint 'Ali ﷺ grew up she married 'Abdullâh bin Ja'far bin Abi Tâlib ؏. And Umm Kulthom married 'Umar bin Khattâb رضي الله عنهما. They had two children Zaid and Ruqayyah. After his wedding 'Umar bin

Khattâb asked the *Muhâjirs* (immigrants) and the Ansâr to congratulate him. They asked him for the reason. He said since he had married Umm Kulthoom, the daughter of 'Ali bin Abi Tâlib ﷺ, I had established links with the family of the Prophet ﷺ, and this was a very great honor for me. And everyone wished him happiness and blessed him on this great occasion.

❀❀❀❀❀

Imâm Ahmad was once asked what he thought of 'Ali and his family members. He said their position in history is unparalleled. According to what the Noble Qur'ân tells us Allâh Almighty had cleaned them of every kind of sin, impurity of faith, disobedience to the Divine Will and social evils.

Ibn 'Abdullâh writes that whenever the Prophet ﷺ came back from any journey or after taking part in a battle, he would first go to the his Mosque in Al-Madinah and pray two *Rak'ât* (units), then he would visit Fâtimah ﷻ and then visit the wives in his household.

There is a miraculous incident related in Al-Bidâyah wa An-Nihâyah, once a lady sent Fâtimah ﷻ a couple of pieces of bread and some roasted meat. She put this in a large plate and covered it with cloth. Then she sent a message to her father to come and have his meal at her house. When he arrived she removed the cloth and to her astonishment she found the plate full of bread and plenty of meat. She understood that this abundance and plenty had come from Allâh. She praised Almighty Allâh and asked Allah to mention and bless His Prophet ﷺ and started to serve the meal to him, beginning with Allâh Almighty's Name. When he saw such a huge amount he smiled and asked who had sent it all. She promptly said Allâh gave it to her and He provides sustenance to whom He pleased without limits. He smiled and thanked Allâh Almighty that He had daughter to speak like Maryam. Then the Prophet ﷺ ate of the meal with his daughter, son-in-law and the two grandchildren. Yet there was so much food still left over that it was sent to the Mothers of the Believers. They also ate their fill and then it was distributed among the neighbours.

❀❀❀❀❀

'Abdullâh bin 'Abbâs 🌸 says that when *Surat An-Nasr* was revealed the Prophet 🌸 sent for Fâtimah 🌸 and told her that Allâh had intimated to him that his life on earth was now drawing to a close. Islâm was spreading and hordes of people were now turning to it. When Fâtimah 🌸 heard this she started to weep at the thought of separation from her beloved father. Then he told her that from among his family members she would be the first to meet up with him. At this she started smiling. When he fell ill and his condition started to deteriorate, she could not bear to see his suffering. He then told her that after that day he would never have to suffer again, as he felt he was about to leave for a better Hereafter.

In his book *Asad Al-Ghâbah*, Ibn Atheer writes that after the Prophet 🌸 passed away no one ever saw Fâtimah 🌸 smile. And her grief remained visible on her face till she passed away, six months later.

"To Allâh we belong and to Him we return." (2:56)

'Ali 🌸 and her four children – Hasan, Hussian, Zainab, and Umm Kulthoom رضي الله عنهم were left to mourn her death at a very young age. She was given her final bath and shrouded by 'Ali, Asmâ' bint 'Omais and Salamah Umm Râf' رضي الله عنهم and buried at night in *Jannatul Baqi'*. 'Ali, 'Abbâs, and Fadhal bin 'Abbâs رضي الله عنهم placed her into her final resting place. Thus the leader of the virtuous women of Paradise set out on her journey to Paradise.

"O the one in (complete) rest and satisfaction! Come back to your Lord – well pleased and well pleasing. Enter you then among My (honored) servants, and enter you My Paradise."

Fâtimah bint Asad رضي الله عنها

The Prophet ﷺ said:

"I gave my shirt to be used as a part of her shroud, so that she would be dressed the dress of Paradise."

Fâtimah bint Asad رضي الله عنها

Fâtimah bint Asad رضي was the mother of 'Ali bin Abu Tâlib رضي, and the mother-in-law of the Prophet's daughter Fâtimah bint Muhammad صلى. Her grandsons, Hasan and Husain رضي الله عنهما are to be the leaders of the youths of Paradise. Besides 'Ali رضي, she had two other sons. One was Ja'far Tayyâr رضي who was a famous General. He led the forces of Islâm in the battle of Mu'tah and was martyred in the same battle.

The Prophet صلى was an orphan child, his father died before his birth; his mother also died when he was very young. His paternal uncle, Abu Tâlib, had in a sense adopted him. And Fâtimah bint Asad رضي, Abu Tâlib's wife, looked after him like her own. She protected him as closely as the heart is in the human breast.

When he grew up and proclaimed himself to be the Prophet and Last Messenger of Allâh, she still stood by him. All the relentless persecution did not deter her in any way. She was exceptionally fond of her son Ja'far رضي, but for the sake of Islâm she bore the separation from him and his wife, Asmâ' bint 'Omais رضي الله عنها when they migrated to Abysiniah on the Prophet's orders with the first group of migrant Muslims.

Fâtimah bint Asad رضي being one of the first to swear allegiance to Islâm and its concept of the Oneness of Allâh صلى, faced the economic and social boycott of the Shi'ab Abi Tâlib for those three terrible years. She was also a member of the privileged group who migrated to Al-Madinah. Her family could be traced to the Hâshmi dynasty, as could the Prophet's.

❀❀❀❀❀

Fâtimah bint Asad bin Hâshim bin Abd Munâf bin Qasi Hâshmi ﷺ – that was her lineage. 'Abdul Muttalib, who was a very discriminating man had assessed her nature, her intelligence and her capabilities from the very beginning and proposed for her for his son, Abu Tâlib. When the Prophet ﷺ was told by Allâh to spread the Message of Islâm among his kith and kin, it was Fâtimah bint Asad ﷺ who immediately accepted this invitation and swore allegiance and entered the fold of Islâm. When the Prophet's grandfather, 'Abdul Muttalib, passed away, the guardianship of the orphan Muhammad ﷺ passed on to Abu Tâlib. His wife, Fâtimah bint Asad ﷺ, looked after him, loving him as if he were her own. He remembered in his later life that she would go hungry to feed him. He respected her so highly that whenever she visited him he would stand up and receive her with great love, addressing her as 'Mother'.

His uncle too loved him deeply. Muhammad ﷺ in his childhood was so well mannered and so fastidious about his personal cleanliness that Abu Tâlib would hold him up as an example to his other children. Normally boys would be dirty and tousled from playing rough games with the other boys, but Muhammad ﷺ was always dignified with a neat appearance. People were impressed when they saw him. Abu Tâlib liked all the children to eat together because he felt that whenever Muhammad ﷺ ate with other children, food would be sufficient and when the children ate alone they would remain hungry. Abu Tâlib often told his nephew that he was specially blessed, as there was plenty when he was around.

Fâtimah bint Asad ﷺ did not spare any pains and looked after the Prophet ﷺ in his infancy, boyhood and youth. Once in his childhood he accompanied his uncle on a business trip to Syria. Some very unusual and surprising incidents took place on the journey, and Abu Tâlib described these to his wife Fâtimah bint Asad ﷺ when they came back. She was also very moved and impressed.

The same was the case with Maisarah, the slave of Khadijah ﷺ. He was amazed at some of the strange signs he witnessed on that first business trip to Syria with him. His courtesy, his humane treatment of people, his business acumen, the enormous profit made as well as some of the strange supernatural happenings, the prediction of the monk, Nestor, all these he narrated to Khadijah 🌸. Nestor, a Jewish monk, noted for his knowledge of religion had predicted that he would be exalted to prophethood by Allâh. Maisarrah told her about the Prophet 🌸 and his reputation for honesty and intelligence. She was impressed by what she heard and the more she came to know Muhammad 🌸 the more she liked and respected him. And, finally, she proposed marriage, rejecting the offers of marriage from the foremost leaders of the Quraish.

When the Prophet 🌸 placed the invitation to a religion with a new and rational perspective before the Quraish of Makkah, the worshippers of all the false idols in the Ka'bah were infuriated. They could not dream that the Prophet 🌸 would dismiss their gods as useless helpless creatures, and they became his bitter enemies for propagating a new faith that did away with their traditional and inherited practices. They adopted a very antagonistic attitude and swore to crush him and Islâm. During this period they resorted to the most cruel and sadistic forms of torture to make the converts give up the new faith and return to their old barbaric practices and rituals. It was only the power and influence of Abu Tâlib that prevented them from doing any harm to Muhammad 🌸. He stood by him with all his love and carried out the responsibilities of a guardian faithfully by giving him his protection. No enemy could dare to do anything to him as long as he was under the mantle of his uncle's protection.

Fâtimah bint Asad 🌸 cooperated with Abu Tâlib wholeheartedly and she was a mother pure and simple where the safety and well being of Muhammad 🌸 was concerned. No wonder he loved and respected her so highly. Considering the dangerous conditions which developed for the Muslims in Makkah, he thought it was better that the Muslims migrate to Abyssiniah where the ruler Najâshi was known to be tolerant and hospitable. The leader of this first group of migrants was Ja'far bin Abi Tâlib 🌸, the brother of 'Ali 🌸, and the favorite son of Fâtimah bint Asad 🌸. She loved him more than the others because he resembled Muhammad 🌸 very much, and was extremely intelligent.

He seemed to have inherited the family's mastery over language and was also an eloquent speaker who could win people over to his viewpoint. It was with this same skill that he had won over Najâshi when the Quraish appealed to him to surrender the Muslims to them.

❈❈❈❈❈

The Quraish now decided to restrict the Muslims to one small area, besiege them and boycott them. Social and economic sanctions were imposed, and these three years were perhaps the toughest that the followers of Islâm faced. Economically, it was certainly the worst ever. Children could be heard on all sides sobbing with hunger, and the elders looked on helplessly with tears in their eyes. To satisfy their hunger they started eating the leaves of trees and grass; they even sucked on wet skins to slake their thirst. Fâtimah bint Asad ﷺ passed this terrible period with fortitude and patience, and did not waver in the smallest degree. Ten years after the first revelation to Muhammad ﷺ, appointing him the Messenger of Allâh ﷺ, this harsh siege was finally lifted. It was in the same year that the Prophet's wife and most faithful supporter, Khadijah ﷺ passed away. The pangs of separation from her were very strong for the Prophet ﷺ. He had not yet recovered from her loss, when he was dealt another terrible blow – his best ally, Abu Tâlib, also passed away. This year is known as 'The Year of Sorrows' in Islâmic history.

The torture and torment, atrocities and cruelties reached such proportions that Allâh ﷺ finally ordered the Prophet to migrate to Al-Madinah. Fâtimah bint Asad ﷺ was among these migrants. When the Prophet's daughter Fâtimah ﷺ married 'Ali ﷺ, there were two Fâtimah in the family, a mother-in-law and daughter-in-law. 'Ali ﷺ narrated how one day the Prophet ﷺ gave him a very large expensive sheet and told him to divide it between the Fâtimahs. At that time there were four Fâtimahs in the family.

Fâtimah bint Asad ﷺ

Fâtimah bint Muhammad ﷺ

Fâtimah bint Hamzah ﷺ

Fâtimah bint Shaibah ﷺ, who was the wife of 'Aqeel bin Abi Tâlib ﷺ, the brother of 'Ali ﷺ.

'Ali 🕮 says he did as the Prophet 🕮 told him and divided it among the four Fâtimahs in his family.

❀❀❀❀❀

Anas bin Mâlik says that when the Prophet 🕮 got news of the death of Fâtimah bint Asad 🕮 he immediately went to her house, sat beside her and prayed for her.

"My dear mother, may Allâh keep you under His Protection. Many times you went hungry in order to feed me well. You fed me and clothed me on delicacies that you denied yourself. Allâh 🕮 will surely be happy with these actions of yours. And your intentions were surely meant to win the goodwill and pleasure of Allâh 🕮 and success in the Hereafter."

He gave his shirt to be used as part of her shroud, saying he prayed to Allâh to forgive her and give her the dress of Paradise.

When the grave was prepared the Prophet 🕮 himself examined it and with his own hands placed her into the grave.

Thus Fâtimah bint Asad 🕮 was one of the few blessed people in whose graves the Prophet 🕮 himself examined. Their names are given below:

Khadijah 🕮

'Abdullâh Mazni 🕮 – very well known as *Zulbajâdain*.

Fâtimah bint Asad 🕮.

His son, born by Khadijah 🕮, who died in his infancy.

Fâtimah bint Asad 🕮 is that great lady for whom he gave the glad tidings that she would be blessed with a place in Paradise.

He said that he shrouded her with his shirt, praying that Allâh would give her the dress of Paradise.

Allâh pleased with them and they pleased Allâh.

Umm Roomân رضي الله عنها

> The Prophet ﷺ said:
>
> "If any person wants to see a beautiful virgin of Paradise, he can see Umm Roomân."

Umm Roomân رضي الله عنها

She was the wife of Abu Bakr Siddique ☘ and the mother of 'Aishah ☘. Thus she was the Prophet's mother-in-law. Her son, 'Abdur-Rahmân bin Abu Bakr Siddique ☘ was an excellent horseman, and master strategist in war. It was she who taught him the meaning of valor and courage. Her real name was Zainab, but she came to be known by her family name. She was a patient and tolerant lady who did not jump to hasty conclusions, but gave matters deep thought. This was evident in the way she handled the incident when people of loose tongues and small minds accused 'Aishah ☘ of adultery. When her husband explained to her the teachings of Islâm she did not linger with doubts about giving up the religion of her forfathers. She immediately saw the greatness of Islâm and accepted it. When the Prophet ☘ saw her attributes – physical and spiritual – he likened her to a celestial spirit of Paradise.

❀❀❀❀❀

Fâtimah bint Asad ☘ was brought up in an area of the Arabia known as Sarât. When she grew up she married a young man from her tribe named 'Abdullâh bin Hârith bin Sakhbarah Azdi. She had a son by him, who was named Tufail bin 'Abdullâh. They then moved to Makkah, where he became the partner and companion of Abu Bakr Siddique ☘. However, soon after this 'Abdullâh bin Hârith passed away, and his widow and son were left with no support. Seeing her precarious condition Abu Bakr Siddique ☘ married her. Umm Roomân ☘ was very happy in her marriage and soon, a son, 'Abdur-Rahmân ☘ and a daughter, 'Aishah ☘ were born. Before he came into the fold of Islâm, Abu Bakr Siddique ﷺ was married to Qateelah bint Abdul-'Uzzâ by whom he already had a daughter Asmâ' ﵂, and a son, 'Abdullâh. Just before the migration to Al-Madinah, Abu Bakr Siddique ﷺ married Asmâ' bint 'Omais, and by this marriage he again had a son, Muhammad bin Abu Bakr ﷺ. Then he married Habibah bint Khârejah and had a daughter whom he named Umm Kulthoom.

Umm Roomân ﵂ had accepted Islâm in its earliest days. It is written in *Tabaqât Ibn Sa'd* that Umm Roomân ﵂ accepted Islâm in the very early days in Makkah. She swore allegiance at the hand of the Prophet himself and then migrated with the blessed group of emigrants.

When she to witness the terrible atrocities committed by the Quraish against the Muslims she would suffer and weep for the innocent victims; but she gained courage when she saw the moral strength and exemplary sacrifice of her husband for the cause of Islâm. She drew inspiration from him and found peace in his presence.

The Prophet ﷺ also used to exhort his faithful followers not to waver, but to be patient and hold steadfast to their faith, for they would surely in the Hereafter be rewarded with Paradise. Bilâl ﷺ, the first *Mu'dhdhin* of Islâm, was often the worst sufferer. Both he and Khabâb bin Aratt رضي الله عنهما were encouraged and inspired by the Prophet ﷺ; he told them how in the earlier ages those faithful to the One True Allâh also suffered. There were the faithful who did not recant even when their bodies were cut in two with a saw. When he saw the suffering of the family of Yâsir ﷺ, he said to them,

> 'O family of Yâsir! be patient, for your final destination and resting place will be Paradise.'

During this long period Umm Roomân ﵂ remained an image of patience, forbearance courage and bravery. Most of her time was spent in earnest supplications and prayers to Allâh. When she saw her husband's devoted efforts for the propagation of Islâm she expressed her admiration and gave him moral support. She devoted her time to the nurturing of her children in the traditions of Islâm. The Prophet ﷺ often used to visit the house of his illustrious follower, Abu Bakr Siddique ﷺ. He would advise Umm Roomân ﵂ to keep encouraging and instilling the love of goodness in 'Aishah ﵂. Khadijah ﵂ passed away three years before the migration of the Prophet 🌸 to Al-Madinah. The Prophet 🌸 spent a year as unmarried person. He then married 'Aishah 🌼 at the command of Allâh as delivered by the Angel Jibril 🌸.

One day he told 'Aishah 🌼 that on three consecutive nights he saw her in his dreams. The Angel Jibril brought a picture of hers wrapped in a silken cloth, and told him that this was an image of his bride. When he removed the cover he saw that it was her image. 'Aishah 🌼 was elated to hear that she was chosen to be the Prophet's wife by Allâh 🌸 himself. Khawlah bint Hakim told him there were two proposals for him, that of 'Aishah 🌼 bint Abu Bakr Siddique 🌸 and Saudah bint Zam'ah 🌼. He accepted both, and thus Umm Roomân 🌼 had the honour of becoming his mother-in-law.

When the Prophet 🌸 was ordered by Allâh 🌸 to migrate to Al-Madinah he went to the house of his closest friend and Companion, Abu Bakr Siddique 🌸. Without any questions or hesitation he prepared to accompany the Prophet 🌸. He packed a few things and took all the cash there was in the house. He left his father, wife and children in the trust and care of Allâh and set off for an unknown and unseen destination.

It was a very tough time for Umm Roomân 🌼; she was separated from her husband; and there was a lack of money for household expenses, since he had taken all the available cash with him. But what predominated all other thoughts in her mind were supplications to Allâh 🌸 for the safe arrival of the Prophet 🌸 and her husband in Al-Madinah. On reaching their destination safely, the Prophet 🌸 sent Zaid bin Hârithah and Abu Râfi' رضي الله عنهما to bring his family, Abu Bakr Siddique 🌸 sent 'Abdullâh bin Ariqat and wrote to his son 'Abdullâh to bring his family. Umm Roomân and 'Aishah رضي الله عنهما got on one camel's back. On the way, the camel suddenly seemed out of control and started to jump and almost threw its riders. Umm Roomân 🌼 was worried about her beloved daughter 'Aishah 🌼 and started calling out, 'O my daughter, O my dear little bride!' Just then someone called out that they should let go of the reins, and when they did so the camel calmed down and stood still. So the mother and daughter were saved from the impending danger.

When they reached Al-Madinah they stayed at the house of Abu Bakr Siddique 🌸 arranged for his family. And it was from this house that

'Aishah 🌺 left as a bride to the Prophet's house. Thus this house became the focal point for the revelations of Allâh 🌺. Umm Roomân 🌺 expressed great happiness at the thought that her daughter would be one of thoes who joined the ranks of the blessed Mothers of the Believers. What other greater honour could she want for her family?

❀❀❀❀❀

When the hypocrites, wrongfully accused 'Aishah 🌺, the whole of Al-Madinah seemed to have been gripped by a gigantic tremor and a wave of and confusion swept through the Muslim population. How could they reconcile themselves to their Prophet's wife having committed a cardinal sin?

The whole of Al-Madinah was flooded by this slanderous gossip that 'Aishah 🌺 was a woman of loose character. When she came to know of it from the mouth of Umm Mastah herself that her son was the originator of this scandal, she was heartbroken and appalled at the sheer spite of the man. She took the permission of the Prophet 🌺 and went to her parents. They also corroborated the story she had heard and she could not stop the flood of tears. Her sympathetic and loving mother was also an image of grief. Then the Prophet 🌺, who was himself very upset, came to see her. When he saw her weeping he told her that if she sinned she should ask Allâh for His forgiveness, because he is Merciful; if she had not sinned she should not grieve, for Allâh 🌺 would surely absolve her and forgive her. 'Aishah 🌺 asked her mother to respond to him, but her mother remained quiet. She then appealed to her father, Abu Bakr Siddique 🌺, to give a convincing reply to the Prophet 🌺 but he too remained silent. Finally she said that if she denied that she was guilty – and Allâh 🌺 knew she was innocent – Muhammad 🌺 would not believe her; if she admitted the guilt, may be he would be satisfied, but then her admission of guilt would be contrary to facts. The best answer would be the answer of the father of Yusuf 🌺, when he was helpless before his sons –

> "So patience is most fitting. And it is Allâh Whose help can be
> sought against that (lie) which you describe." (12:18)

She says she was so disturbed that day that even though she tried hard, she just could not remember the name of Ya`qub 🌺, the father of Yusuf 🌸. Even as this conversation was being carried on the *Âyât* of clarification were revealed to the Prophet 🌸. When the revelation was over he was covered in beads of perspiration; he then turned to 'Aishah 🌸 with a happy smile and recited the *Âyât*.

Her parents were proud and relieved; and they asked their daughter to thank her husband, but 'Aishah 🌸 replied that she was grateful to her Allâh 🌸 for He exonerated her. This relief, with the specially revealed *Âyât* of Allâh 🌸, increased her worth in the heart of her husband.

Umm Roomân 🌸 was a lady who spent her nights and days in prayer, meditation and supplications to Allâh 🌸. Her earnest desire was to win the goodwill of Allâh 🌸 and His Messenger 🌸. She was a dutiful wife who stood by her husband at all times. She noted what her husband had to say about prayers. Once when he entered the house he found her praying and told her that the body should express an attitude of calmness and tranquility. A calm and still posture helped to perfect concentration in prayer, he said.

'Ali bin Bulbân Muqaddasi in his book *Tohfah As-Siddique fi Fadhâ'il Abi Bakr Siddique* and Imam Thahbi in his book *Siyar Al-A'lâm An-Nublâ'* says that one day both Abu Bakr Siddique 🌸 and his wife, Umm Roomân 🌸, went to visit the Prophet 🌸. He asked them the purpose of the visit. They both simultaneously requested him to offer supplications to Allâh 🌸 for 'Aishah 🌸.

Then he prayed to Allâh 🌸 to forgive 'Aishah 🌸 bint Abu Bakr both inside and outside such a forgiveness that would leave no sin. Both her parents looked very happy with this perfect supplication.

Then he told them that this was his prayer for all those who accepted Islâm after his being named Messenger of Allâh, and remained steadfast in their belief.

Prophet 🌸 respected Umm Roomân 🌸 very much, and she in turn gave first priority to doing things that pleased him. So life was very pleasant, and everyone was happy fulfilling their obligations to man and his Creator. One day the Prophet 🌸 praised Khadijah 🌸 at great length extoling her many virtues. 'Aishah 🌸 felt a very strong twinge of feminine jealousy; involuntarily she said that he was talking of

Khadijah 🌸 as if there was no other woman on earth but she. The Prophet 🌿 did not like this at all, and his face reddened with a terrible anger. When Umm Roomân 🌸 heard of this she went to the Prophet 🌿 and tried to apologize for 'Aishah 🌸 telling him that she was still very young that he should not take her seriously. Very curtly, addressing 'Aishah 🌸, he asked her if she had not said that there was no other woman on the face of the earth besides Khadijah 🌸? He swore by Allâh 🌿 that this great lady had believed him when the tribe of 'Aishah 🌸 had denied that he was the Messenger and Prophet of Allâh. She gave him the great gift of children, which was not the case with 'Aishah 🌸.

Umm Roomân 🌸 listened in complete silence because she knew that all that he spoke was by the command and revelation of Allâh 🌿. He did not speak of his own accord, his words were always based on revelations of Allâh.

🌸🌸🌸🌸🌸

Tradition has it that Umm Roomân 🌸 passed away in the year 6th after Hijrah. During her burial, the Prophet 🌿 asked Allâh 🌿 to forgive her. Doubtless this was a great honour for her. It was on this occasion that he said that if any person wanted to see a beautiful celestial virgin of Paradise, he could see Umm Roomân 🌸. Thus these words are an indication that she will, Allâh Willing, be in Paradise in the Hereafter. May Allâh 🌿 fill her grave with radiance. Another tradition regarding the death of Umm Roomân 🌸 is however more reliable. It says that she died after the passing away of the Prophet 🌿.

Verily the words of Allâh 🌿 are true,

> "Verily, those who believe and do righteous deeds, and humble themselves before their Lord, they will be dwellers of Paradise to dwell therein forever." (11:23)

Sumayyah bint Khabât رضي الله عنها

> The Prophet ﷺ said:
>
> "O People of Yâsir! Be patient because your destination is Paradise."

Sumayyah bint Khabât رضي الله عنها

Three brothers set out from Yemen to go to Makkah. They heard about this city and wanted to experience its culture and to partake of its various social activities. One was named Yâsir and the other two were named Hârith and Mâlik. The latter two left to return home to Yemen after some time, but Yâsir liked live there so much that he decided to stay on permanantly. According to the custom of the time he got the sponsorship and support of Abu Huthaifah bin 'Abdullâh Makhzoomi, and became his companion and partner. As they got to know each other better, they took a liking to each other. Abu Huthaifah had a very intelligent and sensible slave girl in his house, Sumayyah. In due course of time she got married to Yâsir.

It was a happy marriage and soon they had a son whom they named 'Ammâr. Abu Huthaifah was a very kind, loving and generous man, and he liberated the family from his bondage; but he continued to keep good terms with them and very often helped them with cash as well. Yâsir had two more sons, whom he named 'Abdullâh and Hareeth. The latter was murdered before the advent of Islâm, and with this tragedy it seemed ill fortune started to haunt the family.

Sumayyah bint Khabât ‎‎ was one of the first seven people to be enlightened by Islâm and swear allegiance to the Prophet ‎‎. She is among the foremost of the greatest women Companions. Islâm is unique in the sense that a person's value does not depend on colour, race, language, sex or nationality. The norms are purity of heart and goodwill towards all. As Allâh says,

"Verily, the most honorable of you with Allâh is that (believer) who is most pious." (49:13)

Thus, a person who wishes for his fellow human beings what he wishes for himself, who is kind to his fellow human beings for the sake of Allâh 鑅, is the one who fulfills the conditions of the test set by Him.

The seven people who first accepted Islâm were the following:

1. Abu Bakr Siddique 鑅.

2. 'Ali bin Abi Tâlib 鑅

3. Khadijah 鑅.

4. Zaid bin Hârithah 鑅.

5. Sumayyah bint Khabât 鑅.

6. 'Ammâr bin Yâsir 鑅.

7. Bilâl bin Abi Rabâh 鑅.

The Quraish of Makkah could harm the Prophet 鑅 because of the power and position of his uncle Abu Tâlib. Abu Bakr Siddique 鑅 was also a very powerful man because of the wealth of his tribe and his own personal influence. But the common Muslim, whether man or woman was not spared any imaginable torture or torment.

❀❀❀❀❀

Sumayyah bint Khabât 鑅, her husband and her son 'Ammâr were very often the targets for the cruelty of the Quraish. On one occasion as the Prophet 鑅 was passing by the marketplace he saw all three members of the family being put through the worst form of torture possible. But he was so helpless, that there was no way he could rescue them. He could only console them and said,

'Be patient O family of Yâsir!, for your final destination is Paradise.'

'Uthmân 鑅 also narrated that the Prophet 鑅 used to say these words to comfort the family. Once 'Ammâr managed to escape and reach the Prophet 鑅. He then asked him when this persecution of the innocent

Muslims would end, and when they would be able to breathe peacefully. He said that things were going way beyond all limits. The Prophet 🌼 then comforted him with a prayer to Allâh 🌼 to protect and save the family of Yâsir from the fire of Hell.

Abu Jahl gave Sumayyah bint Khabât 🌼 the worst kind of punishment, but she did not waver even for a second and remained as steady as a rock. He tried to pressure her, cajole with her and threaten her to recant, but she bluntly refused. He could not accept the fact that she could resist him so stubbornly, and in out of rage he thrust his spear into her. This proved to be a fatal blow, and she died. Thus, Sumayyah bint Khabât 🌼 had the distinction of being the first woman martyr of Islâm. This incident took place seven years before the Hijrah. Then her husband also fell victim to the torture of the Quraish, and he also died. After the martyrdom of both the parents, 'Ammâr took a special place in the affections of the Prophet 🌼. He used to address him lovingly as Ibn Sumayyah 🌼. He often spoke of the family of Yâsir in the highest terms of praise.

'Abdullâh bin Mas'ood 🌼 says the Prophet 🌼 once said that when dissensions and disputes appeared among the people Ibn Sumayyah would always stand by the right and just.

This family sacrificed their lives, all in order to nourish the truth, and also to earn rewards for the Hereafter. It is about people like these that Allâh says,

> "Verily, Allâh has purchased of the believers their lives and their properties for (the price) that theirs shall be the Paradise. They fight in Allâh's cause, so they kill (others) and are killed. It is promise in truth which is binding on Him in the Taurât and the Injeel and the Qur'ân. And who is truer to His covenant than Allâh? Then rejoice in the bargain that you have concluded. That is the supreme success." (9:111)

Umm Harâm bint Malhân رضي الله عنها

The Prophet ﷺ once said:

'From among my *Ummah* (followers) an army will sail on the sea as a king sits on his throne.'

Umm Harâm asked him if she would be one among them. He answered that she would be one of the foremost among them.

Umm Harâm bint Malhân رضي الله عنها

Umm Harâm came from a noble family. Her sister was the mother of Anas bin Mâlik. Her two brothers, Harâm bin Malhân and Saleem bin Malhân, took part in the Battles of Badr and Uhud. She was also related by marriage to Abu Talhah, another distinguished Companion. Her husband was 'Amr bin Qais bin Zaid, and her son was Qais bin 'Amr bin Qais – these were two eminent Companions of the Prophet who were martyred at the Battle of Badr. After her husband's death she married 'Obâdah bin Sâmit, a distinguished General of the Muslim army. She had a son by this marriage, Muhammad bin 'Obâdah bin Sâmit.

Generosity, benevolence and the spirit of sacrifice were an innate part of this noble lady's nature. Her ambition was to be martyred in the cause of Islâm, and in pursuit of this consuming desire she left no stone unturned. She lived on the outskirts of Al-Madinah, in the small town of Qubâ. When the Prophet migrated to Al-Madinah, he stopped at Qubâ to rest before proceeding. She was the first among the *Ansâr* woman to not only accept Islâm, but also announce it; and she did so before the migration of the Prophet. Umm Harâm was a very wise and balanced person, God fearing just and pious. She held a very high position among the women of the *Ansâr*. The Prophet would often visit her house and rest there if he was tired. Whenever the Prophet stopped at her place she felt grateful for his presence and she considered serving him to be the greatest honour.

❀❀❀❀❀

Anas bin Mâlik ﴾ narrated that once he was at his house when the
Prophet ﷺ came there. His mother and her sister were also there. He
told them to rise and he would lead them in a special prayer; it was
not the time for one of the obligatory prayers. After prayers he made a
supplication to Allâh ﷻ to bless the family both in this world and the
Hereafter.

Umm Harâm ﵂ was first married to 'Amr bin Qais bin Zaid. They had
a son whom they named Qais. As mentioned earlier both of them were
with the Prophet ﷺ at Badr. At the Battle of Uhud they fought with great
courage and were martyred. After that Umm Harâm bint Malhân
﵂ married the famous General 'Obâdah bin Sâmit ﵂; they had son
whom they named Muhammad bin 'Obâdah. 'Obâdah bin Sâmit ﴾ was
a member of all the three delegations which had the honour of going to
Makkah before the migration to personally pledge allegiance to Allâh ﷻ
and His Messenger. The first delegation had six members; the second
had twelve and the third had seventy-two members.

'Obâdah bin Sâmit ﴾ was an exemplary husband and father. He was a
loving father to 'Abdullâh bin 'Amr who had been born to Umm
Harâm ﵂ by her first husband. The same love and care he gave to his
own children he gave to his wife's children of the previous marriage.
Muhammad bin 'Obâdah ﴾ was a member of the congregation when
the *Âyah* to change the direction (*Qiblah*) for prayers to the Ka'bah
from *Masjid- al-Aqsâ* was revealed. Thus he had the privilege of facing
both the '*Qiblahs*' in this one prayer.

❀❀❀❀❀

Traditions attributed to Umm Harâm ﵂ have been quoted by such
noteworthy Companions of the Prophet ﷺ as 'Obâdah bin Sâmit, Anas
bin Mâlik, 'Omair bin Aswad, 'Atâ bin Yasâr and Ya'li bin Shadâd bin
Aws رضـي الله عـنـهم. The feelings of love respect and reverence for the
Prophet ﷺ almost reached a peak of perfection in the heart of Umm
Harâm ﵂. Whenever he visited either her house or the house of her
sister Umm Sulaim, their happiness knew no bounds. She would
prepare special delicacies for him and arrange a comfortable bed for
him to rest. The atmosphere was such that the Prophet ﷺ too would
feel a real sense of peace and joy when he called on her. When he was

asked if there was a special reason why he visited her house so often, he replied that he felt a great sense of pity for the family ever since he saw two of her brothers being martyred in the battle of Bi'r Ma'oonah. Ever since then, he said that he visited her to see to her needs and comfort her.

The *Ansâr* were noted for their spirit of sacrifice, generosity and hospitality, and Umm Harâm 🕸️ was an embodiment of this spirit. This spirit is glorigified in the Words of the Noble Qur'ân.

"And those who, before them (emigrants), had homes (in Madinah) and had adopted the Faith, love those who emigrate to them, and have no jealousy in their breasts for that which they have been given, and give them (emigrants) preference over themselves even though they were in need of that. And whoseover is saved from his own covetousness, such are they who will be the successful." (59:9)

Allâh was so pleased with the sympathy, generosity and sacrifice displayed by the *Ansâr* for the migrants of Makkah that Allâh immortalized their selfless character in His Qur'ân. There was no difference between men or women in this display of selflessness. And it seemed Umm Harâm 🕸️ was blessed in more than ample measure with this typical generosity of spirit. The family was fortunate to have the blessings and goodwill of the Prophet 🌸. What more can one ask for in this world? When he passed away he was very happy with her for the exceptional services she rendered.

❀❀❀❀❀

During the caliphate of 'Uthmân bin 'Affân, in the year 27th after Hijrah, Mu'âwiyah bin Abu Sufyân 🕸️ was given permission to conquer the is Island of Cyprus. To reach there a naval force was readied. This was the first time in Islâmic history that such a measure was taken. 'Obâdah bin Sâmit 🕸️ was accompanied by his wife Umm Harâm 🕸️. Accompanying the General Mu'âwiyâh with his wife Fâkhtah bint Qurdhah رضى الله عنها.

'Omair bin Aswad 'Ansi writes that he visited 'Obâdah 🕸️ who was staying in the coastal area of Hamas. He met Umm Harâm 🕸️ who told him that she had heard the Prophet ﷺ say that some of his people would journey on the sea for the purpose of *Jihâd* (war in the cause of Allâh). She asked him if she would be one among them, and he replied in the affirmative. She was really elated at this because it had been her earnest desire to take part in *Jihâd*. By the grace of Allâh ﷻ the Muslims were victorious. After her journey by sea Umm Harâm ﵂ got on to a mule to travel on land, but unfortunately the mule bacame frightened of something and she fell down. She sustained a serious neck injury that cost her her life. Thus she attained the martyrdom which she always desired. She was buried in Cyprus.

Umm Harâm ﵂ is that fortunate women Companions who took part in this naval venture and attained martyrdom, and proved herself worthy of the blessed tidings of the Prophet ﷺ about her place in Paradise.

She lived her life as a praiseworthy lady on land and attained the best end to a well-lived life as martyr of the first naval venture of Islâm.

Allâh will be pleased with them and they with Him.

Asmâ' bint Abu Bakr Siddique رضي الله عنها

The Prophet ﷺ said:

"You will be bestowed two waist collars in exchange of one."

Asmâ' bint Abu Bakr Siddique رضي الله عنها

S he was related to the Prophet ﷺ by his marriage to her sister 'Aishah ﷺ. Her father, Abu Bakr Siddique ﷺ, was the close Companion and trusted friend of Muhammad ﷺ. Her grandmother was Umm Al-Khair Salmâ bint Sakhr Her father's sisters were such eminent women Comapanions as Fardah, Qareebah and Umm 'Amer رضــي الله عـــهن. Her paternal grandfather was Abu Quhâfah. Her husband, Zubair bin 'Awâm ﷺ, was a Companion of the Prophet ﷺ. Her son, 'Abdullâh bin Zubair ﷺ, was another eminent Companion of the Prophet ﷺ. She was the lady who so bravely and calmly carried the burden of the Prophet's secret migration to Al-Madinah in the dead of night with her father. She was the one who packed up their food and other little items necessary for that historic journey. On that occasion the Prophet ﷺ blessed her with the auspicious news of Paradise in the Hereafter. When the enemy came to question her, she remained calm and did not betray any nervousness or fear by so much as the blinking of an eye. Her life is worthy of study, coming as she did from a background where each and every member of the family was a trusted confidant and Companion of the Prophet ﷺ

❀❀❀❀❀.

Asmâ' ﷺ was born twenty-seven years before the migration of the Prophet ﷺ to Al-Madinah. Her mother's name was Qateelah bint 'Uzâ and her father, Abu Bakr ﷺ, married her before the advent of Islâm; Asmâ' ﷺ was born when he was only twenty-one years old. Asmâ' ﷺ and 'Abdullâh ﷺ were born of this marriage. For a long time her mother did not accept Islâm; finally after the conquest of Makkah she pledged allegiance to the Prophet 鏺. Asmâ' 鏺 entered the fold of Islâm because of the influence and teachings of her father.

Piety, farsightedness, intelligence, courage and integrity, generosity – all the qualities praised by Islâm could be found in this one person. When her father and the Prophet 鏺 took refuge in the cave of Thour after leaving Makkah to migrate to Al-Madinah, it was she who went in the wilderness to deliver fresh food to them. As soon as they left on their journey, Abu Jahl came to the house of Abu Bakr Siddique 鏺 looking for them, breathing fire and fury. He asked her where her father was. She answered that she did not know. He gave proof of his barbaric nature by slapping her hard; but so as not to betray her secret she faced him with steadfastness, courage and tolerance.

鏺鏺鏺鏺鏺

Asmâ' 鏺 came to be known by the title *Thât An-Natâqeen*. There is an interesting little episode about how she got this name. In Arabic the belt, or girdle worn by women around the waist is called a *Natâq*. When the Prophet 鏺 and Abu Bakr Siddique 鏺 prepared to set off for Al-Madinah, Asmâ' 鏺 packed the eatables into a leather bag, but there was no rope with which she could tie up the mouth of the bag. So she divided her girdle into two and used one part to tie up the leather bag. The Prophet 鏺 blessed her and said that in place of this one girdle that she sacrificed, she would get two in Paradise. So, he implied that she would go to Paradise. In this manner the Prophet 鏺 gave the news of a glorious Hereafter to his faithful Companions.

鏺鏺鏺鏺鏺

After her father and the Prophet 鏺 left, Asmâ' 鏺 was left with her blind and aged grandfather, Abu Quhâfah. When he realized that his son had migrated he was sad. Then he was worried whether he had left any cash for expenses. She narrated that they had about four or five thousand Dinârs in the house and her father had taken it all for the expenses of the journey. But she comforted the old man saying there was plenty in the house, and nothing was lacking. In order to convince him she collected some pebbles that were of the size of Dinârs; these she put in a pot and spread a cloth over them. Then she

guided his old hands over the cloth; Abu Quhâfah was very pleased
that his son had not neglected them. Asmâ' 🌸 had done this for the
old man's peace of mind; but in truth Abu Bakr Siddque 🌼 with a
strong faith in Allâh, had taken his all to spend in the way of Allâh
and His Messenger.

🌸🌸🌸🌸🌸

Her husband, Zubair bin bin 'Awâm 🌼, the Prophet's friend and
Companion was the son of Safiyyah bint 'Abdul Muttalib. When He
migrated to Al-Madinah, he owned a house in which he lived, a
sword and a horse. It was the duty of Asmâ' 🌸 to tend to the horse
and feed him. One day she was walking home with a bundle of hay on
her head when the Prophet 🌺 saw her. He immediately made his
camel sit down so that he could let her ride. But she was embarrassed
and thought it would displease her husband who was a very proud
man. So she refused the offer and preferred to walk. When she told
her husband about it, he said she should have got on to the camel, it
would have been less shameful than walking with a bundle of hay.

When Asmâ' 🌸 was migrating to Al-Madinah, near the valley of Qubâ
she went into labor, and gave birth to a son 'Abdullâh bin Zubair. This
was a very special occasion for the Muslims. For a very long time no
sons had been born among their people. The disbelievers were very
happy and they used to gossip among themselves that now the
Muslims would be rooted out. All the Muslims were excited, as was
the Prophet 🌺. He picked up the baby in his arms and congradulated
the family. Then he bit off a little piece of a date, softened it in his
mouth and gave it to the baby. This was an honor that made the
family feel very proud.

🌸🌸🌸🌸🌸

When 'Abdullâh bin Zubair 🌼 grew up he was learning, understanding and courage personified. Later his mother came to live with
him. When he moved to Makkah she also accompanied him. He did
not accept Banu Omayyah as the caliph and tried to set up his own
caliphate; he succeeded in winning the support of most people since
they acknowledged him to be a powerful, learned and brave man.
However, when 'Abdul Malik bin Marwân ascended the throne, he

took over some of the provinces. He sent Hajjâj bin Yusuf as his representative to Hijâz. Hajjâj took command of the Syrian forces and besieged, attacking it from all sides; an intense battle ensued between the two forces.

At this critical juncture, 'Abdullâh bin Zubair ﷺ went to see his mother. When she told him that she was sick, he replied that human beings could find peace and rest after death. She smilingly asked him if he wished her to die. She said she wanted him to live and wanted to live herself, because she had to see the end result of his struggle. If he were martyred she would accept it with patience and fortitude, and if he routed his enemy in this battle she would be happy.

A desperate battle was being waged now in Makkah itself and 'Abdullâh bin Zubair's army was facing defeat. He went to see his mother who was at the mosque and asked her if he should surrender. She replied that if he was in the right he should not worry about dying. He said he feared that the enemy would cut up his body after death. She answered it was irrelevant what they did with the body. Once a goat is slaughtered the skinning cannot cause it any pain. She added that fear of death should not stand in the way of a truly courageous man. Death with honour was better than a life of peace with dishonour. A disgraceful peace did not suit a young hero like him. So 'Abdullâh bin Zubair ﷺ returned to the battlefield with renewed ardour and advanced through the ranks fighting courageously; but since they were outnumbered he died the death of a martyr. The cruel Hajjâj bin Yusuf hung up his body for all to see, and did not take it down even after three days. On the third day the aged mother went to try and recover the body of her valiant and noble son. Since she lost her eyesight due to age she could only feel her way around. Sighing, she asked, if the time had not yet come for her son to get down from his horse. She faced this great torture with characteristic strength and fortitude.

When Hajjâj saw the mother standing near the son's body he sent a messenger to bring her to him. She answered with scornful hatred that she would not go to see her son's murderer. When Hajjâj bin Yusuf got the message, he was filled with rage and told the messenger to go and tell her that if she did not come by herself, she would be dragged into his presence by her hair. She answered him with supreme indifference that she would not go to see the despicable ignoble man; this was her final decision, and he could do anything he wished. When Hajjâj saw his threats were ineffective he went to see her. He asked her if she had seen what he had made of her son. She replied that he had ruined her son's life in this world, but her son had ruined him for eternity. She added that she had heard the Prophet 🌸 saying that a man would appear from the tribe of Banu Thaqeef who would be a liar and a cruel and ignoble barbarian. Today she had seen him for herself. Hajjâj bin Yusuf left silently.

One day when she went to the Haram (sanctuary) in Makkah, she heard Hajjâj bin Yusuf addressing the gathering from the pulpit. Even in her extreme old age she had not lost her spirit; boldly she went and stood next to him. When he saw her he said her son had spread disbelief and atheism in the House of Allâh 🌸 and so He gave him a terrible punishment. Asmâ' 🌸 promptly answered that her son was never an atheist; he was a pious, learned man who always prayed to Allâh 🌸, worked for the welfare of the Muslim *Ummah* and was a standard bearer of integrity and honesty. You, on the other hand, was known to be a liar, a hypocrite and a treacherous man. He should fear the wrath of Allâh 🌸, for it hit man when he was least expecting it to strike. Hajjâj, pretending he had not heard her, continued his speech and said,

> "I admit that 'Abdullâh bin Zubair was an excellent member of the *Ummah*, but he had a burning desire for power. Thus he created differences among the people and caused trouble right there in the House of Allâh 🌸, so he met a terrible end. You know Adam 🌸 was much greater and more highly respected as Prophet of Allâh than 'Abdullâh bin Zubair. Allâh 🌸 gave him a tranquil and peaceful life in Paradise. But when he disobeyed the Command of Allâh and ate the fruit of the forbidden tree he was thrown out of Paradise. Doubtlessly Paradise is a far better place than the sanctuary of the Ka'bah."

Then in a thundering voice he asked the people to rise up and get ready for prayers. 'Abdullâh bin 'Umar 🌸 was present and he said in a loud voice,

"O Hajjâj! if I call you a hypocrite and a liar it will not be contrary to facts. I swear by the Majesty and the Wrath of Allâh ﷻ that 'Abdullâh bin Zubair ﷺ never took any step in his whole life that went contrary to the injunctions of Allâh ﷻ. I now testify in public that 'Abdullâh bin Zubair ﷺ was a God fearing man who fasted and prayed at nights. He always stood by what was right and stood by it.

Then he went to the body of 'Abdullâh bin Zubair ﷺ that was still hanging there and in a grief-stricken trembling voice said,

"Peace be upon you O Abu Khubaib, Peace be upon O Abu Khabeeb."

Khabaib was the family name of 'Abdullâh bin Zubair ﷺ. Then looking at the body he said that he warned 'Abdullâh ﷺ not to get involved in a struggle for power. The most respected people often lost their prestige struggling for power. Then he prayed to Allâh ﷻ to grant him a place in His Merciful Paradise.

After a few days Hajjâj threw the body into the graveyard on the instructions of 'Abdul Malik bin Marwân. When Asmâ' ﷺ heard this news she sent for the body, had it bathed and had the congregational prayer for the dead conducted. Finally, she buried her beloved son's body.

Hajjâj bin Yusuf received a message from the court of Syria saying that he should personally visit Asmâ' ﷺ and ask her if there was any request or if she needed anything. The government would be happy to oblige her. Hajjâj went to her house to pass on the message of the governor of 'Abdul Malik bin Marwân. Asmâ' ﷺ flew into a terrible rage; she told him in a thundering voice that she did not need anything and shouted at him to get out of her house; she said she kicked his offer in his face. She asked if the shameless scoundrel had come to prick her wounds. She said he was a burden on this earth, and she considered him an unfortunate and impious man.

❀❀❀❀❀

Asmâ' ﷺ would pray with full concentration. Zubair bin 'Awâm ﷺ relates that when he came home one day he saw her praying and weeping; she kept on repeating these words from the Qur'ân again and again:

"Allâh has blessed us and saved us the torture of the burning winds." (52:27)

When he saw her thus lost in the presence of Allâh ﷻ, he left the house and went to the market. He came back much later and still found her still lost in prayer.

Asmâ' ﷺ had a very sharp memory. If she heard anything even once she would never forget it. Like 'Aishah, Umm Salamah and Asmâ' bint Yazid bin Sakan Ansâriyah رضي الله عنهن, she also has many *Ahâdith* attributed to her. Many Companions and successors would come to her for guidance and verification of *Ahâdith*. 'Abdullâh bin Zubair, 'Urwah bin Zubair, 'Abdullâh bin 'Abbâs, Fâtimah bint Manthar bin Zubair and 'Abdullâh bin Keesân رضي الله عنهم are some of the noteworthy ones.

Asmâ' bint Abu Bakr Siddique ﷺ died in the year 73th after Hijrah. She was almost a hundred years old, but even at that age she had a full set of teeth and a sharp memory.

Allâh will be pleased with them and they with Him.

Umm Sulaim bint Malhân Ansâriah رضي الله عنها

The Prophet ﷺ said:

"When I entered the Paradise, I heard someone's footsteps – It was explained to me that she was Ghameesâ bint Malhân."

Keep in mind that Ghameesâ is the name of Umm Sulaim Ansâriah رضي الله عنها. She is also called Ramisâ', Sahlah, and Ramlah but nickname overcame the name.

Umm Sulaim bint Malhân
Ansâriah رضي الله عنها

L earning, courage, patience and fortitude, steadfastness of purpose and generosity of heart and mind – these are the qualities common to all the women Companions who are the subject of this book.

Umm Sulaim 🌸 is no exception. She too came from an illustrious family who sacrificed its all for Islâm. Her son was the famous Companion Anas bin Mâlik 🌸 and her brother was the eminent Companion Harâm bin Malhân 🌸.

Her first marriage was unhappy; there were constant quarrels between husband and wife because she became a Muslim. Her husband, Mâlik bin Nadhar, tried his very best make her recant and give up the new religion to which she had vowed allegiance, but he failed and she remained loyal to her new faith. On the other hand she started persuading her son, Anas 🌸, as well to convert to Islâm, under the most trying circumstances. He said she was now spoiling his son. She replied that she was not spoiling him; on the other hand she was teaching him the meaning of true and everlasting success for the Hereafter. Her persistence finally paid off, and Anas read the words signifying acceptance of Allâh as the One Supreme Being and Muhammad 🌸 as His Messenger.

There were frequent violent scenes in the house, but she stood her ground, patiently and calmly. She told him that he just could not perceive the nature of the treasure she found. She said that it was a treasure for all time, a light that illuminated her heart. Her husband said she was without any religion, and she replied courageously that by accepting Islâm she had accepted the True religion and hence she would be successful even in the Hereafter.

Finally her husband left her and migrated to Syria where he was murdered. Dedicating her son to the service of the Prophet ﷺ, she requested him to pray for her son. The Prophet ﷺ then prayed for Anas ؓ for increase in knowledge and riches. The Ansâri ladies used to call her Sehla, Ghameesâ', Rameesâ' Ramlah and Sahlah, but finally she came to be known only as Umm Sulaim.

In Al-Madinah there was a handsome young man called Abu Talhah, who was also the leader of his tribe. He had not yet converted to Islâm, though many people were influenced by the teachings of Mus'ab bin 'Omair ؓ. Abu Talhah knew that the widow, Umm Sulaim ؓ had many admirable qualities. Her integrity, her loyalty, her courage - all these appealed to him, and he sent her a proposal of marriage. She said it was not possible because she was a Muslim and he was a disbeliever. When he insisted she asked him what kind of a man he was; sometimes he worshipped trees growing in the earth, at other times he worshipped stone idols which other people carved out. She asked him if he had ever considered how these things could solve his problems when they were themselves helpless.

When Abu Talhah heard these arguments he had no answer. He tried his best to persuade her, but she was adamant. She told him that normally a proposal from a man of his stature would not be rejected, but she was helpless. She dedicated her life to Islâm and he was, up to that time, deprived of this great blessing. Finally, he asked her if she would marry him if he converted to Islâm. She was very happy at this; she said the *Mahr* for her would be his acceptance of Islâm.

Umm Sulaim ؓ then told Anas ؓ to arrange for her marriage. Thâbit bin Aslam Bannâni, the famous successor and scholar says this was an excellent *Mahr* (Bridal dowery) and unique in the history of Islâm. The Prophet ﷺ often used to visit her and prayed for prosperity and the blessings of Allâh for her.

After her husband's murder in Syria she dedicated her son, Anas ؓ to the service of the Prophet ﷺ. Anas ؓ lived the next ten years of his life in his service, and these were the best years of his life. Umm Sulaim ؓ requested the Prophet ﷺ to supplicate to Allâh ﷻ for an increase in knowledge and for his prosperity, both in this world and the next.

And Allâh 🕸️ answered his prayers in ample measure. Anas 🕸️ lived to the age of a hundred and three and had eighty children. He had a magnificent palace in Basrah and huge beautiful gardens. He was a fastidious man who loved to dress well and dye his hair with henna. Among his sons, many became learned scholars. After his death he became an heir to the gardens of Paradise.

🕸️🕸️🕸️🕸️🕸️

Umm Sulaim 🕸️ had a happy second marriage and soon the couple was blessed with a son, Abu 'Umair. One day the Prophet 🕸️ visited the house and found Abu 'Umair looking very dejected. He asked why the little boy was upset. Umm Sulaim 🕸️ told him that his pet bird, which he loved to play with, had died. The Prophet 🕸️ caressed him and tried to console him lovingly.

After some time Abu 'Umair fell sick, and one night his temperature shot up very high and he passed away. Umm Sulaim 🕸️ displayed exemplary patience and control. She did not inform anyone or scream and shout in her grief. She did not want to upset her husband when he came home after a hard day's work. On his return home, he asked her how the child was and she told him he was better then before. Then she served him dinner and chatted with him. When he had enjoyed himself in her company in peace and tranquillity, late in the night she brought up the topic. She said she wanted to ask him a question. He asked her what she wanted to know. She asked him whether if a person entrusted one with something, and then came to claim it, should one return it? He answered that certainly one should return it gladly. Then she took him to the room where the son was lying in a peaceful eternal sleep. She removed the sheet from his face and said in a trembling voice that Allâh 🕸️ had taken back the son He had entrusted to their care.

Abu Talhah 🕸️ was shocked and asked her why she had not informed him as soon as he had come home. In the morning they went to see the Prophet 🕸️ and told him what happened the previous night. He prayed for Allâh's blessings and prosperity for the couple. And soon another son was born to them. Anas 🕸️ carried him in his lap to the Prophet 🕸️; he softened a piece of a date and gave it to the newborn, and named him 'Abdullâh. He prayed that Allâh 🕸️ grant him prosperity. And by the grace of Allâh 🕸️ when he grew up and married he had nine sons;

all of them were memorizers of the Qur'ân.

❀❀❀❀❀

Anas ❀ narrates that his mother had a goat. One day she made ghee from its milk and collected it in a little leather bowl. When it was full she sent it as a gift for the Prophet ❀ with her adopted daughter. The Prophet ❀ told his family to empty the bowl and return it with the little girl. She brought back the empty bowl and hung it by a nail on the kitchen wall.

Umm Sulaim ❀ saw that the bowl was still hanging and it was full – in fact it was overflowing and dripping. She asked her daughter why she did not carry out her instructions. The little girl said that she had taken the ghee to the Prophet's house as instructed and brought back the empty bowl and hung it. Umm Sulaim ❀ was amazed by this mystery.

She went to the Prophet's house and told him about this strange incident. He said the little girl brought the gift which he accepted. And she left his place with an empty bowl.

Umm Sulaim ❀ swore by Allâh ❀ Who sent him as a Messenger of the one True Religion that the bowl was full and dripping even then. The Prophet ❀ then told her that she should not be amazed; she had sent a gift for Allâh's Prophet ❀, so He in turn had sent a gift for her. She should eat it and feed others also with it. Umm Sulaim ❀ says she emptied this bowl of ghee into a larger vessel. It lasted them for two months and others also ate from it.

❀❀❀❀❀

Anas narrates that one day Abu Talhah ❀ came home and told Umm Sulaim ❀ that the Prophet ❀ sounded very weak, possibly he was hungry. If there was some food in the house they could have the honour of having him over for a meal. She answered that she had some bread wrapped up in cloth. Abu Talhah ❀ went to the mosque and invited the Prophet ❀ to join him.

He accepted and invited the people sitting there to join him at the house of Abu Talhah ❀. All of them rose to go with the Prophet ❀. When Abu Talhah ❀ saw this he became nervous, because he did not have enough food for so many people. When he went home he expressed this fear to his wife Umm Sulaim ❀. She smiled and told him not to worry; they would just put out all the food they had in the house. And this was what she did. The Prophet 🌺 came in and made a supplication to Allâh 🌺 for plenitude. Then he asked Abu Talhah 🌺 to call in ten people from outside. So ten people came in to a satisfying meal. After they finished he asked Abu Talhah 🌺 to call in ten more. And so it went on till about seventy or eighty had taken their fill of the delicious food. And there was food still left over!

When the Prophet got married to Zainab bint Jahash 🌸, Umm Sulaim 🌸 made a special dish of dates and ghee and sent it to him as a gift. And after the battle of Khaiber when he married Safiyyah 🌸 it was Umm Sulaim 🌸 who dressed her up as a bride. She also played a very active role in the battlefields of Islâm. Anas 🌺 says that in the Battle of Uhud his mother and 'Aishah 🌸 used to fill leather bottles with water and give it to the thirsty wounded soldiers. Umm Sulaim 🌸 was pregnant at the time but that did not deter her in any way. She took an active part in the Battle of Hunain as well. She carried a spear and when Abu Talhah 🌺 saw this he told the Prophet 🌺 about it. He asked her why she was carrying a spear. She answered that if any enemy soldier came before her she would slit his belly. The Prophet 🌺 smiled at her spirit.

Anas 🌺 narrated that once the Prophet 🌺 came to visit them. My mother, her sister and I were at home. He told them that he would lead the prayer in their house that day. After praying he made special supplications to Allâh 🌺 to bless them, both in this world and in the Hereafter.

Anas 🌺 reported that the Prophet 🌺 used to visit them often. When someone asked him for the reason, he said he felt pity for her ever since he saw her brother, Harâm bin Malhân 🌺 killed before his eyes. He participated in the two crucial battles of Badr and Uhud. In the year 4th after Hijrah he was fighting in the Battle of Ma'oonah, when the enemy took an opportune moment to trap him and hit him from the back with a spear which pierced through his heart. His last words have become immortal in Islâmic history. He said,

" I swear by the Sustainer of the Ka'bah I have become successful."

His brother Sulaim bin Malhân 🌺 also was martyred in the same battle.

In *Sahih Muslim*, the Book of *Fadhâ'il* talks about the beads of perspiration of the Prophet 🌺. One afternoon the Prophet 🌺 went to visit Umm Sulaim 🌸; she was out and he dropped off to sleep while waiting for her. When she came home she found him sleeping and in the heat his perspiration was dripping on a small piece of leather. She was very happy to see him in her house and started collecting the beads of perspiration in a small bottle to preserve them. The Prophet ﷺ woke up to find her doing this. He asked her what she was doing. She replied she was collecting the drops of his perspiration to put them into some perfume. If the Prophet ﷺ passed on a road or street he left a trail of perfume in the atmosphere and people would sense that he had passed that way. When Anas ﷺ realized he was dying he made a will that some of these drops should be added to the water with which his body would be bathed.

On the occasion of the final pilgrimage, when the Prophet ﷺ shaved his head, Abu Talhah ﷺ collected his hair and took it back to Al-Madinah. There he gave it to Umm Sulaim ﷺ to preserve it. She put it away safely as a memento.

Anas ﷺ mentioned that one day when the Prophet ﷺ visited their house he took a drink of water from a leather bowl kept in the courtyard. His mother cut out the section that his lips had touched and preserved it as well.

On another occasion when he visited them Umm Sulaim offered him dates and ghee. He said she should put them away as he was fasting that day. He stood in a corner of the room to pray, then he spent a long time making supplications to Allâh ﷻ to bless the members of the family both in this world and the next. Umm Sulaim ﷺ then requested him to pray for her son. He prayed so long for his welfare both here and in the Hereafter that Anas ﷺ felt he must have asked Allâh ﷻ for the best possible good for him in both this world and the next.

Once the Prophet ﷺ told them that when he entered Paradise, he could hear someone's footsteps ahead of him. When he asked who it was, he was told that was Ghameesâ' bint Malhân , or Umm Sulaim ﷺ. So she heard directly from the Prophet ﷺ of the joyful tidings of the Paradise which awaited her after this earthly life.

Allâh will be pleased with them and they with Him.

Umm 'Ammârah
Naseebah رضي الله عنها

The Prophet ﷺ said:

"O Allâh! Make this family my friends in Paradise."

Umm 'Ammârah Naseebah رضي الله عنها

Umm 'Ammârah ﷺ was also Ansâriah. She was from the famous Banu Najjâr tribe, that was an offshoot of the Khazraj tribe. Her two sons had been martyred and her brother 'Abdullâh bin Ka'b ؓ was a Companion of the Prophet ﷺ in the Battle of Badr. She was renowned for her courageous exploits in the battlefields. She was a faithful and loyal wife, and a loving mother, also remarkable for her patience and forbearance. Also she was very learned in the Qur'ân and *Hadith*. Her life makes pleasurable and instructive reading for the growth and development of one's faith.

❀❀❀❀❀

The fortunate *Ansâr* in Al-Madinah who were converted to Islâm by the teachings of Mus'ab bin 'Omair went to a particular mountain pass to pledge allegiance to Allâh ﷻ and His Messenger ﷺ for the second time. There were about seventy-two men and two women, and the Prophet ﷺ had also reached there. One of the women was Umm 'Ammârah ﷺ and the other was Umm Munee' Asmâ' bint 'Amr bin 'Adi. The former narrates that her husband, Ghazyah bin 'Amr, told the Prophet ﷺ that these two women also wanted to swear allegiance on his palm. He said it was all right, but for these women too the terms would be the same as for the men. He said that the only difference would be that he took the men's palms in his palm, but he did not shake hands with women. This incident of the swearing of allegiance is called *Bai't-ul-'Aqabah thaniah* (second oath) in Islâmic history. When Umm 'Ammârah ﷺ returned to Al-Madinah after taking this oath of allegiance, she devoted herself to the education and training of women in accordance with the teachings of Islâm.

Umm 'Ammârah ﷺ was married the first time to Zaid bin 'Asim Mâzni. She had two sons by him - 'Abdullâh and Habib رضي الله عنهما. Both were among the Companions of the Prophet ﷺ. A boy Tameem, and a girl Khawlah, were born from her second marriage which was to Ghazyah bin 'Amr Mâzni.

❀❀❀❀❀

In his book *Siyar A'lâm An-Nublâ'*, Imam Thahbi writes that Umm 'Ammârah ﷺ took part in the Second *Bai't-ul-'Aqabah*, the Battle of Uhud, the Battle of Hunain, the war of Yamâmah, and the Treaty of Hudaibiyah. Her skill with the sword in the battle of Uhud astonished those who saw her. The Prophet ﷺ said that in whichever direction he turned in the battlefield he could see her defending and protecting him.

She herself describes a very critical stage in the battle of Uhud. The *Mujâhideen* of Islâm were on the verge of defeat and they were scattering. She, along with her two sons, and husband tried to surround the Prophet ﷺ in order to ward off and repel any attack on him. She had a sword in one hand and a shield in the other. If the enemy had been on foot and not on horseback, they would have slain all of them. When one of the enemies attacked her she warded off the attack with her shield; she then pulled at the bridle of the horse to turn it around. Taking this opportunity, she plunged her sword into the horse's back. The wounded horse fell, taking the rider with him. Seeing this, the Prophet ﷺ called out to 'Abdullâh bin Umm 'Ammârah ﷺ to help his mother. And together she and her son finished off the enemy soldier.

'Abdullâh bin Umm 'Ammârah ﷺ relates how during the battle of Uhud the enemy made a forceful thrust against them. The *Mujâhideen* scattered before them and he and his mother moved close to the Prophet ﷺ to defend him from all quarters. The Prophet ﷺ called out to him to attack the enemy. He threw a stone at the disbeliever; it hit the eye of the horse he was riding. The horse fell to the ground somersaulting. He threw another heavy stone and the enemy died. The Prophet ﷺ looked pleased, and then he noticed that Umm 'Ammârah ﷺ was bleeding from the shoulder; he asked 'Abdulâh ﷺ to bandage his mother's wound and said that they were a truly great family.

He invoked Allâh's blessings on them, and prayed that they should be his friends in Paradise as well.

Both Umm 'Ammârah 🕮 and 'Abdullâh 🕮 were overjoyed when they heard these auspicious words from the lips of the Prophet 🕮. At the same time they were inspired to greater heights of heroism and returned to the attack with renewed vigour. His next victim injured him on the left arm with his sword, and a fountain of blood gushed out. The Prophet 🕮 told him to immediately bandage his wound. When Umm 'Ammârah 🕮 saw her son bleeding profusely, she bandaged his arm and told him not to lose courage but continue with his attack on the enemy. The Prophet 🕮 smiled when he saw the heroism and courage of both mother and son, and said,

'From where can anyone get courage like you, O Umm 'Ammârah 🕮 ?'

Umm 'Ammârah 🕮 was standing in front of the Prophet 🕮 with a naked sword when the same man came before them. The Prophet 🕮 pointed out to her that this was the man who injured her son. She struck a powerful blow cutting off his leg. The man fell face down; a few other *Mujâhideen* leapt on him and killed him.

The Prophet 🕮 was very impressed with this display of strength and courage by Umm 'Ammârah 🕮. He smiled and thanked Allâh 🕮 who gave her that success and had soothed her grief and avenged her by the death of the enemy before her very eyes.

'Umar bin Khattâb 🕮 says that the Prophet 🕮 once told him that in the Battle of Uhud wherever he turned, whether to the right or to the left, he saw Umm 'Ammârah 🕮 fighting to defend him.

During this battle she sustained at least twelve major wounds; the deepest one, the one on her shoulder being inflicted by a disbeliever named Ibn Qumiah. It was so deep that she fainted; and it took a year for it to heal. When she regained consciousness her first question was about the well being of the Prophet 🕮, rather than about her own sons or husband. When she learned that he was fine, she thanked Allâh 🕮. Besides the battle of Hunain and the conquest of Makkah, Umm 'Ammârah 🕮 fought valiantly in the battle against Musailamah

Kaththâb. She sustained eleven wounds and her arm was cut. Her son, Habib bin Zaid Ansâri was martyred in this battle, slain by Musailamah himself.

Her other son, 'Abdullâh bin Zaid ♣ was martyred in the Battle of Hurrat. This war was fought in in the year 63th after Hijrah, on stony black ground to the east of Al-Madinah. Stony black ground is called *Harrah* in Arabic, and it is to be found on three sides of Al-Madinah. 'Abdullâh bin Zaid ♣ was that great Companion who took part in many wars and the one, who murdered Musailamah Kaththâb with his sword. Wahshi bin Harb, who martyred Hamzah bin 'Abdul Muttalib ♣ was also among those who murdered Musailamah Kaththâb. After the battle of Uhud when the Muslim troops returned to Al-Madinah under the leadership of the Prophet ﷺ, he announced that they should get ready to march to a place called, *Hamrâ' Al-Asad*, to chase the pagans. The *Mujâhideen* spent just one night in Al-Madinah. Umm 'Ammârah ﷺ also got up to join them, energized as she was by her ardour to fight the pagans, but weakened by her serious injuries she could not make it. As soon as the Prophet ﷺ returned he asked her brother, 'Abdullâh bin Ka'b Mâzni about her sister's welfare. When he heard that her wounds were healing he breathed a sigh of relief and thanked Allâh ﷻ for His Divine Mercy.

❀❀❀❀❀

Umm 'Ammârah ﷺ and some other women also took part in a war with the Banu Quraidhah. The Prophet ﷺ gave them part of the booty taken during this war. These were the terms of equality practised by the Prophet ﷺ. She was also active during the Treaty of Hudaibiyah. She related how they set out from Al-Madinah to perform *'Umrah* under the leadership of the Prophet ﷺ. They were stopped at Hudaibiyah because the Quraish did not want the Muslims to enter Makkah. 'Uthmân bin 'Affân ♣ was appointed ambassador and sent to Makkah to negotiate. Since his return was delayed, rumours spread that he had been martyred. At the command of Allâh the Prophet ﷺ sat under a tree and people started swearing allegiance to Allâh ﷻ and His Messenger.

Those who were armed took hold of their weapons. Most people came unarmed as they set out for *'Umrah*. Umm 'Ammârah ﷺ says she had a stick and she stuck a knife in her belt, to defend herself in case of enemy attack. As it turned out the news about the death of 'Uthmân bin 'Affân ✿ turned out to be a false rumour. And a pact was made with the enemy that came to be known as the Treaty of Hudaibiyah. This treaty is mentioned in the Qur'ân in the following words,

"Indeed, Allâh was pleased with the believers when they gave the pledge to you under the tree: He knew what was in their hearts, and He sent down calmness and tranquillity upon them, and He rewarded them with a near victory. And abundant spoils that they will capture. And Allâh is Ever All-Mighty, All-Wise." (48:18-19)

Twenty women took part in the Battle of Khayber; one of them was Umm 'Ammârah 🌸. Once again when the Muslim army triumphed women were given a share of the booty of war. Umm 'Ammârah 🌸 got expensive dresses and jewellery and two dinars. In the Battle of Hunain as well she had fought valiantly and received some part of the booty. A man of the tribe of Banu Huwâzin entered the battlefield on camel back, waving a flag. She hit the camel from the back so violently that it stumbled and fell; the rider also fell, she attacked him so that he never recovered.

The Prophet ﷺ sent Umm 'Ammârah's son, Habib bin Zaid ✿, as his representative to Musailamah Kaththâb, in order to bring him to the right path. Breaking all norms of diplomacy, this low down man captured Habib ✿ and tied him to a pillar. He then asked him,

"Do you testify that Muhammad is the Messenger of Allâh?" When he answered in the affirmative, he asked him if he also testified that he, Musailamah, was also the messenger of Allâh ﷺ.

Habib ✿ replied that he was deaf and could not hear him. He kept on repeating the question again and again. And Habib ✿ kept on repeating the same answer. Then this cruel man cut off each part of his body, one by one, and gradually martyred him. When Umm 'Ammârah 🌸 got this news about her son she displayed exemplary patience. The Prophet ﷺ consoled the family and prayed for them.

During his caliphate, Abu Bakr Siddique ✿ sent the army to test the challenge of the army of Musailamah. Umm 'Ammârah 🌸 was also in the army. She was about sixty years old at the time, and her son

'Abdullâh bin Zaid ﷺ was also with her; he was one of those who finally killed this man. During this battle her arm was cut off and she sustained eleven injuries. Khâlid bin Waleed ﷺ, the General of the army boiled some oil and immersed her arm in it to cure her wounded arm; but for Umm 'Ammârah ﷺ her happiness at the death of Musailamah, was much greater than her grief at the loss of her arm.

During the caliphate of 'Umar bin Khattâb ﷺ, some beautiful and exclusive sheets were sent to him. One of these sheets was exceptionally beautiful and large as well. Some of the companions suggested that it should be sent as a gift to Safiyyah bin 'Obaid, the wife of 'Abdullâh bin 'Umar رضي الله عنهما. But 'Umar bin Khattâb ﷺ said that he knew of someone even better than her and praised by no less a person than the Prophet ﷺ. He then sent it to Umm 'Ammârah ﷺ.

Once Umm 'Ammârah ﷺ told the Prophet ﷺ that in the Noble Qur'ân only men were mentioned and women were often deprived of any importance. Then this *Âyah* was revealed.

"Verily, the Muslims men and women, the believers men and women, the men and the women who are obedient (to Allâh), the men and women who are truthful, the men and the women who are patient, the men and the women who are humble, the men and the women who give *Sadaqât* (i.e. *Zakât* and alms), the men and the women who observe fast, the men and the women who guard their chastity (froillegal sexual acts) and the men and the women who remember Allâh much with their hearts and tongues, Allâh has prepared for them forgiveness and a great reward (i.e. Paradise)." (33:35)

Umm 'Ammârah ﷺ held a very special place among the women Companions. When the Prophet ﷺ saw the valour and sacrificing spirit of the whole family – husband, wife, and sons – in the most intense part of the battle of Uhud he prayed that Allâh ﷺ might have Mercy on that family.

Umm 'Ammârah ﷺ requested him to pray that they should have the good fortune to be with him in Paradise. It was then that he prayed that they should be his friends in Paradise.

Allâh will be pleased with them and they with Him.

Ar-Rabee' bint Ma`uwth رضي الله عنها

The Prophet ﷺ said:

"Whosoever participated in the Pledge of Rizwân, are the holders of Paradise."

Ar-Rabee' رضي الله عنها participated in the Pledge of Rizwân so she is a lady of Paradise.

Ar-Rabee' bint Ma`uwth رضي الله عنها

Rabee' ﷺ was the daughter of Ma'uwth bin 'Afrâ' and her uncles (her father's brothers) were Mu'âth bin 'Afrâ' and 'Auf bin 'Afrâ' رضي الله عنهم. All the three sons of 'Afrâ' were at the battle of Badr. In the Noble Qur'ân, Allâh has said:

> The Prophet's Companions were granted forgiveness at the battle of Badr.

In the battlefield at Badr, 'Utbah bin Rabee'ah, Shaibah bin Rabee'ah, and Waleed bin 'Utbah had come forward for the pagans to challenge the forces of the Muslims. From among the Muslims the three sons of 'Afrâ' ﷺ came forward to meet the challenge. The Makkan champions said arrogantly that people worthy of them and tribe chiefs should be sent to oppose them. The Prophet ﷺ called these three brothers back and sent his uncle, Hamzah bin 'Abdul Muttalib, 'Ali bin Abi Tâlib and 'Obaidah bin Hârith رضي الله عنهم to face these arrogant men. These three riders launched such a powerful attack that the three heroes of the pagans were shattered. In a second the pride of these Makkans was laid low in the dust. Licking their wounds they were dispatched to death and their place in Hell.

❀❀❀❀❀

'Abdur-Rahmân bin 'Auf ﷺ relates that in the field of Badr the son of 'Afrâ' Ma`uwth ﷺ, came to him and asked him in a whisper which one was Abu Jahl and where he was. He had barely answered him when his brother came running to him and asked the same question.

'Abdur-Rahmân bin 'Auf ﷺ asked them why they were looking for Abu

Jahl. They replied that they had heard that he always cursed the Prophet ﷺ; they were determined that on this day they would either chop off his head or be martyred themselves. On hearing this 'Abdur-Rahmân bin 'Auf ؓ was very happy. As they were speaking they saw Abu Jahl riding up in all his pride and glory. Pointing out to him 'Abdur-Rahmân ؓ told them that this was their prey. They both leapt and made such a powerful attack that he fell from his horse. They again struck at him so that he could not rise up. Then 'Abdullâh bin Mas'ood ؓ reached there and prepared to lop off his head. Even at this stage his pride was such that he requested them to cut him off lower in the neck, so it would look like the head of a chieftain. He said that he wished he had been slain by a strong young person rather than by these farmers. The Prophet ﷺ prayed for Ma`uwth bin 'Afrâ' and Mu'âth bin 'Afrâ'. All the three sons of 'Afrâ' ؓ were present at the *'Aqabah thaniah.*

🌸🌸🌸🌸🌸

'Afrâ's daughter, Ar-Rabee' ؓ was married to a famous prominent businessman, Ayâs bin Bakeer. She had a son by this marriage, Muhammad bin Ayâs.

Rabee' bint Ma`uwth ؓ was the daughter of a well-known family. The Prophet ﷺ used to visit her house sometimes, and always gladly accepted any gift she offered him. She was justifiably proud of this great honour. She relates that on the day she was married the Prophet ﷺ visited her house and sat on the bed. Young girls were singing to the accompaniment of the *Daf* [1] and the Prophet ﷺ enjoyed their singing.

When they started saying that a Prophet who knew things about the future was sitting in their midst.

Prophet ﷺ stopped them, and gently told them that no one had knowledge about the unknown, except Allâh ﷻ. Leaving out this phrase they could continue with their singing.

This shows that it is not a wrong for the young girls of the family to get

---

[1] Similar to a tambourine without cymbals or bells.

together and sing on a joyous occasion like a marriage to express their happiness.

❁❁❁❁❁

Rabee' bint Ma`uwth 🌸 used to serve the Prophet's favorite dishes when he visited her house. Once she served him ripe dates that he relished. On that day he gave her some gold and silver ornaments he received from Bahrain. He asked her to accept them and wear them.

Rabee' bint Ma`uwth 🌸, a lady who had been assured a place in Paradise, was indeed fortunate to receive such a gift from the Prophet 🌸 himself. It is a *Sunnah* (way) of the Prophet 🌸 to exchange gifts, which increase affection and pleasant feelings of mutual regard between people exchanging them.

She was also fortunate in that the Prophet 🌸 often used to come to her house to make the ablution, offer prayers, have a meal and then rest for a while. So Rabee' bint Ma`uwth 🌸 used to acquire knowledge about many points of religion. Many Companions used to value her and often request her to relate *Ahâdith* and the knowledge she gained from her experiences. Rabee' bint Ma`uwth 🌸 relates that when the Prophet 🌸 visited her, he would ask her to get some water. She would arrange for it and then help him to perform the ablution for prayer. She describes the correct procedure that she learnt from watching him. He would wash his hands three times, then wash his face three times. He would rinse his mouth once and clean his nose by drawing in water. Next he washed his arms up to the elbows three times. Then he would wipe his head by drawing his palms over from the front of his forehead to the back of the nape of his neck, then back to the forehead. Then he would insert his fingers into the outer and inner parts of his ears. Then he washed each foot three times.

❁❁❁❁❁

Abu 'Obaidah bin Hamd bin 'Ammâr bin Yâsir 🌸 says that he once asked Rabee' bint Ma`uwth 🌸 to describe how the Prophet 🌸 looked.

She said that he looked as bright as the sun.

She compared his face to the sun, because it shone like the sun and also because sunshine eached every corner of the earth, like the message of the Prophet.

During the Prophet's days women had the privilege of taking part in wars as well. They would nurse the wounded and quench the thirst of the soldiers in the battlefields. It is mentioned in *Sahih Al-Bukhâri* that Khâlid bin Thakwân narrated from Rabee' bint Ma`uwth that she took part in the wars. She would bandage and nurse the wounded, give water to the *Mujâhideen*, carry the wounded, the dead and convey them to Al-Madinah. She was part of the congregation which swore the oath of allegiance in the year 6th after Hijrah which become famous in Islâmic history as *Bai'at Ridhwân*. Thus she heard of her succession to Paradise in the Hereafter from the lips of the Prophet ﷺ himself. This is a greater distinction than any other in this world.

❀❀❀❀❀

Rabee'ah bint Ma`uwth ◈ was a woman of mature understanding, farsighted and quick-witted. One day Abu Rabee'ah's wife, Umm 'Ayâsh came to her door selling perfumes. In the course of conversation she said, she would not sell any perfumes to her because she was the daughter of the man who killed the leader of her tribe. Rabee'ah bint Ma`uwth ◈ was enraged and asked the woman to get out of her house, her perfume was worse than any stink. She shouted to her to get out of her sight.

Later in life, during the caliphate of 'Uthmân bin 'Affân ◈, Rabee' bint Ma`uwth ◈ and her husband developed some differences. She asked him to take everything she had and give her *Khula'*[1], as she did not want to remain his wife any longer. He agreed and left taking everything with him. It is said he did not leave even a sheet in the house. When the complaint went to 'Uthmân bin 'Affân ◈ he said nothing could be done as he was within his rights according to the *Shari'ah*. Nothing could be taken back from him. Even people of the highest caliber sometimes have to face such unexpected critical times in their life.

---

[1] The release from the marriage tie obtained by a wife upon the return of the dowery.

People of modern times who talk so loudly about women's liberation and women's rights should remember this law of Islâm. If a woman just cannot tolerate life with her husband she can demand separation or divorce. She can settle the matter trough mutual agreement or go to a court of law. Only in this case, in the language of *Shari'ah*, it is called *Khula'*, and not *Talâq*, or divorce. Just as a man has the right to *Talâq*, so a woman has the right to *Khula'*. These two possibilities are there for both the partners in a marriage to ease the tension caused by conflicts in family life. Separation, it is said in the Noble Qur'ân, is not the ideal way but it is permitted. It is the least desirable, yet best possible way under the worst marital circumstances. If this escape route had not been there, both partners would live life as if it were a war. And that is not the best environment, either for them or their children. Thus, such rules of the *Shari'ah* (Islâmic legeslation) are a blessing for the common problems of everyday society.

There are twenty-one *Ahâdith* associate with Rabee'ah bint Ma`uwth 🌸. 'Aishah bint Anas bin Mâlik, Sulaimân bin Yassar, Khâlid bin Thakwân, 'Abdullâh bin Muhammad bin Aqeel, Abu 'Obaidah Muhammad bin 'Ammâr bin Yassir رضــي الله عـــهم - some of the most famous followers of Islâmic *Shari'ah* (Islâmic legeslation) - are some of those who have narrated her words.

After living a long eventful life, Rabee' bint Ma`uwth 🌸 passed away in the year 45th after Hijrah during the caliphate of Mu'âwiyah bin Sufyân 🌸.

Allâh will be pleased with them and they with Him.

Faree'ah bint Mâlik رضي الله عنها

The Prophet ﷺ said:

"Whosoever participated in the Pledge of Rizwân, are the holders of Paradise."

Faree'ah participated in the Pledge of Rizwân so she is a lady of Paradise.

Faree'ah bint Mâlik رضي الله عنها

S he was the daughter of the great Companion, Mâlik bin Sinân bin 'Obaid Ansâri Khudri ﷺ. It was about him that the Prophet ﷺ said:

"Whosoever wants to see a person of Paradise, then they should look at her."

Her brother was Abu Sa'eed Khudri ﷺ, the *Mufti* (scholar) of the Grand Mosque at Al-Madinah. He was an extremely learned man, and an authority on *Hadith*. He was also a *Mujâhid* and General of the Muslim army and had been a ruler of a province. One thousand one hundred and seventy *Ahâdith* are attributed to him. Another brother from her mother's side was a General too. He was Qatâdah bin Nu'mân Ansâri ﷺ, who had taken part in the battles of Badr and Uhud.

On one occasion his eye was injured by the enemy and came out of its socket. When the Prophet ﷺ saw this he thrust it back with his hand; it went back to its original position and his vision became sharper than before.

❀❀❀❀❀

The father of Faree'ah bint Mâlik, Mâlik bin Sinân bin 'Obaid Ansâri Khudri رضي الله عنهما, was one of the greatest and foremost Companions, and a personality who, the Prophet ﷺ said, was of Paradise. He could not take part in the Battle of Badr, but in Uhud he was martyred defending the life of the Prophet ﷺ. When he went to the Prophet ﷺ to volunteer for the Battle of Uhud he was accompanied by his son, Sa'd,

that is, Abu Sa'eed bin Khudri ﷺ. He was very young and the Prophet
ﷺ did not give him permission to go to war. He started to weep and
his sister, Faree'ah bint Mâlik ﷺ, embraced him affectionately, and
wiping his tears asked him to be patient and wait for the right time.
Abu Sa'eed bin Khudri ﷺ grew up to shine in world of knowledge
and learning and occupy the post of *Mufti* (The delieverer of formal
legal opinions) of Al-Madinah.

When Mâlik bin Sinân bin 'Obaid Ansâri Khudri ﷺ met the Prophet ﷺ
he spoke to him in a very eloquent manner and said that they were
setting out to test their strength against the disbelievers. They would
either triumph by the Grace of Allâh ﷺ or be martyred. Both the likely
alternatives were good for a true Muslim, both would bring victory to
him. At the time when the fighting was at its most intense, he
earnestly adopted the best defensive position to protect the Prophet ﷺ.
Finally, he lost his life in the way of Allâh ﷺ, fulfilling this most
demanding duty. At this critical juncture in the battle the world saw
the Prophet ﷺ, injured in his face and bleeding. Mâlik bin Sinân bin
'Obaid Ansâri Khudri ﷺ sucked the blood from the wound. Thus the
blood of the Prophet ﷺ mingled with his own.

As soon as the Prophet ﷺ reached Al-Madinah after the Battle of Uhud
he was met by Abu Sa'eed bin Khudri ﷺ. He immediately recognized
him and asked if he was Sa'd bin Mâlik. When the latter noticed the
encouraging and affectionate tone of the Prophet's greeting, he drew
nearer to him. The Prophet ﷺ condoled with him and told him to be
patient and brave. He said his father's martyrdom would earn
blessings for him. When he returned home, Abu Sa'eed bin Khudri ﷺ
gave his sister, Faree'ah bint Mâlik ﷺ, the news regarding their father,
and the injunctions of the Prophet ﷺ about how to accept his loss. She
accepted her father's martyrdom with equanimity, courage and patience
as advised by the Prophet ﷺ, taking it as a matter of pride to be
addressed by the Prophet ﷺ. She expressed happiness that he returned
safe and sound. At the time of her father's martyrdom there was no
means of sustenance in the house for the family. But the children
displayed exemplary patience. They practised patience as advised by
the Prophet ﷺ, and did not ask anyone for aid. They heard him say that
a person who is content and trusted in Allâh, is made wealthy by Him;

one who wishes to be pure and chaste, Allâh 🕮 makes him pure; one who restrains himself, is granted patience and fortitude by Allâh 🕮. As a result of following the injunctions and teachings of the Prophet 🕮 the family became wealthy and prosperous beyond belief.

Faree'ah bint Mâlik 🕸 was married to Sahl bin Râfi' bin Bashir Khazraji. He was killed by some of his slaves near Al-Madinah. This tragedy left her grief-stricken. After the murder of her husband she wanted to go back to her parents' house. She consulted the Prophet 🕮 as to what course of action was permitted by the *Shari'ah*, and if she could do so. He said that she should continue to stay in her house till she completed the perscribed waiting period. It should be noted that when a woman's husband dies she should observe a period of mourning for four months and ten days. Faree'ah bint Mâlik 🕸 says that she obeyed the Prophet 🕮 and stayed in her house for the prescribed period, and after that she devoted her full life to the service and propagation of Islâm. She was one of those who took part in the *Bai'at Ridhwân*.

The Prophet 🕮 said about these people that none of them would go to Hell. In other words, they would all go to Paradise.

During the caliphate of 'Uthmân bin 'Affân 🕸 a lady's husband died. The matter of her place of residence during the period of her *'Iddat* came under consideration. Faree'ah bint Mâlik 🕸 was summoned to the court of the caliph. She was asked what the Prophet 🕮 had told her when she was in a similar situation regarding the place where she should pass the period of *'Iddat*. What she said was accepted in the court and applied to the lady in question.

Faree'ah bint Mâlik 🕸 had a very good memory. If she heard the command of the Prophet 🕮 even once, she would immediately learn it and retain it in her memory. In their study of traditions and *Ahâdith*, many great scholars would approach her for authentication or reference. Especially in the matter of observance of *'Iddat*; she has the distinction of being the predominant authority regarding the rules to be observed.

Those learned in *Fiqh* in Al-Madinah, Syria, Iraq and Egypt gave their *Fatwâ* on *'Iddat* based on what she said. Hâfidh Ibn Qayyam in his famous book, *Zâd Al-Mi'âd*, has written that the famous interpreter of the *Shari'ah*, Muhammad bin Sireen, writes that a woman was sick when her husband died. People moved her from her husband's place to her parents' house. When the learned people of the community came to know of this, they all said she should be moved back to her husband's house. She should pass the days of her *'Iddat* there. So she moved back. This was done based on the life and experience of Faree'ah bint Mâlik ﷺ.

One thousand four hundred people wento perform *'Umrah* in the year 6th after Hijrah and were stopped by the Quraish at Hudaibiah. They gathered under a tree to swear allegiance to Allâh ﷺ and His Messenger. They also swore to take revenge for the death of their emissary, 'Uthmân bin 'Affân ﷺ, who was sent by the Prophet ﷺ to Makkah to negotiate with the enemy. Rumour had it that he was killed by the Quraish. The ardour and spirit of sacrifice of these people appealed so much to Allâh ﷺ that He promised Paradise for all of them.

It was an honour of which they could be truly jubilant and proud. Surely such a promise is given to only the very fortunate, and Faree'ah bint Mâlik ﷺ was one of them.

Allâh will be pleased with them and they with Him.

Umm Hishâm bint Hârithah bin Nu'mân رضي الله عنها

Jâbir bin 'Abdullâh ※ narrated that Allâh's Messenger ﷺ said:

"Those who participated in the Pledge of Rizwân will never go to Hell."

Umm Hishâm bint Hârithah participated in the Pledge of Rizwân therefore, she is a lady of Paradise.

Umm Hishâm bint Hârithah bin Nu'mân رضي الله عنها

Like the other women Companions whom participate in the *Bai't
Ridhwân* she was one of them, so she ensured a place in
Paradise for her spirit of sacrifice and selflessness. Loyal and
faithful, learned and knowledgeable in matters of religion, she was
pious and very particular about cleanliness – especially about ablution
and prayer. She had the good fortune to be the neighbour of the
Prophet ﷺ in Al-Madinah. She was the daughter of another noteworthy
Companion, Hârithah bin Nu'mân ﷺ. He was a very wealthy man
and one of the leading and well-known personalities of the city. Her
father had given away several houses as gifts for the use of the
Prophet ﷺ. In fact, in praise of this Companion the Prophet ﷺ said:

> He had given me so many houses that I felt embarrassed to ask
> him for a new one.

Umm Hishâm bint Hârithah ﷺ was, like her father, a great
personality, and an exemplary character.

❊❊❊❊❊

When the Prophet ﷺ came to Al-Madinah after his migration from
Makkah he enjoyed the hospitality of Abu Ayub Ansâri ﷺ for almost
six months. Their next door neighbour was Hârithah bin Nu'mân ﷺ.
His daughter, Umm Hishâm bint Hârithah ﷺ, often used to cook and
send food for the esteemed guest, the Prophet ﷺ. Whenever he
contracted a marriage he needed a new house. And it was Hârithah
bin Nu'mân ﷺ who gave him his own home and moved on to another

house himself. The Prophet ﷺ felt ashamed that he was put to so much trouble and had to move so often.

'Allamah Yâqut Hamwi in his book, *Mu'jam Al-Baldân*, writes that Hârithah bin Nu'mân ؊ was the first Companion to be fortunate enough to offer so many houses to the Prophet ﷺ. He was also extremely obedient to his mother, hence Allâh ﷻ gave him such a high status in life. 'Aishah ؅ narrated that the Prophet ﷺ once said that when he entered Paradise he heard someone reciting the Noble Qur'ân beautifully. He asked who this might be and he was told it was Hârithah bin Nu'mân ؊. He then said that thus were the good people, who were obedient to their mothers.

Hârithah bin Nu'mân ؊ was so exalted that he actually had the good fortune to see the Angel Jibril ؅ twice. He says that he saw him twice with his own eyes. When the Prophet ﷺ left to battle with Banu Quraidhah he saw him in the guise of another Companion of the Prophet ﷺ, Dahyah Kalbi ؊. This was in *Jannatul Baqi'*. The second time he saw him was in the battlefield, during the Battle of Hunain when he was busy talking to the Prophet ﷺ. When he passed by the two of them silently, the Angel Jibril ؅ asked the Prophet ﷺ who he was.

He replied that it was Hârithah bin Nu'mân ؊. Then he said he was one among the hundred persons who, Allâh ﷻ had said, would be blessed with the food of Paradise. Also if he had greeted me today, he would have returned his greetings, said the Angel. This noble Companion also had the honour of taking part in the Battle of Badr.

Umm Hishâm bint Hârithah ؅ was a descendant of noble families from both sides. Her mother, Umm Khâlid bint Khâlid bin Ya'eesh was from the Banu Mâlik tribe. She had the privilege of swearing allegiance to Islâm with the Prophet ﷺ. She was married to Hârithah bin Nu'mân ؊. She had five children by him – 'Abdullâh, 'Abdur-Rahmân, Saudah, 'Umrah and Umm Hishâm – who filled the house with love and liveness. All of them had the good fortune of accepting Islâm. This whole family served the Prophet ﷺ in a remarkable manner. Umm Hishâm bint Hârithah ؅ visited the Prophet's house very often; thus she had the golden opportunity of meeting and mixing with the Mothers of the believers and observing them from close quarters on many an occasion. And the close social contact with these ladies of noble character deeply influenced her.

On the days of '*Eid* and on Fridays, the Prophet 🌸 would recite *Surah Qâf* of Noble Qur'ân. Umm Hisham 🌸 had learned it by heart from listening to him. She had a very sharp mind and a remarkable memory. She also remembered many *Ahâdith* by heart. Her sister, 'Umrah, Muhammad bin 'Abdur-Rahmân bin As'ad bin Zurâh, Yahyâ bin 'Abdullâh and Habib bin 'Abdur-Rahmân have narrated *Ahâdith* from her.

❀❀❀❀❀

In the year 6th after Hijrah when the Prophet 🌸 announced his intention to set out for Makkah for '*Umrah*, one thousand four hundred companions – both men and women prepared to accompany him. This group of pure-minded people set out on this sacred journey, but they were stopped at Hudaibiyah by the Quraish, who restricted their entry into Makkah. The Prophet 🌸 sent 'Uthmân bin 'Affân as his emissary to negotiate with the Quraish. They did not send him back for a long time and rumours spread that he had been killed by them. When this news reached the Prophet 🌸 he was very sorrowful and upset. He said that they could not return to Al-Madinah without avenging the murder of 'Uthmân bin 'Affân 🌸. He sat down under a tree; all his Companions – men and women – gathered around him and swore the oath of allegiance; they also swore to battle with the Quraish to avenge the murder of their delegate. *Bai't Ridhwân* was the name given to this historic event. Allâh 🌸 gave his approval to this convention and also foretold for them victory in the future. As he says in *Surat Al-Fath*,

> "Indeed, Allâh was pleased with the believers when they gave the pledge to you (O Muhammad 🌸) under to you: He knew what was in their hearts, and He snet down almness and tranqillity upon them, and He rewarded them with a near victory." (48:18)

The Companions and Women Companions present there on this occasion of historic and religious significance are also remembered in Islâmic history as the 'Companions of the Tree'. As it turned out 'Uthmân bin 'Affân 🌸 did not have to stay there for very long, and the Quraish sent Abu Yazid Sohail bin 'Amr as their representative to Hudaibiyah to where the Prophet 🌸 was encamped with his Companions. On the basis of some terms a peace treaty was concluded here. This came to be known as the Peace Treaty of Hudaibiyah. When Makkah was taken by the Muslims he converted to Islâm. He became a devout Muslim, zealous with prayers, *Zakât*, sacrifice and charity.

When he recited the Noble Qur'ân he would start weeping and sobbing. When the Prophet ﷺ passed away there was an upheaval; many of the people in Makkah started to recant; and return to their old ways. At this critical point in time, Abu Yazid Sohail bin 'Amr stood up and addressed the Quraish in a thundering voice:

"O Quraish! You should be ashamed. You were the last to enter into the fold of Islâm, and you are the first to leave this strong circle? Remember Islâm will ultimately triumph. Its light will spread as far and wide as the light of the sun and the moon, taking the whole world in its embrace.

Stop, O Quraish! And do not become unfaithful apostates. You will ruin yourself both in this world and the next."

Listening to his sincere and moving advice, the people of Makkah then held on firmly to Islâm.

Abu Yazid Sohail bin 'Amr took part in the War of Yarmouk and died as a martyr.

The Prophet ﷺ gave the good news of life eternal in Paradise for all of the one thousand four hundred people, who were the 'Companions of the Tree'. The Prophet ﷺ said that those who took part in the *Bai't Ridhwân* were promised that not one of them would go to *Jahannum*. Thus, Umm Hishâm bint Hârithah ﷻ was also given the glad tidings of Paradise.

There was one misguided hypocrite Jadd bin Qais among these 'Companions of the Tree', who owned a very expensive red camel. According to the tradition in *Sahih Al-Bukhâri*, this man was separated from the pure-hearted members of this group. The words of the *Hadith* are,

"All those people who swore allegiance under the tree will certainly go to Paradise, except the man with the red camel."

This promise of Paradise in the life Hereafter is the greatest reward, the parallel of which cannot be found in this world. Fortunate are those who received this promise from Allâh ﷻ and His Messenger ﷺ. And when Umm Hishâm bint Hârithah ﷻ left this world this is the treasure she carried with her.

Allâh will be pleased with them and they with Him.

Umm Salamah Asmâ' bint Yazid bin Sakan Al-Ansâriah رضي الله عنها

The Prophet ﷺ said:

"Who participated in the Pledge of Rizwân will never go to Hell."

Asmâ bint Yazid رضي الله عنها got the honor of participating the Pledge of Rizwân.

Umm Salamah Asmâ' bint Yazid bin Sakan Al-Ansâriah رضي الله عنها

atient, with complete faith in Allâh, pious, wise and God fearing – these were some of the qualities of Umm Salamah Asmâ' bint Yazid Ansâriah ﷺ. But, above all it was her courage that inspires a reader of the biographies of these women Companions. Daring in the extreme, she was so brave that with the pole of her tent she killed nine Roman soldiers in the battle of Yarmook. Her statements were well considered, therefore she was always eloquent and convincing. It was almost as if she was casting a spell when she spoke. Her phrases were in beautiful sequence like a string of pearls, and her tone was well modulated and sweet sounding. On one occasion she appeared before the Prophet ﷺ as a representative, rather as an attorney to plead for the cause of women. She addressed him very respectfully and said,

> "Today I have come into your presence to plead the case for women. Allâh ﷺ sent you as His Prophet ﷺ for all mankind – men and women. We women also have had the privilege and honour of swearing allegiance to Allâh ﷺ and you. We also follow your teachings and your *Sunnah* (ways). We women live within our houses and fulfill our duties. We are absorbed in looking after our husbands and fulfilling their needs. We see to the upbringing of our children and to the daily function of the household. Men, however have more opportunities for earning rewards from Allâh ﷺ because they can do things which we, as

women, cannot do. Men attend the congregational prayers in the mosques and special Friday prayers. They participate in the special prayers for the dead; they also have the privilege of taking part in the *Jihâd*. When they go for *Jihâd* we are left at home to protect their property and look after the family. Are we not also equally deserving of reward from Allâh?"

The Prophet ﷺ was very moved and impressed by her eloquently presented and rational plea. He turned around to his Companions and asked them if they had ever heard anyone else express a better question regarding religion.

Simultaneously they all answered that she was truly excellent. The Prophet ﷺ then turned around to the lady and answered her.

'Please go and tell the ladies whom you represent that by doing your duty by your husbands in a pleasant manner, keeping in mind what will make them happy, and following them faithfully, you will please greatly Allâh ﷻ and He will give you the same rewards as have been promised to men.'

She was so happy on hearing this good news that she rose from the meeting, reciting the words – *Lâ ilâha illallâh, Allâhu-Akbar*. She rushed to give her friends the good news she had just received from Allâh's Messenger ﷺ.

She narrated that once she was sitting with her friends when the Prophet ﷺ passed by. When he saw them he addressed them, saying:

They should not be ungrateful to their benefactors. Since she was bolder than the rest of her friends she asked him to be more specific and clarify what he meant by his statement. He said,

'A woman lives with her parents, then she gets married and Allâh ﷻ blesses her with children. At times when she gets annoyed with her husband she says that she never got any happiness in his house. This is a display of sheer ingratitude to her husband. Every Muslim woman should try to avoid saying such things.'

Talking about the status and position of a husband he said,

'If I were to order a person to prostrate before another human being, I would ask a wife to prostrate before her husband.'

🌸🌸🌸🌸🌸

'Amr bin Qatâda 🌸 relates that among the ladies of the *Ansâr*, the first to pledge allegiance to Allâh 🌺 and His Messenger and recite the words of testimony were Umm Sa'd bin Mu'âth, Kabthah bint Râfi', Umm Salamah Asmâ' bint Yazid, and her sister Hawâ' bint Yazid Ansâriah رضــي الله عنــهن. And they all had the privilege of doing this personally with the Prophet 🌺. This was not a trifling thing. One who gains this opportunity is very fortunate indeed, and he or she should be justifiably proud.

Umm Salma Asmâ' bint Yazid Ansâriah 🌸 narrates that when the Prophet 🌺 got married to 'Aishah 🌸, she was the one who helped to get the bride ready. When the Prophet 🌺 arrived she offered him a glass of milk. He had some of it and then gave the rest to 'Aishah 🌸; she was feeling very shy and did not take the glass. So Umm Salamah 🌸 told her.

This was a golden opportunity which did not come everyday; she should accept it and not feel bashful.

'Aishah 🌸 narrated that she was so nervous and shy that her hands were trembling. She took the glass and started drinking the milk.

The Prophet 🌺 told her to give some to her friends as well as to the other ladies who were present. All of them started laughing and said that they had no desire to have the milk.

He joked with them saying that lies and hunger should not be joined together.

🌸🌸🌸🌸🌸

Umm Salamah Asmâ' 🌸 says that one day the Prophet 🌺 came to their house when it was the time for *Maghrib* prayers. In the courtyard of their house they made a small mosque and he prayed there. Then she offered him some bread and some soup she cooked. She said that she swears by Allâh 🌺 in whose Hand is her soul, that there were about forty people who sat down for the meal; there was just a little bread and the soup was in a small leather bowl, but everyone had a hearty meal and there was still a lot of food left over. Then the family too ate their fill. She says that she cleaned the bowl and put it away in a safe place. She says that whenever anyone in the family fell sick, she would give him water in that bowl and he would be cured. Sometimes for plenitude they would use the bowl to drink water and their needs would be fulfilled.

❀❀❀❀❀

During the battle of the Trenche Umm Salamah Asmâ' bint Yazid ﺭﺿ sent his favorite dish of dates and gee to the Prophet ﷺ. At the time he was with the Mother of the believers Umm Salamah ﺭﺿ. She took as much as she wanted and then she sent a general invitation to the *Mujâhideen* who were taking part in the war to come and partake of it. Everyone had their fill, but there was still the same quantity of food left over.

Jâbir bin 'Abdullâh ﺭﺿﻲ ﺍﻟﻠﻪ ﻋـﻨـﻪ, had also given a dinner; there too the same thing happened. Another such incident of plenitude and blessings of Allâh ﷻ took place when Umm Sulaim ﺭﺿ served a meal to the Prophet ﷺ.

Umm Salamah Asmâ' bint Yazid ﺭﺿ narrated that in the lifetime of the Prophet ﷺ she was divorced. There was no precedent for the *'Iddat* of a divorced woman before this. When she got divorced the following Verse of the Noble Qur'ân was revealed:

> "And divorced women shall wait for three menstrual periods." (2:228)

In the matter of knowledge and learning Umm Salamah Asmâ' ﺭﺿ occupied a very high position. Among the women Companions her position was after that of the Mother of the believers 'Aishah ﺭﺿ and the Mother of the Believers Umm Salamah ﺭﺿ. There are eighty-one *Ahâdith* associated with her name. One of the *Ahâdith* narrated by her says,

> 'The Prophet ﷺ said verily, Allâh forgives all the sins and it does not bother Him.'

Umm Salamah Asmâ' bint Yazid ﺭﺿ was a very patient person and thankful to her Lord under all circumstances. During the Battle of Uhud her father, Yazid bin Sakan, her brother, 'Amer bin Yazid bin Sakan, and her uncle, Ziyâd bin Sakan رضي الله عنهم were all martyred. When she was told about it, she asked for news about the Prophet ﷺ. After she herself saw him arriving, she thanked Allâh ﷻ, and said:

"As long as he was all right and well, all other troubles faded into insignificance, and the greatest of difficulties were of minor consequence."

In short, looking at the various events of her life, one realises her greatness. The food she served in the Battle of Uhud became the occasion of one of the miracles of the Prophet ﷺ. She had the distinction and pride of being a member at the signing of the Peace Treaty of Hudaibiyah. She was among the Companions of the Tree at the *Bai't Ridhwân*. She took part in the Battle of Khaiber. At the Battle of Yarmouk she killed nine enemy soldiers with just the pole of her tent. At the Battle of Uhud she was given the good news of eternal life in the Hereafter in Paradise for the tribe Banu 'Abdul-Ashahal. Among those martyred was her father as well. About these people, the Prophet ﷺ had said that the whole family had met together in Paradise, and intercession was accepted for all of them. In the light of this statement it can be said that she also would go to Paradise.

She lived to a ripe old age, and died during the caliphate of Yazid bin Mu'âwiyah. She had moved to Damascus in the latter part of her life. It was there that she died. She was buried near the Saghir Gate of Damascus.

Allâh will be pleased with them and they with Him.

Umm Sa'd Kabshah bint Râfi' Ansâriah رضي الله عنها

The Prophet ﷺ said:

"O Umm Sa`d رضي الله عنها! Be Happy and give the good news to your family that their all martyrs have entered in Paradise and their intercession has been accepted for their family."

Umm Sa'd Kabshah bint Râfi' Ansâriah رضي الله عنها

Her name was Kabshah bint Râfi' Ansâriah and she was the mother of a great *Sahâbi*, Sa'd bin Mu'âth رضي الله عنه. When Abu Sa'eed Khudri رضي الله عنه started digging his grave he said that the earth gave out perfumed air as of saffron or musk. The Prophet ﷺ said that the very throne of Allâh ﷻ was elated at his arrival in Paradise. He was the chieftain of the Banu Abdul-Ashahal tribe, and when he accepted Islâm the whole tribe did so too, because he was held in such high esteem for his learning and knowledge.

❀❀❀❀❀

Usaid bin Hudhair, the leader of the Aws tribe, came to know that a young man, Mus'ab bin 'Umair رضي الله عنه, came from Makkah and with his magical eloquence he was attracting people to himself. Once a person heard him, he became his constant Companion. One day Usaid came to know that he was sitting in a garden and people gathered around him. Also present there was As'ad bin Zurârah. He went there in full pride and arrogance, holding a small spear in his hand. Glorying in his power and position, he spoke in a haughty tone to Mus'ab bin 'Umair رضي الله عنه, asking who had given him permission to spread trouble in their peaceful city. He said if he dared to enter his neighbourhood he would be the worst person to deal with and he himself would be responsible for the consequences.

Mus'ab bin 'Umair رضي الله عنه, was a dignified and patient man, with steadfast faith in Allâh 🌸. He addressed him politely and patiently, calling him brother, and said that he should just spend a few minutes with him and listen to what he had to say. If he liked what he heard he could accept it; on the other hand if what he heard did not appeal to him he could reject it. This sounded reasonable to Usaid bin Hudhair and he agreed. After all, the world accepted him as a learned man, and he was also a poet whose mastery over his language was well-known. He thrust his spear in the ground and sat down next to Mus'ab 🌸 to listen to what he had to say.

Mus'ab bin 'Umair 🌸 started by reciting the first *Surah* of the Noble Qur'ân, *Surat Al-Fâtihah*. He did so in such a moving and appealing tone that Usaid bin Hudhair, for whom the meaning and content were totally lucid and new, could not help but exclaim,

> "These are not the words of a human being. These are surely Divine and True Words. If you have brought this message and these Verses for the people of Al-Madinah, please address them openly. No one will prevent you from spreading the Message. Please also do me the favor of accepting me into the fold of Islâm."

As soon as he swore his pledge of allegiance to Islâm, his way of thinking changed. He went back and sent Sa'd bin Mu'âth on some pretext to listen to Mus'ab bin 'Umair 🌸. In the very same manner, arrogantly and angrily, he also went one day to meet Mus'ab 🌸. The cousin of Sa'd bin Mu'âth 🌸 happened to be sitting there, and softly he whispered to him the identity of the person approaching them; he then asked him to talk to him, as he was a very influential leader of his tribe. If he accepted Islâm, then so would the whole tribe of Banu 'Abdul-Ashahal. As they were speaking, Sa'd bin Mu'âth, strode up angrily. Mus'ab bin 'Umair 🌸 again spoke very politely and humbly to him, appealing to him to at least patiently listen to him. If he did not like what he heard he, Mus'ab 🌸, would leave. After all it was not his land, and he was a stranger there without any power. When Sa'd 🌸 heard this refined and cultured man appealing to him so politely, he calmed down, and sat next to him to listen to what he had to say. Mus'ab bin 'Umair 🌸 spoke first about the principles of Islâm that made it a great religion. Then he recited Various Verses of the Noble

Qur'ân. Sa'd bin Mu'âth 🕸 also was overcome by this new approach to life and its values. He immediately swore the oath of allegiance and converted to Islâm. That very evening he gathered the members of his tribe and asked them,

> "O Banu Abdul-Ashahal, do you accept me as your leader?"

They all answered in the affirmative, saying he was a leader who was loved by them. They acknowledged him to be a highly learned man. Then, becoming intensely emotional he appealed to them that if they did not swear allegiance to Allâh 🕸 and His Messenger 🕸 he would not talk to any one of them.

All the members of his tribe, men and women, had pledged allegiance to Islâm by the evening. When such a large number of people entered the fold of Islâm the whole of Al-Madinah, echoed to the cries of *Allâhu-Akbar* (Allâh is the greatest). The mother of Sa'd bin Mu'âth 🕸 was the first to accept Islâm and the city experienced its first spring season, as it were, of this great religion. The emissary of the Prophet 🕸 moved from the house of As'ad bin Zurârah 🕸 to that of Sa'd bin Mu'âth 🕸. And his house was filled with the blessings of Islâm.

🕸🕸🕸🕸🕸

The eloquence, the hard work and the sincere efforts of Mus'ab bin 'Umair 🕸 bore fruit and the Islâmic revolution took over the city of Al-Madinah. At this stage Allâh 🕸 commanded His Messenger, Muhammad 🕸 to migrate from Makkah to Al-Madinah, which today is known as the Prophet's City. When the new converts to Islâm heard that he was going to settle there in their midst, they could not contain their joy. The ladies of the two most prominent tribes of the city, Aws and Khazraj, started looking forward to his arrival excitedly. Umm Sa'd 👧 was the foremost among the ladies. She earnestly wished he should stay at her house, just as his emissary, Mus'ab bin 'Umair 🕸 had.

Anas bin Mâlik 🕸 narrates that the display, by both the *Ansâr* men and women, of such love, respect and sincere happiness moved the Prophet 🕸 deeply. He repeated emotionally three times,

> 'By Allâh you people are dearer to me than any others.'

Prophet ﷺ stayed at the house of Abu Ayub Ansâri ﵏. But he said about the houses in Al-Madinah that among the houses of the *Ansâr*, the best were those of Banu Najjâr. Then those of Banu 'Abdul-Ashahal; then those of Banu Hârith bin Khazraj, then those of Banu Sâ'dah; in other words, all the houses of the *Ansâr* were the best.

Sa'd bin Mu'âth ﵏ says that when the Prophet ﷺ reached Al-Madinah and started accepting the oath of allegiance from the people of the city, his mother, Umm Sa'd ﵂ was the first among the Ansâri women to do so. With her were Umm 'Amer bint Yazid bin Sakan and Hawâ bint Yazid bin Sakan رضي الله عنهما.

Umm Sa'd ﵂ was a very dignified, forbearing, courageous, God-fearing and pious lady. Her two sons, Sa'd bin Mu'âth and 'Amr bin Mu'âth رضي الله عنهما took part in the Battle of Badr. She nursed the wounded *Mujâhideen* and carried around the battlefield large water bags made of leather to quench their thirst. She took an active part in the Battle of Uhud. When she heard that her son, 'Amr bin Mu'âth ﵏, had been martyred she went swiftly to the area where intense fighting was going on. She thanked Allâh ﷻ for protecting the Prophet ﷺ, and said her grief for her son was lessened when she saw him safe and sound.

Prophet ﷺ condoled with her on her son's death and tried to console her. 'Amr bin Mu'âth ﵏, had thrust himself into the enemy ranks, moved by the spirit of *Jihâd* and also killed Dharâr bin Khattâb by his sword. In the Battle of Uhud twelve people from Umm Sa'd's tribe, 'Abdul-Ashahal were killed, and thirty were injured.

In the battle of the Trenches the Prophet ﷺ had taken safety precautions for the ladies and they stayed in the fort of Banu Hârithah. 'Aishah ﵂ narrated that Umm Sa'd ﵂ was also with them. When she looked outside she saw Sa'd bin Mu'âth ﵏ wearing very little armour, carrying a spear, reciting war poetry and advancing triumphantly. She pointed out to his mother, Umm Sa'd ﵂, that he was wearing very little armour; It would have been better if he had worm a larger one. His arms were outside it an unprotected. The enemy could injure him. And it happened exactly as she feared. Habbân bin 'Arqah let loose an arrow which pierced the main artery in his arm and blood gushed out. Seeing this, Habbân bin 'Arqah guffawed happily and said that it was a gift from him. Sa'd bin

Mu'âth 🌸 cursed him saying his face should burn in *Jahannum*.

Since it was a very deep wound it was very painful. The Prophet 🌸 had the tent of Sa'd 🌸 pitched inside the sanctuary at Al-Madinah so that he could be nursed and attended too more easily. When he saw that the blood had not stopped flowing, he had the wound branded with a hot iron. This stopped the bleeding completely, but it became swollen. One day after the war of Banu Quraidhah was over, a goat happened to walk across his wound. This reopened the wound that burst with blood gushing out. He became very weak, and finally died with his head in the lap of the Prophet 🌸.

Asmâ' bint Yazid bin Sakan 🌸 says that when Sa'd bin Mu'âth 🌸 died his mother broke into uncontrollable tears. The Prophet 🌸 condoled with her and asked her to be patient. Her son was such a great person, he said, that Allâh 🌸 smiled when he saw him and His *'Arsh* (Throne) welcomed him gladly.

When all the forts of the Banu Quraidhah were finally conquered the booty of war was distributed equally among all the soldiers – men and women – who fought in the war. Among them was his father's sister, Safiyyah bint 'Abdul Muttalib, Umm Sa'd bin Mu'âth, Umm 'Ammârah, Umm Saleet, Sameerah bint Qais and Umm-ul-'Alâ رضي الله عنهن.

❀❀❀❀❀

Umm Sa'd bin Mu'âth 🌸 is that fortunate lady who heard from the Prophet 🌸 himself that she would go to Paradise. A *Hadith* narrated by Anas bin Mâlik 🌸 says that the Prophet 🌸 said:

> "If a person lost three sons or daughters and remained patient, and made the intention of earning reward from Allâh 🌸, then he or she would enter Paradise."

A woman rose up and asked about a person who lost two sons or daughters, and he answered in the affirmative.

She later wished that she had asked about one child also. Umm Sa'd bin Mu'âth 🌸 is that lady who bore patiently the loss of two sons in the cause of Allâh.

In the battle of Uhud she saw the Prophet 🌸 on horseback and moved swiftly towards him. Her son, Sa'd bin Mu'âth ﷺ, was holding the reins of the horse and he pointed out to the Prophet ﷺ that his mother was approaching. He reined in his horse and greeted her warmly and said:

> O Umm Sa'd ﷺ! be pleased and pass on the glad tidings to her family that the martyred members of her family were gathered in Paradise, and intercession for them had been accepted.

When she heard this, Umm Sa'd ﷺ was very happy. Who could possibly weep and mourn for the dead after hearing that they were already in Paradise? Then she requested the Prophet ﷺ to pray for those of the family left behind. The Prophet ﷺ offered the supplication to Allâh to remove grief and sorrow from their hearts and make their troubles pass away.

After her two sons were martyred Umm Sa'd ﷺ spent most of her time in prayer and remembrance of Allâh and she continued to earn this reward till the end of her life.

Allâh will be pleased with them and they with Him.

Umm Munthir Salamâ bint Qais رضي الله عنها

The Prophet ﷺ said:

"Those who participated in the Pledge of Rizwân are the holders of Paradise."

Umm Al-Munthar Salamâ رضي الله عنها participated in the Pledge of Rizwân, so she is the holder of Paradise.

Umm Munthir Salamâ
bint Qais رضي الله عنها

Umm Munthir ﷺ was a notable daughter of the tribe of Banu Najjâr. And she was the sister of a very eminent Companions, Saleet bin Qais ﷺ. He participated in the battles of Badr. She had the privilege of being a member of the congregation, when the Âyah regarding the change of Qiblah or direction of prayer, was revealed during the middle of prayer. She was also a distant aunt of the Prophet ﷺ, who had great regard for her tribe. Whenever a member of the tribe fell ill he would visit them.

One of the men of the Banu Najjâr tribe was sick. He went to see him and addressing him as maternal uncle, asked him to recite the words,

'None has the right to be worshipped except Allâh.'

The man said that he was not his maternal uncle, but his paternal uncle.

The Prophet ﷺ smiled and said all he had to do was to recite the Kalimah once.

He asked if it would be better and more beneficial for him. He said that it would be not just better but very much better. His life would be better both in this world and in the Hereafter.

Umm Munthir Salamâ bint Qais ﷺ was the great lady who had accepted the invitation of Mus'ab bin 'Umair ﷺ to accept Islâm. She came to be known by her son's name as Umm Munthir ﷺ. Her original name was Salamâ bint Qais 👒. Her two sisters, Umm Sulaim bint Qais and 'Umairah bint Qais also accepted Islâm and swore allegiance to it in the presence of the Prophet 👑.

*****

In no time the women of Al-Madinah were accepting Islâm and pledging allegiance personally to the Prophet 👑. When the women requested that they wanted to do so in the Prophet's presence, he agreed, though he did not touch their palms, when swearing them in. But he made some conditions before swearing them in. He told the women that they should abstain completely from the following six things.

1. They should not accept any other but Allâh as worthy of worship.

2. They should not steal.

3. They should not commit adultery.

4. They should not kill their children.

5. They should not slander or accuse a person falsely.

6. They should not be disobedient to the commands recommended by Allâh.

Umm Munthir 👒 relates that when the Ansâri women gathered to take the pledge, she was among them. They repeated all the six points with the Prophet 👑 when they swore allegiance to Islâm.

The Prophet 👑 also told them they should not deceive their husbands.

Umm Munthir Salamâ bint Qais 👒 was married to Qais bin Sa'sa' bin Wahab; so her father's name was Qais and so was her husband's. But she came to be known by her son's name as Umm Munthir 👒.

*****

After the Battle of Ahzâb the war of Banu Quraidhah took place. In this battle the *Mujâhideen* besieged Banu Quraidhah for twenty-five[1]

---

[1] By some accounts the siege lasted fifteen days.

days. Since they were allies of the Aws, the Jews of Banu Quraidhah appealed to their leader, Sa'd bin Mu'âdh 🌸, for his judgement on the egoistic and arrogant Banu Quraidhah and how they should be punished. Sa'd bin Mu'âdh 🌸 declared that the warmongers among them should be beheaded, their children should be taken prisoner and their property should be confiscated. The sentence meted out by him was carried out. At the time he gave his judgement he was lying injured in the tent which had been put up in the courtyard of the Prophet's Mosque.

Realising that the situation was critical Rafâ'ah bin Samwâl Qurdhi appealed to Umm Munthir Salamâ 🌸 to give him refuge, and appeal to the Prophet 🌸 for his safety. He said that he would not forget this favor for the rest of his life. Feeling sorry for him, Umm Munthir Salamâ 🌸 gave him shelter and requested the Prophet 🌸 to accept him since she had given him refuge. He agreed and fixed a bail for Rafâ'ah. Thus he was saved from certain death. One day Umm Munthir Salamâ 🌸 told the Prophet 🌸 that her refuge prayed regularly and also ate camel meat. He smiled and answered that if he said his prayers it would be benefit him; but if he remained loyal to his own faith and did not accept Islâm it would be of no use. Some time later Rafâ'ah converted to Islâm swearing the oath of allegiance.

This great act of goodness would certainly be recorded among her other good deeds. If she had not given him refuge and if she had not appealed for his life to the Prophet 🌸, he might have died as a disbeliever and gone to the eternal Fire of Hell in the Hereafter.

Among Banu Quraidhah there was a lady, Rehânah bint Zaid bin 'Amr, whom the Prophet 🌸 took as a slave for his household. According to some accounts he married her and she became one of the Mothers of the Believers. The wedding ceremony took place in the house of Umm Munthir 🌸. When the Prophet 🌸 came back from his Farewell Pilgrimage, she passed away and had been buried in *Jannatul Baqi'*.

The Prophet 🌸 sometimes used to visit Umm Munthir Salamâ bint Qais 🌸. He would have his lunch and rest for a while there. She used to cook very well and the Prophet 🌸 enjoyed eating at her place. She would make special dishes on Fridays because he would drop in with some of the Companions for a meal.

Umm Munthir ﷺ was one of those fortunate fourteen hundred Companions of the Tree at the *Bai't Ridhwân* for whom Allâh ﷻ promised Paradise. As the *Hadith* in *Sahih Muslim* says,

'No one among them, who swore allegiance under the tree will go to *Jahannum*.'

Umm Munthir ﷺ left this world when both Allâh and His Prophet Muhammad ﷺ were well pleased with her.

Allâh will be pleased with them and they with Him.

Umm Waraqah bint 'Abdullâh bin Hârith Ansâriah رضي الله عنها

The Prophet ﷺ said:

"Umm Waraqah! Dwell in your House, Allâh will give you the death as a martyr."

Umm Waraqah bint 'Abdullâh bin Hârith Ansâriah رضي الله عنها

The *Ansâr* of Al-Madinah were standing on the outskirts of their city, looking with impatient eyes towards the road approaching from Makkah.

Men, women, girls and boys, the young and the old were waiting for the arrival of their beloved Prophet ﷺ who was migrating from his city to theirs at their invitation and at the command of Allâh ﷻ. Suddenly someone shouted, "Here they come!" And all the young girls and women burst into a song of praise of Allâh ﷻ and a welcome to His Messenger.

Among these Ansâri women was Umm Waraqah bint 'Abdullâh ﷜. She was a learned, scholarly, pious and modest lady, who was well known among the women Companions as one who spent her nights and days in prayer and meditation. She used to recite the Noble Qur'ân beautifully; it was second nature for her to spend a lot of time meditating on the meaning of its Verses.

The Prophet ﷺ valued her highly and he told her to lead the family in congregational prayers. The courtyard of the house was converted into a mosque; with the permission of the Prophet ﷺ they had a *Mu'ththin* to give the call to prayers. 'Abdur-Rahmân bin Khallad says that he saw the *Mu'ththin*, who was a very aged man. Thus Umm Waraqah bint 'Abdullâh ﷜ was appointed by the Prophet ﷺ to be an *Imâm* and lead the prayer for ladies.

❀❀❀❀❀

Besides her thirst for knowledge of the Qur'ân, *Shari'ah* (Islâmic legeslation) and *Ahâdith*, Umm Waraqah ﷺ had a burning desire to die a martyr in the cause of Islâm. When it was announced that the army should prepare to leave for the battle of Badr, Umm Waraqah ﷺ went to the Prophet ﷺ and volunteered her services to tend to the wounded in the battlefield. She told him that it was her earnest desire to die in the cause of Islâm. The Prophet ﷺ could see her enthusiasm and ardour, but he told her to stay at home and she would attain martyrdom there. She went back happily because it was her duty to yield to the command of the Messenger of Allâh ﷺ.

The Prophet ﷺ, would sometimes take along some of his Companions and visit the house of Umm Waraqah ﷺ. He would tell them to accompany him to the house of the lady who was a living martyr. He would ask about her welfare, rest for awhile and then offer supplications to Allâh ﷺ for her well being and return. Allâh ﷺ revealed to his beloved Messenger that Umm Waraqah ﷺ would die the death of a martyr in her own home. Nobody could understand how this would take place with her sitting in her house, but they were sure it would definitely happen, as this news had been given to them by their Truthful Prophet.

Umm Waraqah ﷺ herself was waiting every moment to see how this auspicious event, which would be the fulfillment of her greatest dream, take place. She waited patiently, for it would give her eternal life and a place in Paradise. When would it take place? How exactly would it take place? What shape would it take? How would it be possible to become a martyr sitting in the house? Lost in these thoughts she passed her nights and days. The Prophet ﷺ passed. Abu Bakr Siddique ﷺ succeeded and he also passed away; 'Umar Farooq ﷺ became the Caliph.

Umm Waraqah ﷺ had two slaves working for her, a girl and a man. She told them that after her death they would be free. One day they got together and decided that they were tired of waiting for this old lady to die. They planned that they would kill her while she lay asleep and escape to freedom. They were so tempted by the thought of freedom that they forgot to consider their future as well as life in the Hereafter.

In the dead of night as Umm Waraqah 🌸 lay in a deep sleep, they killed her, covered her body with a sheet and crept away from the house silently. As day broke and the sun came up, the neighbours missed the sound of the beautiful recitation of the Noble Qur'ân by Umm Waraqah 🌸 which used to fill the air early in the dawn. When they entered the house they were shocked to see her lying in the sleep of death. Then they saw that both the slaves – man and the girl – were missing. They realised that they must be the criminals. 'Umar bin Khattâb 🌸 ordered that people should be sent out to search for them. Finally when they were found hiding. When they were brought before the Caliph in the court, they admitted their guilt and were put to death.

Thus the Prophet 🌸 was proved right, that Umm Waraqah 🌸 would die a martyr's death in her own home, and attain Paradise.

"Verily, the pious will be in the midst of Gardens and Rivers. In a seat of truth, near the Omnipotent King (Allâh, the One, the All-Blessed, the Most High, the Owner of Majesty and Honour)." (54:54-55)

Umm Aiman bint Tha'labah رضي الله عنها

> The Prophet ﷺ said:
>
> "Whosoever wishes to marry a lady of Paradise, then he should marry Umm Aiman رضي الله عنها."

Umm Aiman bint Tha'labah رضي الله عنها

Her real name was Barakah bint Tha'labah, but she came to be known by her son Aiman's name as Umm Aiman 🌸. She was the lady who played the role of mother and took care of the young boy, Muhammad 🌸 when his mother Âminah bint Wahab passed away while travelling from Makkah to Al-Madinah. The Prophet 🌸 used to address her as 'mother' and said she would go to Paradise in the Hereafter. She was a lady who was like a member of the Prophet's family over the years. When Khadijah 🌸 passed away, she was deeply affected and wept for her. She was the one who bathed and shrouded her, and prepared her body for burial. When the Prophet's daughter, Zainab 🌸 passed away, again she was as grief-stricken as any member of the family. She also prepared her body for burial, with the help of Mother of the Believers Saudah 🌸 and the Mother of the Believers Umm Salamâ 🌸. She took part in the Battles of Uhud, Khaiber and Hunain. She also had the distinction of migrating twice – once to Abyssiniah and again to Al-Madinah.

❀❀❀❀❀

She had been a slave of the Prophet's father, 'Abdullâh bin 'Abdul Muttalib. She was originally from Abyssiniah. According to the tribal customs prevailing in the Arabia of the time, the Prophet 🌸 spent his early years with the tribe Banu Sa'd. He was nursed by Halimah Sa'diah, and was brought up by her. When he was five years old he was returned to Makkah to his mother. When he was six years old his mother decided to take him to Yathrib to meet his grandparents who were from the tribe of Banu Najjâr. The slave girl Barakah bint Thu'labah also accompanied them. On the way back when they reached Abwâ', his mother suddenly fell ill and died. They then buried her there.

Barakah bint Tha'labah consoled the little boy, and tried her best to fill the gap of his mother.

When the Prophet 變 grew up to be a young man he freed her and married to 'Obaid bin Zaid Khazarji. When Umm Aiman converted to Islâm differences developed between them. He was not willing to swear the oath of allegiance and accept Allâh 變 and His Messenger; and so they separated.

By her first husband, 'Obaid, she had a son, Aiman. Thus she became known as Umm Aiman. He grew up to be a very prominent Companion and was martyred in the Battle of Hunain. Her second marriage was to Zaid bin Hârithah 變. He was the General of the Muslim army and was martyred in the battle of Mu'tah. They had a son, Usâmah bin Zaid 變, who was another great General of the Muslim army.

When the Prophet 變 married Khadijah 變 he asked Umm Aiman 變 for Zaid bin Hârithah 變 to serve him. She was very happy to give her son to him. The Prophet 變 was aware of her exemplary character, noble manners and purity of heart. He said that whosoever wished to marry a lady of Paradise should marry Umm Aiman 變.

When Zaid bin Hârithah 變 heard this statement of the Prophet 變, based not on her looks, but on her character, he developed a liking for her and was only too happy to marry her. Their son, Usâmah bin Zaid 變, because of his praiseworthy character the was loved deeply by the Prophet 變. Zaid bin Hârithah 變 became famous because of the Prophet's love for him; so also his son, Usâmah bin Zaid 變, he became famous as the Prophet's favorite.

❀❀❀❀❀

The Prophet 變 had great respect for Umm Aiman 變, and regarded her as his mother. Sometimes because of her nature, she would become insistent and stubborn. The Prophet 🕌 would then be very respectful and patient and try his utmost to please her.

Anas bin Mâlik 🙏 says that the *Ansâr* of Al-Madinah gave their date orchards to the Prophet 🕌; he in turn distributed them among the *Muhâjirs* (migrants) from Makkah. When the Muslims triumphed over Banu Quraidhah and Banu Nadheer, the Prophet 🕌 started returning their property to the generous *Ansâr* owners. Anas bin Mâlik 🙏 relates that when he went to take back his orchards from Umm Aiman 🙏, she refused point blank. On the other hand, she tied a cloth around his neck, jerked him and said that it was out of the question, that she would not return the orchards to him anyway. When the Prophet 🕌 saw this he tried to persuade her to return the orchards. He said he would give her something of the same value in exchange, but she did not agree. Then he offered her something double the value; still she refused. Then he went on to offer three times the value and so on. At last, he offered her something ten times the value of the orchards, and she finally agreed. And Anas bin Mâlik 🙏 got his date orchards back.

The Prophet 🕌 often visited her. As soon as he saw her he would say that she was a reminder of his family and she was his mother who deserved respect.

'Aishah 🙏 narrates that one day when all of them were seated together, the Prophet 🕌 drank some water. Umm Aiman 🙏 asked him to fetch some water for her too.

'Aishah 🙏 asked in a rather shocked tone if she was asking the Messenger of Allâh 🕌 to get some water for her.

She said, "Why not? I have served him often." He fetched the water for her and offered it to her in a very respectful manner.

Anas bin Mâlik 🙏 narrates that he would sometimes visit Umm Aiman 🙏 with the Prophet 🕌. She would express great pleasure on their arrival and serve delicious food and drinks. If the Prophet 🕌 refused to partake of it for some reason, she would be very angry and offended. She would ask him why he did not eat or drink. The

Prophet 🕊 would smile at her getting upset in this manner. Sometimes it would so happen that he was fasting.

Anas bin Mâlik ⟡ said that one day, she started kneading dough to make some bread. He asked her what she was doing. She answered she was making some bread for him as was the custom in her country, Ethiopia. Usâmah ⟡, resembled his mother rather than his father. So the hypocrites used to taunt him, saying that he was not really the son of Zaid bin Hârithah ⟡. This used to upset the Prophet 🕊 very much. 'Aishah said that once, the Prophet 🕊 entered the house looking very happy and smiling. She asked him if there was any special reason for this. He answered that something strange had happened. He said Zaid bin Hârithah and Usâmah bin Zaid رض الله عنهما were lying asleep with their faces covered, but their feet could be seen from under the sheet. Majzaz Madalji, an expert in physiognomy saw them sleeping and said,

> "Looking at the bone structure of the feet: It seems that father and son are sleeping."

The Prophet 🕊 said he was very pleased to hear this.

❀❀❀❀❀

Some miracles associated with Umm Aiman 🌸 are to be found in books of history. In *Tabqât Ibn Sa'd* it is mentioned that during her migration from Makkah to Al-Madinah, she experienced such severe thirst that she thought she would die. There were no signs of water in the vicinity. Suddenly she saw a bowl of water tied with an extremely beautiful pure white rope, descending gradually towards her from the sky. It came near her face and stopped. She put her lips to it and drank her fill to her heart's content. This cool water from the heavens was enough to ward off hunger, thirst and disease for the rest of her life. After that, she says she never experienced thirst for the rest of her life. Though she fasted during the hottest months possible she never experienced a desire for water. Abu Nu'aym Asbahâni, a noted biographer and historian, has mentioned this incident in his book *Hiliyat-ul-Awlia'*. He says Umm Aiman 🌸 was a God-fearing, good-hearted, pious woman of pure character who fasted during the day and spent her nights in prayer.

❀❀❀❀❀

Under the guidance of the Prophet 變 she played an active role in *Jihâd*. She was active in various battles. In the battle of Uhud she gave herself up completely to nursing the wounded and providing water to the thirsty *Mujâhideen* in the battlefield. In the battle of Khaiber she was one of the twenty women who fought against the enemy. When her son did not take part in this war because his horse was sick she called him a coward.

A devotee of the Prophet 變 and a poet of Islâm, Hassân bin Thâbit 錄 wrote poetry on this occasion, and elaborated on this point. The horse of Aiman 錄 had eaten poisoned grain and he could not take part in the battle because he had to tend to it.

In the battle of Hunain this same courageous and fearless warrior Aiman 錄 was martyred proving his valor as a warrior of Islâm. When the Muslim army was losing ground a few of the Companions – Abu Bakr Siddique, 'Umar Farooq, 'Ali bin Abi Tâlib, 'Abbâs bin 'Abdul Muttalib, Abu Sufyân, Hârithah bin Nu'mân, Usâmah bin Zaid and Aiman bin 'Obaid رضي الله عنهم were those noteworthy Companions who stood their ground with the Prophet 變. They did not falter and displayed unmatched loyalty and bravery.

During the battle of Hunain the Muslim army faced a very critical situation, the army panicked and scattered and the *Mujâhideen* were on the verge of running away from the battlefield. It seemed that the earth that was spread out so wide was now closing in on them. At this stage when all seemed lost, the Prophet 變 displayed extraordinary courage and said –

'I am the Prophet no lie.

I am the son of 'Abdul Muttalib.'

He meant that he was standing steadfast in the field of battle and at that critical stage it was no trivial matter.

Umm Aiman 樂 lost her son Aiman 錄 in this battle, but she was a role model in patience and acceptance of the Will of Allâh.

During the battle of Mu'tah Zaid bin Hârithah ☙ was appointed
General of the Muslim army. The Prophet ﷺ said if Zaid bin Hârithah
☙ was martyred, then Ja'far bin 'Ali Tâlib ☙ should be made General.
If he also was martyred, then 'Abdullâh bin Rawâhah should take his
place, and if he was martyred then the *Mujâhideen* should choose
anyone they thought suitable. And it was Allâh's Will that all three of
them were martyred one by one. Umm Aiman ﷺ bore the loss of her
husband with great fortitude and asked her son, Usâmah ☙ too to
bear the loss of his father bravely.

Umm Aiman ﷺ being sometimes pronounced some words in the
Ethiopian dialect. When the Prophet ﷺ heard her pronounciation of
certain words he would just smile pleasantly and correct her. She
could not say *Assalâm-u-Alaikum* and would invariably say *Assalâm la
Alaikum*. He told her gently one day to just say *Salâm*, as the meaning
became the opposite the way she said it. In the same way she
mispronounced certain expressions in supplications to Allâh ﷻ; so he
told her to keep silent.

She was a very straightforward person with absolutely no malice; she
was very soft-hearted, sincere and sympathetic. On returning from the
Battle of Bani Mustalaq when the hypocrites spread slanderous gossip
regarding the character of 'Aishah ﷺ, she vouched unhesitatingly for
the purity of her character. This endeared her and increased her worth
in the eyes of 'Aishah ﷺ. It is recorded in history books that 'Aishah ﷺ
said about Umm Aiman ﷺ,

"My eyes and my ears have the best impressions about her."

The Prophet ﷺ prepared an army to crush the power and might of
the Romans in Palestine; Usâmah bin Zaid bin Hârithah ☙ was
appointed General of the Army. Such Companions as Abu Bakr
Siddique and 'Umar Farooq رضــــي الله عــهما were also asked to serve
under him. Some of the *Mujâhideen* were not happy with this
appointment. But the Prophet ﷺ remained very firm about his
decision and said that Usâmah bin Zaid ☙ would retain that
position as he deserved it. He sent for Usâmah bin Zaid ☙ and told
him to start on his journey in the Name of Allâh. The army had
hardly reached Jaraf near Al-Madinah when Umm Aiman ﷺ sent a

messenger to say that the Prophet 🌸 was very ill. The army stopped and camped at Jaraf. When Usâmah 🌸 reached Al-Madinah, the Prophet 🌸 passed away. It seemed that Umm Aiman 🌸 could not withstand this sorrow.

Involuntarily, plunged in grief, she burst into tears. The people there were taken by total surprise; they had never heard anything like it before. She had nurtured him in his childhood and held him in her arms; she had seen him grow into a fine young man – a young man who then wore the mantle of the Prophet of Allâh 🌸. She witnessed him as a young bridegroom, when he wed Khadijah 🌸. She also underwent the tortures and cruelties inflicted by the Quraish and the polytheists of Makkah against him and the new converts. She experienced the days when Makkah was like the Final Day of Judgement. She saw those historic days when he ruled over the newly founded Muslim Islamic state. And best of all she saw the miraculous revelations of Allâh's radiance. All the golden pages of his life seemed to pass before her eyes.

A few days after the death of the Prophet 🌸 Abu Bakr Siddique and 'Umar Farooq رضي الله عنهما went to visit Umm Aiman 🌸 to console with her. She started to cry remembering the Prophet 🌸. They asked her why she was crying though she knew very well that he was in a far better world than this one with Allâh 🌸. She said that although she indeed knew this, she was crying because the revelations from Allâh 🌸 had come to an end with his passing away. Hearing this they also started weeping.

One day Mu'âwiyah bin Sufyân 🌸 talking to Usâmah bin Zaid 🌸 praised his mother highly. Zaid 🌸 agreed saying that she was more blessed than even his mother, Hind. Mu'âwiyah bin Sufyân 🌸 accepted the truth of this statement and said he was right. Then he said Allâh 🌸 also said so and quoted the following *Âyah:*

> "Verily, the most honorable of you with Allâh is the most pious among you." (49:13)

🌸🌸🌸🌸🌸

She had looked after the Prophet 🌸 from his childhood and given him a mother's love and care after Aminah bint Wahab's death. The Prophet 0 loved and regarded her highly; his Companions also treated her with great respect.

Sahih Muslim records that Umm Aiman tidied just six months after the passing away of the Prophet H But some others disagree and say that she died during the caliphate of 'Uthman bin 'Affan She lived to a ripe old age.

Allah will be pleased with them and they with Him.

CPSIA information can be obtained
at www.ICGtesting.com
Printed in the USA
BVHW052349060223
658028BV00011B/337

9 781643 543765